J GREGORY A. JOHNSON
7838 DEVONSHIRE WAY
BOULDER, CO 80301-4115

D0210887

MERGERS
AND
ACQUISITIONS
FROM A TO Z

MERGERS AND ACQUISITIONS FROM A TO Z

Strategic and
Practical Guidance for
Small- and Middle-Market
Buyers and Sellers

Andrew J. Sherman

AMACOM

American Management Association

New York • Atlanta • Boston • Chicago • Kansas City • San Francisco • Washington, D.C.
Brussels • Mexico City • Tokyo • Toronto

This book is available at a special
discount when ordered in bulk quantities.
For information, contact Special Sales Department,
AMACOM, a division of American Management Association,
1601 Broadway, New York, NY 10019.

This publication is designed to provide accurate and authoritative
information in regard to the subject matter covered. It is sold with the
understanding that the publisher is not engaged in rendering legal,
accounting, or other professional service. If legal advice or other expert
assistance is required, the services of a competent professional person
should be sought.

Library of Congress Cataloging-in-Publicaton Data

Sherman, Andrew J.
    Mergers and acquisitions from A to Z: strategic and practical
guidance for small- and middle-market buyers and sellers / Andrew J.
Sherman.
        p.   cm.
    Includes index.
    ISBN 0-8144-0376-X
    1. Consolidation and merger of corporations.   2. Small business—
Mergers.   I. Title.
    HD58.8.S484   1998
    658.1'6—dc21   97-52037
                                                          CIP

© 1998 Andrew Sherman.
All rights reserved.
Printed in the United States of America.

This publication may not be reproduced,
stored in a retrieval system,
or transmitted in whole or in part,
in any form or by any means, electronic,
mechanical, photocopying, recording, or otherwise,
without the prior written permission of AMACOM,
a division of American Management Association,
1601 Broadway, New York, NY 10019.

Printing number

10   9   8   7   6   5   4   3   2

This book is dedicated to
Max and **Susie Joffe**
and
M. Gary Goldman
I thank them for their never-ending support.

Contents

List of Exhibits

List of Boxed Materials

Acknowledgments

As with most of my books, there are usually many people to thank and not enough room on the page.

First, I would like to thank all of my emerging growth clients who have over the years allowed me to work with them on merger and acquisition transactions of all shapes and sizes.

Next, the wonder team at AMACOM Books, whose steady support and excellent editing made this book possible: Jacquie Flynn, Kate Pferdner, Carole Berglie, Desiree Rivera, and Ray O'Connell.

My fellow shareholders at Greenberg Training also deserve a big thanks, particularly the attorneys in the Corporate and Securities Department, who represent some of the nation's finest business lawyers.

The organizational and administrative support of Michele Lewis and Samantha Ferrell kept me focused and efficient, and I could not have completed this project without their assistance.

Finally, my heartfelt gratitude goes out to my wife, Judy, and to my children, Matthew and Jennifer, who continue to tolerate me when I say "OK, just one more book . . ." but share in my excitement when it is finally published.

MERGERS
AND
ACQUISITIONS
FROM A TO Z

Introduction

During the turbulent 1980s, nearly half of all U.S. companies were restructured, over 80,000 were acquired or merged, and over 700,000 sought bankruptcy protection in order to reorganize to continue operations. The general public's perception of the go-go eighties, however, was depicted in Michael Douglas's portrayal of Gordon Gekko, the corporate raider on Wall Street who declared "Greed is good." This era featured swashbucklers and Rambo tactics to gain control over targets. The 1990s have proved to be equally or even more dynamic in terms of companies evolving through upsizing and growth, downsizing, rightsizing, spinoffs, rollups, divestitures, consolidation, and growth, but with a different focus on postclosing synergies, operating efficiencies, increases in customer bases, strategic alliances, and market share and access to new technologies. The *Kiplinger Washington Letter* (June 28, 1996) estimated that, in 1996 alone, there will have been at least 10,000 mergers and acquisitions, if you count the 4,000 or so reported or announced transactions together with the typically unreported 6,000 transactions estimated in the small and midsize market. The total value of the 4,000 reported transactions is nearly $600 billion, and probably closer to $800 billion when you estimate the unreported transactions by many small and mid-size companies. Yet with so many dollars changing hands, there remains a very limited number of readily available resources for business executives and professional advisors to turn to for legal and strategic guidance.

This book is intended to be such a resource. There is no more complicated transaction than a merger or acquisition. The various issues raised are broad and complex, from tax and securities laws to antitrust and corporate laws. The industries affected by this emerging trend and rapid activity are also diverse, from banking and computer software companies to retailing and health care forums. It seems that virtually every executive of every major industry faces a buy or sell decision at some point during his or her tenure as leader of the company. As we will see in the chapters to follow, the strategic reasons for considering such transactions are also numerous, from achieving economies of scale, to mitigating risk via diversification, to satisfying shareholder hunger for steady growth and dividends. The federal government's degree of intervention in these transactions varies from administration to administration, depending on the issues and concerns of the day.[1] During the Reagan-Bush years, the government took a passive role, generally allowing market forces to determine whether a given transaction would have an anticompetitive effect. In recent years, the Clinton administration has taken a more proactive approach, with more intervention by the U.S. Department of Justice and the Federal Trade Commission, such as a refusal to provide the necessary approval for the proposed merger of Staples and Office Depot in mid-1997. The focus is more on international competitiveness, and if the proposed transaction will enhance the "surviving entity's" ability to compete in global markets, then the transaction is likely to be approved, provided it does not have a monopolistic or anticompetitive effect on domestic markets.

This book will *not* focus on the mechanics of the mega-mergers of recent years, such as Walt Disney's purchase of Capital Cities/ABC for $19 billion, the Nynex–Bell Atlantic deal valued at $21 billion, or the Westinghouse-Infinity merger. Nor will it be an analysis of 1996 and 1997 mega-deals such as Time Warner's acquisition of Turner Broadcasting, Wells Fargo's acquisition of First Interstate Bancorp, Britain's merger of Guinness PLC and Grand Metropolitan PLC (which created the world's seventh-largest food and beverage company), or Boeing's acquisition of McDonnell Douglas Corporation. Nor will it address the recent trend by overseas companies to buy in to the U.S. market via acquisitions in the banking, computer, and telecommunications industries, such as

---

1. Under certain circumstances, the federal government must approve the proposed merger or acquisition, under a statute known as the Hart Scott and Rodino Act. For more information on the act, see Chapter 6.

the recent $30 billion to $40 billion bidding war by GTE, British Telecomm, and Worldcom to obtain control over telecommunications giant MCI, the nearly $3 billion acquisition of Stop & Shop grocery chain by Royal Ahold (a Dutch food retailing group), or the $770 million purchase of Helene Curtis, one of the last independent U.S. personal-care products companies, by the Anglo-Dutch conglomerate, Unilever PLC. These international conglomerates have looked at U.S. companies as either an expansion of their market share and brand recognition, such as in the Unilever deal, or, as in the case of the Royal Ahold acquisition, a chance to establish a foothold in the U.S. market once its own domestic market had been saturated. There is a definite trend toward mergers and acquisitions on "friendly" terms, such as Worldcom's $13 billion acquisition of MFS Communications or NationsBank's purchase of Boatman's Bancshares for almost $10 billion.

As we approach the new millennium, and as technologies converge and business and home consumers increase their demands for truly integrated products and services, we are likely to see ever greater merger and acquisition activity in the telecommunications, cable television, and computer industries.

When the value of a transaction is $1 billion or more, there is a team of skilled investment bankers and professional advisors quarterbacking the transaction, and in these cases the importance of this book will be less. But what about the thousands and thousands of transactions each year that range from $1 million at the low end to $500 million at the high end? Where do these small and middle-market company executives turn for guidance? For many of these executives, mergers and acquisitions represent a digestible and manageable strategy for business growth. Buying an additional $2.5 million, or even $25 million, in sales or profits may be easier and faster than building it from scratch. Recent years have seen a significant increase in merger and acquisition activity within industries that are growing rapidly and evolving overall, such as in health care, information technology, communications, and software development, as well as in traditional industries such as manufacturing, consumer products, and food services. Many developments reflect an increase in strategic buyers and a decrease in the amount of leverage, implying that these deals were being done because they made sense for both parties, which is different from the highly leveraged, financially driven deals of the late 1980s. The tables in Boxes I-1 and I-2 show the dollar value and number of mergers and acquisitions in 1996, broken down by industry.

In addition, these middle-market transactions in evolving industries have attracted aggressive valuations. For example, in 1995 and 1996, purchase-price multiples for middle-market acquisitions have been at the highest level since the late 1980s, with prices averaging 7.0 times earnings before income and taxes (EBIT) and 6.5 times operating cash flow. The multiples have been highest for companies with the following six characteristics:

1. Significant market share or strong niche position
2. A market with barriers to entry by competitors
3. A strong management team
4. Strong, stable cash flow
5. No significant concentration in customers, products, suppliers, or geographic markets
6. Low risk of technological obsolescence or product substitution

---

Box I-1. Ten Most Active M&A Industries by Dollar Value (1996)

Industry	Value ($ bil)*	% of Total M&A Value	No. of Deals
Radio and TV broadcasting	$61.7	11.2%	173
Commercial banks	55.1	10.0	296
Telecommunications	29.0	5.3	113
Business services	26.1	4.7	963
Measuring, medical, and photographic equipment	25.4	4.6	246
Insurance	24.4	4.4	194
Health services	21.2	3.8	364
Electric, gas, and water utilities	18.8	3.4	77
Oil and gas; petroleum refining	18.1	3.3	242
Investment and commodity firms	15.1	2.7	176

*Values are based on 2,752 deals that disclosed purchase prices.

Box I-2. Ten Most Active M&A Industries by Number of Deals (1996)

Industry	No. of Deals	% of All M&A Deals	Value ($ bil)*
Business services	963	14.1%	$26.1
Health services	364	5.3	21.2
Durable goods wholesaling	317	4.6	12.8
Commercial banks	296	4.3	55.1
Measuring, medical, and photographic equipment	246	3.6	25.4
Computer software	244	3.6	9.9
Oil and gas; petroleum refining	242	3.5	18.1
Real estate; mortgage bankers and brokers	205	3.0	11.9
Insurance	194	2.8	24.4
Metal and metal products	183	2.7	5.9

*Values are based on 2,752 deals that disclosed purchase prices.

Successful mergers and acquisitions are neither an art nor a science but a *process*. A study of deals that close with both buyer and seller satisfied show that the deal followed a sequence, a pattern, a series of steps that have been tried and tested. This book focuses on conveying this process to the reader, as we learn to understand the objectives of both buyer and seller in Chapters 2 and 3, through the process of negotiations and closing in Chapters 4 through 10, to closing and beyond in Chapters 11 and 12. For example, when a deal is improperly valued, nobody really wins. To be successful, a transaction must be fair and balanced, reflecting the economic and tax needs of both buyer and seller, and convey real and durable value to the shareholders of both companies. Achieving this involves a review and analysis of financial statements, a genuine understanding of how the proposed transaction meets the economic objectives of each party, and a recognition of the tax and accounting implications of the deal.

A transaction as complex as a merger or acquisition is fraught with potential problems and pitfalls. Many of these problems arise either in the preliminary stages, such as forcing a deal that shouldn't really be done (the classic attempt to fit a square peg into a round hole); as a result of mistakes, errors, or omissions owing to inadequate, rushed, or misleading due diligence; in not properly allocating risks during the negotiation of definitive documents; or because it became a nightmare to integrate the companies after closing. These pitfalls can lead to expensive and protracted litigation unless an alternative method of dispute resolution is negotiated and included in the definitive documents. This book is designed to share the pitfalls of such transactions, with the hope that buyers and sellers and their advisors can avoid these problems in their future transactions.

Chapter 1

The Basics of Mergers and Acquisitions

The 1990s have had countless examples of companies, such as HFS Inc., and U.S. Office Products, that have grown dramatically and built revenues almost exclusively through an aggressive acquisition program. The wave of consolidations, mergers, acquisitions, and corporate restructurings has reached a record height in the United States and is now poised to sweep through the small and middle-market company sector of our economy. As we approach the year 2000, seasoned executives and entrepreneurs are searching for efficient and profitable ways to increase revenues and win market share. Their options are typically limited either to *internal* revenue growth strategies—hiring more staff, opening more locations, and acquiring other companies with a view toward reaching more customers or selling new lines of products (or both)—or to *external* revenue growth opportunities—franchising, licensing, joint ventures, strategic alliances, and the appointment of overseas distributors, which are available to growing companies as an alternative to mergers and acquisitions as a growth engine. This book focuses primarily on mergers and acquisitions as an internal growth strategy, although toward the end of the book I explore certain external ones as well.

Understanding Key Terms

The terms *merger* and *acquisition* are often confused or used interchangeably by the business media. Consider the following from the *Washington Post* Business section (July 24, 1997), reporting on the Boeing–McDonnell Douglas transaction:

> The Dow's strongest component was Boeing, which rose 2 11/16 to 59 1/16 on news that the European Union endorsed the main points of the aerospace company's proposed $15 billion *acquisition* of McDonnell Douglas. Boeing made some surprise concessions Tuesday to appease the EU, which had threatened to reject the *merger* as anti-competitive. [italics added]

On the surface, the distinction in meaning may not really matter, since the net result is often the same: two companies (or more) that had separate ownership are now operating under the same roof, usually to obtain some strategic or financial objective. Yet the strategic, financial, tax, and even cultural impact of a deal may be very different, depending on which transaction is made. A *merger* typically refers to two companies coming together (usually through the exchange of shares) to become one. An *acquisition* typically has one company—the *buyer*—who purchases the assets or shares of the *seller*, with the form of payment being cash, the securities of the buyer, or other assets of value to the seller. In a *stock purchase* transaction, the seller's shares are not necessarily combined with the buyer's existing company, but often kept separate as a new subsidiary or operating division. In an *asset purchase* transaction, the assets conveyed by the seller to the buyer become additional assets of the buyer's company, with the hope and expectation that the value of the assets purchased will exceed the price paid over time, thereby enhancing shareholder value as a result of the strategic or financial benefits of the transaction.

What's All the Fuss About?

What has driven the merger mania of the late 1990s? What factors have fueled the current resurgence of merger and acquisition activity? There is no one explanation, and the full impact on the economy is complex and remains to be seen, but there are certain themes and trends that have emerged. The eight key reasons deals are getting done today are:

1. Mergers and acquisitions are clearly more strategically motivated than their 1980s counterparts. Jobs are gained, not lost, as a result of these deals. Companies are being built up, not busted up. In fact, access to today's "knowledge worker" and the ability to obtain additional intellectual capital may be the primary motivators for the deal. Many technology companies, such as Cisco Systems, have developed a reputation for aggressively recruiting executive and technical talent. If key employees can't be lured away, then Cisco considers an acquisition as an alternative.

2. The financing behind the deal is more sound and secure than ever before. Buyers are using their stock as currency, and sellers are gladly accepting this form of payment in lieu of or in addition to cash. This forces both parties to work together on a postclosing basis to truly *enhance* shareholder value. In addition, third-party financing is more readily available than ever before, with commercial and investment bankers competing for the right to provide the financing for these transactions.

3. Mergers and acquisitions are being driven in many cases by a key trend within a given industry, such as:
   a. Rapidly changing technology, which is driving many of the deals in the computer industry
   b. Fierce competition, which is driving many of the deals in the telecommunications and banking industries
   c. Changing consumer preferences, which is driving many of the deals in the food and beverage industry
   d. The pressure to control costs, which is driving many of the deals in the health care industry
   e. A reduction in demand, such as the shrinking federal defense budget, which is driving the consolidation in the aerospace and defense contractor industries

The gains in efficiency from reducing excess capacity in these industries have led to much sounder deals, which are having a positive impact on the economy.

4. Some deals are motivated by the need to transform corporate identity following a crisis. For example, after the dust settled, ValuJet began looking for a merger partner that would help effect a change of identity, since the company's reputation was so closely tied to its Florida plane crash and the negative publicity that followed the incident regarding its spotty safety records.

5. Many deals are fueled by the need to spread the risk and cost of:

    a. Developing new technologies, such as in the communications and aerospace industries

    b. Research into new medical discoveries, such as in the medical device and pharmaceutical industries

    c. Gaining access to new sources of energy, such as in the oil and gas exploration and drilling industries

6. The global village has forced many companies to explore mergers and acquisitions as a means to develop an international presence and expanded market share. This market penetration strategy is often more cost-effective than trying to build an overseas operation from scratch.

7. Many recent mergers and acquisitions come about with the recognition that a complete product or service line may be necessary to remain competitive or to balance seasonal or cyclical market trends. Transactions in the retail, hospitality, food and beverage, entertainment, and financial services industries have been in response to consumer demand for "one-stop shopping."

8. Many deals are driven by the premise that it is less expensive to buy brand loyalty and customer relationships than it is to build them from scratch. Buyers are paying a premium for this intangible asset on the balance sheet, which is often referred to as goodwill. In today's economy, goodwill represents an asset that is very important but which is not adequately reflected on the seller's balance sheet. Veteran buyers know that long-standing customer and other strategic relationships that will be conveyed with the deal have far greater value than machinery and inventory.

9. Some buyers even look upon an acquisition as an alternative to starting a new line of business, the goal being to "retrofit" the acquired business on a postclosing basis, making those changes necessary to meet the buyers' long-term objectives.

The motivation for the deal, and the underlying goals and objectives for the transaction on a postclosing basis, often affects the structure of the transaction, pricing and valuation issues, and the ability to obtain necessary third-party or governmental approvals.

Why Bad Deals Happen to Good People

Nobody ever plans to enter into a bad deal. But many good-intending entrepreneurs and business executives enter into mergers and acquisitions that they later regret. Classic mistakes include a lack of adequate planning, an overly aggressive timetable to closing, a failure to really look at possible postclosing integration problems, or, worst of all, synergies that were intended to be achieved turn out to be illusory. As evident in the eight key reasons for today's deals, the underlying theme is the goal of postclosing synergy. What is synergy and how can you be sure to get some? The key premise to *synergy* is that the "whole will be greater than the sum of its parts." But the quest for synergy can be deceptive, especially if there is inadequate communication between buyer and seller, a situation that usually leads to a misunderstanding regarding what the buyer is really buying and the seller is really selling. Every company says that it wants synergy when doing a deal, but few take the time to develop a transactional team, draw up a joint mission statement of the objectives of the deal, or solve postclosing operating or financial problems on a timely basis.[1]

Why Do Buyers Buy, and Why Do Sellers Sell?

In Chapters 2 and 3, we'll look at the basic reasons why a buyer buys and a seller sells in the context of a merger or acquisition. The goal here is twofold: (1) to educate you as a prospective buyer or seller on how to define your own goals and objectives; and (2) to provide some insight into the motivations of the other party to the transaction, which will usually facilitate a more successful and mutually rewarding transaction.

---

1. An excellent book on this topic is *The Synergy Trap* by NYU business professor Mark L. Sirower (Simon & Schuster, 1997), which discusses how companies are losing the acquisitions game by overpaying for assets that never realize the promises of increased performance or competitiveness. The overpaying for synergies that never come to pass ends up costing the shareholders of the buyer dearly, instead of enhancing shareholder value, as originally intended.

Motivations in an Acquisition

For the seller, the key "motivators" in an acquisition (which will be discussed in more detail in Chapter 2) usually include one or more of the following:

- Ownership nearing retirement or ready for an exit
- Inability to compete as an independent
- The desire to obtain cost savings
- Access to the greater resources of the acquiring company

For the buyer, the key "motivators" in an acquisition (which will be discussed in more detail in Chapter 3) usually include one or more of the following:

- Revenue enhancement
- Cost reduction
- Vertical and/or horizontal operational and financial synergies or economies of scale
- Growth pressures from investors
- Underutilized resources
- Intrapreneurs with a large appetite
- A desire to reduce the number of competitors (increase market share)
- A need to gain a foothold in a new geographic market (especially if the current market is saturated)
- A desire to diversify into new products and services

Motivations in a Merger

It is important to note that a merger is a different animal from an acquisition and thus a different set of objectives typically emerges for either party:

- To improve process engineering and technology
- To increase the scale of production in existing product lines
- To acquire the capability to produce subassemblies internally
- To find additional uses for existing management talent
- To redeploy excess capital in more profitable or complementary uses
- To obtain tax benefits

In a classic merger, there is no buyer or seller, though one party may be quarterbacking the transaction or have initiated the contract. Therefore, the culture and spirit of the negotiations are different from those for an acquisition. In a merger, data gathering and due diligence are two-way and mutual, with each party positioning its contribution to the postmerger entity to justify its respective equity share, management, and control of the new company.

Before turning to the details of structuring and negotiating these complex transactions, let's take a look at the individual perspective of both buyer and seller in Chapters 2 and 3. An understanding of each party's goals and objectives is critical to understanding the overall dynamics of the transaction.

Box 1-1. Buyers and Sellers: Different Motivations

Common Seller Motivations	*Common Buyer Motivations*
The desire to retire	The desire to grow
Lack of successors	Opportunity to increase profits
Business adversities	The desire to diversify
Inability to compete	To have a value-driven acquisition strategy
Lack of capital to grow	To buy up competitors
Inadequate distribution system	To use excess capital
To eliminate personal guaranties or other personal obligations	To achieve new distribution channels or efficiencies
No ability to diversify	To diversify into new products or geographic markets
Age and health concerns	Need particular people, existing business, or assets
Need particular amount of money for estate planning	To gain access to new or emerging technologies
Irreconcilable conflict among owners	To efficiently deploy key people or resources
Losing key people or key customers	For strategic fit between buyer and seller's current operations

Chapter 2

Preparing for the Dance: The Seller's Perspective

Two houses in my neighborhood recently went up for sale. The sellers took very different approaches to preparing for the transaction. One couple, who were nearing retirement, began the process almost two years ago. Every weekend they would work on a different part of the house or garden, taking steps to increase the value and hence raise the ultimate selling price. The proceeds represented the bulk of their retirement nest egg, and every dollar of value was critical. Naturally, there were certain items that could not be specifically addressed, such as new wallpaper and paint, because they did not know the needs and wants of the possible buyer. In such cases, steps were taken to make the rooms more generic, so as to appeal to the varying tastes of prospective buyers. The other couple, in their mid-thirties with three young children, seemed as if they started preparing about one week before the first prospective buyer arrived. They were on their way to their next home, and although selling price mattered, it really only affected the size of their next mortgage. In fact, with three wild and destructive kids, it seemed that they were taking steps to decrease the value of the house on a weekly basis! Clearly, their approach to the buyer was "take it as is and perhaps it will meet your needs." Prospective buyers came into the transaction knowing that a lot of time, care, and attention would need to go into the house after closing.

In many ways, these two approaches mirror the attitudes of

sellers of businesses. Some companies become available for sale only after years of planning and preparation, with the sellers laying the groundwork for maximizing value. These sellers take the time to anticipate the needs and wants of different types of buyers, yet they realize that some items must be kept "plain vanilla" because each buyer will have different objectives and motivations. Other companies become available for sale owing to boredom of the founding entrepreneur or competitive or financial factors that may have only recently appeared. Although each circumstance will be different, these sellers simply may not want to make the significant capital investments necessary to continue operations. Or the industry may have become less profitable, or there may be irreconcilable shareholder or management disputes driving the transaction. In these cases, the buyer is likely to be purchasing a "fixer-upper," and the price and valuation will be negotiated accordingly. In rare cases, the "hasty" decision to sell may be for positive reasons, such as an industry being perceived as hot by the financial markets, thereby creating an ability to sell at an inflated price for a limited time. Or a competing business opportunity may have been presented and the company needs to diversify its assets in order to pursue that opportunity.

There are many reasons why a company may want to consider the sale of its business, including:

- The desire of the owner to retire
- Business adversities
- Lack of capital to grow
- Desire to eliminate personal guaranties or other personal obligations
- Age and health concerns
- Irreconcilable conflict among owners
- Lack of successors
- Inability to compete
- Inadequate distribution system
- No ability to diversify
- Money is needed for estate planning
- Key people or key customers have been lost

Box 2-1. The Selling Process and Seller's Decisional Path

Reaching the Decision to Sell
1. Understanding your motivation and objectives
2. Building the foundation for value
3. Timing and market factors

Getting the House in Order
1. Assembling your advisory team
2. Legal audit and housekeeping
3. Establishing preliminary valuation
4. Preparing the offering memorandum
5. Estate and exit planning

Marketing Strategy
1. Targeting qualified buyers
2. Use of third-party intermediaries
3. Narrowing the field of candidates

Choosing a Dance Partner
1. Selecting the most qualified and synergistic candidate (or financial candidate, depending on your objectives)
2. Preliminary negotiations
3. Execution of confidentiality agreement
4. Preliminary due diligence

Fighting It Out
1. Execution of more detailed letter of intent or memorandum of understanding
2. Extensive negotiations and strategic adjustments
3. Structuring the deal
4. Accommodating the buyer's team for legal and strategic due diligence
5. Doing due diligence on the buyer

Preparing for the Closing
1. Preparation and negotiation of the definitive legal documents
2. Meeting conditions to closing
3. Obtaining key third-party consents

The Closing

Postclosing Issues
1. Monitoring postclosing compensation/earn-outs
2. Facilitating the postclosing integration plan
3. Postclosing challenges

Regardless of the seller's specific motivations or timetable, it is critical for it to have an exit strategy and a plan of action in place in order to protect the value of the business it has worked so hard to build. There is usually a direct correlation between the amount of time a seller spends preparing for the transaction and the amount ultimately paid by a buyer for the seller's business.

Preparing for the Sale of the Company

From the seller's point of view, the key to the process is *preparation*, regardless of motivation for selling. This means taking all steps to prepare the company for sale from a corporate housekeeping perspective, anticipating the questions and concerns of a prospective buyer, and preparing your own financial and retirement plan to determine the pricing parameters.

The preparation process begins with a strategy meeting of all members of the seller's team. It is the job of the team to:

- Identify the financial and structural objectives.
- Develop an action plan and timetable.
- Begin preparation of an outline of the offering memorandum.
- Identify the potential legal and financial hurdles to a successful transaction (e.g., begin thinking about what problems may be "transactional turnoffs" to a prospective buyer), such as unregistered trademarks, illegal securities sales, or difficulties in obtaining a third-party consent.
- Develop a definitive "to do" list in connection with corporate housekeeping matters, such as preparation of board and shareholder minutes and maintenance of regulatory filings.
- Identify how and when prospective buyers will be recruited, proposed terms evaluated, and final candidates selected.

STEP 1: Selecting the Seller's Team

One of the most important steps in the preparation process is the selection of a team of advisors to help not only prepare the company for the sale itself but provide assistance to the seller in developing an offering memorandum that will summarize the key aspects of the company's operations, products and services, and personnel and financial performance. In many ways, this *offering memorandum* is akin to a traditional business plan, and serves both as a road map for the seller and an informational tool for the buyer.

When selecting members for the team, a seller should choose people who:

- Know the company, its history, and founders.
- Understand the seller's motivation, goals, and postclosing objectives.
- Are familiar with trends in the seller's industry.
- Have access to a network of potential buyers.
- Have a track record and experience in mergers and acquisitions with emerging growth and middle-market companies.
- Have expertise with the financing issues that will face prospective buyers.
- Know tax and estate planning issues that may affect the seller both at closing and beyond.

At a minimum, the team should include the following members:

1. *Financial advisor/investment banker.* A financial advisor (or investment banker) counsels the seller on issues affecting valuation, pricing, and structure. He or she assists the seller in identifying and evaluating prospective buyers. In some cases, multiple offers may have different structures and different consequences for the seller, so a financial advisor counsels the seller on how to evaluate each proposed transaction.

2. *Certified public accountant.* A certified public accountant (CPA) assists the seller in preparing the financial statements and related reports that the buyer (or buyers) inevitably request. He or she advises the seller on the tax implications of the proposed transaction. The CPA also assists in estate planning and in structuring a compensation package that maximizes the benefits associated with the proposed transaction.

3. *Legal counsel.* The transactional attorney is responsible for a wide variety of duties, including:

a. Assisting the seller in pre-sale corporate "housekeeping," which involves cleaning up corporate records, developing strategies for dealing with dissident shareholders, and shoring up third-party contracts

b. Working with the financial advisor in helping evaluate competing offers

c. Assisting in the negotiation and preparation of the letter of intent and confidentiality agreements such as Exhibit 2-1, which should be signed by all potential buyers who are provided access to the seller's books and records

d. Negotiating definitive purchase agreements with buyer's counsel

e. Working with the seller and the CPA in connection with certain postclosing and estate and tax planning matters

STEP 2: The Legal Audit

The next step in the preparation process is to get the company ready for the buyer's analysis and due diligence investigation. A pre-sale legal audit should be conducted in order to assess the state of the company; it is critical to identify and predict the problems that will be raised by the buyer and its counsel. The legal audit should include corporate housekeeping and administrative matters, the status of the seller's intellectual property and key contracts (including issues regarding their assignability, regulatory issues, and litigation. The goal is to find the bugs before the buyer's counsel discovers them for you (which would be embarrassing as well as costly from a negotiating perspective) and to get as many of the bugs out as possible before the first buyer is considered. For example, now may be the time to resolve any disputes with minority shareholders, complete the registration of copyrights and trademarks, deal with open issues in your stock option plan, or renew or extend your favorable commercial leases. It may also be a good time to set the stage for the prompt response of those third parties whose consent may be necessary to close the transaction, such as landlords, bankers, key customers, suppliers, or venture capitalists. In many cases, there are contractual provisions that can prevent an attempted change in control without such consent. For those bugs that can't be exterminated, don't try to hide them under the carpet. Explain the status of any remaining problems to the prospective buyers and negotiate and structure the ultimate deal accordingly.

The legal audit should include an examination of certain key financial ratios, such as debt-to-equity, turnover, and profitability. The audit should also look carefully at the company's cost controls, overhead management, and profit centers to ensure the most productive performance. The audit may also uncover certain sloppy or self-interested business practices that should be changed before you sell the company. This strategic reengineering will help build value and remove unnecessary clutter from the financial statements and operations.

Even if you don't have the time, inclination, or resources to make such improvements, it will still be helpful to identify these areas and address how the company *could* be made more profitable to the buyer. Showing the potential for better long-term performance could earn you a higher selling price, as well as assist the buyer in raising capital needed to implement the transaction.

STEP 3: Preparing the Offering Memorandum

The third step in the preparation process is to identify a marketing strategy to attract prospective buyers. This strategy should include developing a profile of the "ideal" buyer, identifying how and when buyer will be identified, determining who will meet with potential buyers, and gathering a set of initial materials to be given to potential buyers and their advisors. These initial materials are often referred to as the *offering memorandum*. This offering memorandum should include the following information:

- Overview of the seller's company
- Description of the seller's key products and services
- Description of the company's management team and organizational structure
- Comparison of the advantages and disadvantages of each category of target buyer (e.g., competitor, family member, employee, strategic buyer, financial buyers, or owner/operator)
- Summary of the seller's company's financial performance to date

- Schedule of key customer relationships and intangible assets
- Key hurdles (if any) to accomplishing the sale
- Supplemental materials

As you know, when offering anything for sale, from single products to an entire company, you must present the information truthfully and attractively. You must resist the temptation to paint an overly attractive picture or fail to disclose key problems or challenges that the company faces.

Common Preparation Mistakes

Once you have assembled your team, conducted an internal pre-sale legal audit, and pulled together the "good, the bad, and the ugly" in a detailed offering memorandum, you are ready to start meeting with buyers. To maximize the selling price, however, you must take certain strategic and reengineering steps in order to build value in the company and to avoid the common mistakes made by sellers, as discussed below. To properly reengineer and reposition the company for sale, hard decisions need to be made and certain key financial ratios need to be analyzed in critical areas such as cost management, inventory turnover, growth rates, profitability, and risk mitigation techniques. The next chapter gives some insights into the buyer's perspective, while Chapters 4 through 10 discuss the process itself. But before turning to Chapter 3, take a look at a few of the common preparation mistakes sellers make in getting ready to sell their company.

- *Showing impatience and indecision.* Timing is everything. If you seem too anxious to sell, buyers will take advantage of your impatience. If you sit on the sidelines too long, the window of opportunity or best time in the market cycle to obtain a top selling price may pass you by.
- *Telling others at the wrong time.* Again, timing is critical. If you tell key employees, vendors, or customers that you are considering a sale too early in the process, they may abandon your relationship in anticipation of losing their jobs, their customer or supplier, or from a general fear of the unknown. Key employees, fearful of their

jobs, may not want to chance relying on an unknown buyer to honor their salary or benefits. Vendors and customers will want to protect their interests, too. Yet these key employees and strategic relationships may be items of value in the sale; the buyer may count on their being around after closing the deal. If you wait too long and disclose your news at the last minute, employees may feel resentment for being kept out of the loop and key customers or vendors may not have time to react and evaluate the impact of the transaction on their businesses—or, where applicable, provide their approvals.

▪ *Retaining third-party transactions with people you're related to.* If there are relationships that will not carry over to the new owner, shed these ghost employees and family members. They should follow you out the door once the deal is secured.

▪ *Leaving loose ends.* Purchase minority shareholder interests so that the new owner won't have to contend with their demands after the sale. Very few buyers will want to own a company that still has remaining shareholders, who may present legal or operational risks. It's akin to the real estate developer who needs 100 percent of all of the lots in a development to agree to sell before proceeding with its plans—a lone straggler or two can break the deal.

▪ *Forgetting to look in your own backyard.* In seeking out potential buyers, look for those who may have a vested interest in acquiring control of the company, such as key customers, employees, or vendors.

▪ *Deluding yourself—or your potential buyers—about the risks or weaknesses of your company.* Your credibility is on the line—a loss of trust by the potential buyer usually means that it will walk away from the deal.

Other Considerations for the Seller

The Importance of Recasting

Since privately owned companies often tend to keep reported profits—and thus tax obligations—as low as possible, *financial recasting* is a crucial element in understanding the real earnings history and future profit potential of your business. Buyers are interested in *real* earnings; recasting shows how your business would look if its philosophy matched that of a public corporation, in which earnings and profits are maximized. In presenting the complete earnings history of your company, recast your financial statements for the preceding three years. For example, adjust the salaries and benefits to prevailing market levels (and not overinflated), and eliminate expenses that are avoidable, unusual, or nonrecurring, such as personal expenses, country club dues, and expensive car leases. Recasting presents the financial history of your business in a way that buyers can understand. It translates your company's past into a valuable, saleable future, and it allows sophisticated buyers the means and opportunity for meaningful comparisons with other investment considerations.

Selling the Proforma

The price that a buyer may be willing to pay depends on the quality and reasonableness of the profit projections you are able to demonstrate and substantiate. The profit and loss statement, balance sheet, cash flow, and working capital requirements are developed and projected for each year over a five-year planning period. Using these documents, plus the enhanced value of your business at the end of five years, you can calculate the discounted value of the company's future cash flow. This establishes the primary economic return to the buyer for his acquisition investment.

Prequalifying Your Buyer

It is critical to prequalify the potential buyers, especially if you contemplate a continuing business relationship after closing the deal. Thus, the buyer must demonstrate the ability to meet one or more preclosing conditions, such as availability of financing, a viable business plan for postclosing operations (especially if the seller will be receiving part of its consideration in the form of an earnout), or a demonstration that the postclosing efficiencies or synergies are bona fide. Take the time to understand each potential buyer's postclosing business plan, especially in a rollup or consolidation, where the seller's upside will depend on the buyer's ability to meet its business and growth plans.

Exhibit 2-1. SAMPLE CONFIDENTIALITY AGREEMENT

THIS CONFIDENTIALITY AGREEMENT ("Agreement") is made as of this _____ day of _____, 19_____, by and among Company1, Inc., a _____ corporation ("Company1") and Company2, Inc., a _____ corporation ("Company2") and each of the undersigned representatives of each of Company1 and Company2, respectively (the "Representatives"). Company1 and Company2 are collectively referred to hereinafter as the "Parties."

WHEREAS, the Representatives executing this Agreement shall include, but are not limited to, the following individuals: On behalf of Company1, _____, and on behalf of Company2, _____; provided, however, that any additional Representatives also shall execute a copy of this Agreement;

WHEREAS, Representatives of the Parties intend to meet on _____, 19_____ to discuss certain transactions related to the businesses of the Parties, including a potential purchase and sale transaction between the Parties or other possible combinations of Company1 and Company2 (all of which shall be referred to hereinafter as the "Transaction");

WHEREAS, each of the Representatives, in the course of meetings and discussions relating to the Transaction, may disclose certain confidential and proprietary information regarding each Party's business plans, financial and operational data, services, products, and product development plans;

WHEREAS, each of the Parties desires to protect its proprietary rights and further desires to prevent unauthorized disclosure of any information regarding its individual business plans, financial and operational data, products and services;

WHEREAS, the Representatives collectively desire to prevent unauthorized disclosure by any one of them of any information regarding the Transaction and the business plans, financial and operational data, products and services associated therewith;

WHEREAS, the Parties intend to have the "confidential information" as defined below treated as being confidential and/or proprietary.

NOW, THEREFORE, in consideration of the premises and the mutual covenants contained herein, the parties agree as follows:

1. <u>Definition of Confidential Information</u>. In connection with the Transaction being discussed among the Representatives, each of the Parties and their Representatives may disclose certain information intended to remain as proprietary and confidential, including information regarding business plans, financial data, operational data, product development plans, products and services. The information furnished by either of the Parties or any Representative is hereinafter referred to as "Confidential Information" and such Confidential Information shall belong to the Party furnishing the same (through one or more of its Representatives) and shall be treated as

Confidential Information as provided herein. Confidential Information shall also include all discussions in connection with, and all information in any medium in any way related to, the Transaction.

The term "Confidential Information" shall not include information which was or becomes generally available to the public other than as a result of a disclosure by a Representative or his affiliates, agents or advisors including, without limitation, attorneys, accountants, consultants, bankers and financial advisors (collectively "Affiliates").

2. Use of Confidential Information. The Representatives of a Party shall not use any Confidential Information disclosed by the Representatives of the other Party or pertaining to the Transaction for its own use or for any purpose other than to carry out the discussions between the Parties and to further the evaluation of the Transaction and the business relationship between the Parties.

3. Permitted Disclosure. A Party or its Representatives may disclose Confidential Information if required by a governmental agency or court of competent jurisdiction, or the rules thereof; provided, however, each Party agrees to give to the other prompt notice of the receipt of the subpoena or other process requiring or requesting disclosure of Confidential Information.

4. Proprietary Rights. All Confidential Information furnished by a Party or its Representatives to the other Party or its Representatives shall remain the property of the Party furnishing the same and shall be promptly returned or destroyed at the request of the Party furnishing the Confidential Information.

5. No License or Right to Reproduce. Nothing contained in this Confidentiality Agreement shall be construed as granting or conferring on any Party or its Representatives, any rights, by license or otherwise, to reproduce or use in any other matter any Confidential Information disclosed hereunder by the other Party or its Representatives or pertaining to the Transaction, except to further the Transaction and the business relationship between the Parties.

6. Non-Competition. For a period of one (1) year from the date of this Confidentiality Agreement, no Party nor any of its respective Representatives shall, directly or indirectly, on behalf of itself or himself or any other person, use any Confidential Information disclosed by the other Party or its Representatives or pertaining to the Transaction, except in connection with the furtherance of the Transaction and the business relationship between the Parties.

7. No Further Obligation. Neither the disclosure or receipt of Confidential Information shall obligate a Party to undertake any business relationship with the other Party in connection with the Transaction. The Parties and the Representatives understand and acknowledge that neither Party is making any representation or warranty, express, or implied, as to the accuracy or completeness of the Confidential Information, and that only those representations or warranties that are made in a definitive purchase and sale or merger agreement when, as, and if executed, and subject to such limitations and restrictions as may be specified in such definitive agreement, will have any legal effect.

(continues)

Exhibit 2-1. (continued)

8. No Waiver. Failure to enforce any provision of this Agreement shall not constitute a waiver of any other term herein and any waiver of any breach shall not be construed as a waiver of any subsequent breach. If any provision of this Agreement is held to be invalid, void or unenforceable, the remaining provisions shall continue in full force and effect without being impaired or invalidated. This Agreement shall be construed and governed in accordance with the laws of the State of _____.

9. Termination. This Agreement shall terminate on the earlier of the execution of definitive agreement by the Parties, the unanimous agreement of the undersigned parties, or one year from the date hereof.

10. Entire Agreement. This Confidentiality Agreement embodies the entire understanding among the Parties and their respective Representatives with regard to the Transaction, the Confidential Information and all other subject matter described or contained herein. This Agreement may not be amended, changed, altered or modified in any way, except by a writing signed by the Parties. This Agreement may be executed in a number of counterparts which, when taken together, shall constitute one and the same instrument.

IN WITNESS WHEREOF, the parties hereto have executed this Confidentiality Agreement as of the day and year first above written.

COMPANY2, INC.   COMPANY1 CORPORATION

_____   _____

By: By:

_____, Individually _____, Individually

Chapter 3

Initiating the Deal: The Buyer's Perspective

Business strategists often say that it is cheaper to buy than to build a business. This approach, together with the low interest rates and large pools of capital that have flowed into large and medium-size companies through initial public offerings, both in the United States and abroad, has created a buying frenzy that is likely to continue into the next millennium. Our domestic market has clearly experienced major industry consolidation via acquisitions and rollup strategies. Notwithstanding all of the excitement, the purchase of an existing business is a complex and challenging task. This chapter leads the buyer through the process, with a focus on preparation for the deal and preliminary negotiation tips, as we begin to understand the seller's perspective.

Assembling the Team

Every buyer needs to develop an internal working team, as well as a set of experienced external advisors, such as lawyers, accountants, investment bankers, valuation experts, and in some cases insurance or employee benefits experts. The internal work team should include representatives from the finance, marketing, strategic planning, and operations departments. An effective buyer's team will not only be creative and aggressive, it also will not lose focus on the core fundamentals that drive the acquisition strategy, such as distribution, integration, and expansion of the customer base. There will be cohesive thinking and constant communication among team members and a dedication to increasing shareholder value. As the quarterback, the CEO or appointed leader of the team must clearly define both the responsibilities and the authority of each team member, including who speaks on behalf of the buyer, who contacts prospective sellers, who negotiates with the selected sellers, and so forth. All parameters of operations must be clearly set.

One interesting decision with respect to assembling the team is whether to use a buyer's broker, or investment banker, to find and evaluate sellers or whether the deal flow will be generated internally through networking, industry contacts, and the like. In many cases, the sellers (or at least those who have declared their businesses eligible for sale) may have hired intermediaries. If both sides are paying finder's fees to brokers, the process can get expensive. Nevertheless, using a broker can save valuable time and money; chasing after the wrong sellers or even trying to figure out which companies have expressed an interest in selling can be costly.

Compensation for External Services

There are many different ways to structure the relationship with an intermediary, investment banker, or business broker. Most relationships are based on a commission contingent on a successful transaction (generally in the 5 to 12 percent range and often the responsibility of the seller). However, many intermediaries look for a monthly retainer or the ability to bill for certain services, such as assistance in the preparation of the acquisition plan, as well as coverage of certain expenses, such as phone calls or trips to visit with prospective candidates. These fees and expenses are not usually contingent upon a successful transaction, though some brokers will credit the aggregate of fees paid toward the ultimate commission; therefore these costs should be negotiated carefully. If you do retain an intermediary for small deals, be sure that you have hired a buyer's broker—someone who has the experience and orientation to meet your needs.

The CFO as Broker

A recent trend is for the chief financial officer (CFO) of a medium to large company to take on the role of investment banker in order to develop in-house expertise and save money. In essence, the CFO and his team are responsible for developing new ideas, drafting acquisition plans, interviewing potential candidates, structuring deals, conducting due diligence, analyzing product, doing valuations, and assisting in the negotiation and closing of deals. Keeping these tasks in-house leaves only a handful of jobs that require outside advisors. For example, when Cisco Systems, a computer networking supplier, bought StrataCom for nearly $4 billion, Merrill Lynch was retained to render a fairness opinion, but the lion's share of the valuations and negotiations was conducted by the Cisco team.

Smaller companies doing smaller deals may not have the expertise or resources to bring some of these tasks in-house, but this strategic trend should nevertheless raise some eyebrows as to how many items on an investment banker's or intermediary's proposed list of services are really needed. And the benefits of doing part of the deal with your own staff may extend beyond savings of time and money. There is an argument that the quality and accuracy of the valuations and due diligence may be higher when conducted by industry veterans, who have a keener understanding of the buyer's objectives and the seller's problems. These industry veterans may also be better at forecasting postclosing issues and problems. The do-it-yourself movement appears to be a trend that will be around for some time.

Developing an Acquisition Plan

Mergers and acquisitions often play a key role in a company's ongoing growth planning process. The achievement of certain corporate goals and objectives may involve the external acquisition of assets and resources needed for growth, a step that may be more efficient than internal expansion. A growing company considering an acquisition should always begin with an *acquisition plan,* which identifies the specific objectives of the transaction and the criteria to be applied in analyzing potential target companies.

The acquisition plan also identifies the value-added efficiencies and cost savings that will result from the proposed transaction and answers the fundamental question: *How will the buyer's profes-*

sional management or brand equity enhance the performance or profitability of the seller's company? The possible answers may vary, but generally they include a desire to accelerate growth in revenues and profits, strengthen the buyer's competitive position, broaden existing product lines, or break into new geographic markets or market segments as part of a diversification strategy. The heart of the plan identifies the targeted industries and lists the criteria for evaluating candidates within these targeted industries.

STEP 1: Identify Your Objectives

The first step in developing an effective acquisition plan is to identify key objectives. Although the reasons for considering growth through acquisition will vary from industry to industry and from company to company, certain strategic advantages provided by an acquisition should be considered. The buyer may seek to acquire another company in order to:

- Achieve certain operating and financial synergies and economies of scale with respect to production and manufacturing, research and development, management, or marketing and distribution.

- Obtain the rights to develop products and services owned by the target company. For example, Microsoft acquired WEB-TV in order to establish an ownership position in a method of access to the Internet, a market source that is likely to grow. Original attempts had stumbled owing to inadequate resources, which Microsoft could bring to the negotiating table.

- Provide growth opportunities for a surplus of strong managers, who are likely to leave unless the company acquires other businesses for these managers to operate and develop. The target company may stand to lose a talented management team due to the lack of career growth potential unless it is acquired by a growing business which may offer higher salaries, increased employee benefits, and greater opportunity for advancement.

- Stabilize its earnings stream and mitigate its risk of business failure through diversification of its products and services. For example, Tim Horton's, the largest chain of coffee and donut shops, was acquired by Wendy's International, a major player in the fast-food industry that lacked a presence in the breakfast or baked goods market.

- Deploy excess cash in a tax-efficient project, since both distribution of dividends and stock redemptions are generally taxable events for shareholders.

- Achieve certain production and distribution economies of scale through vertical integration, which involves the acquisition of a key supplier or customer.

- Be able to exploit residual assets that have been undeveloped or underdeveloped by the target company's retiring or burnt-out management team. Top managers may be ready for retirement, or a key manager may have recently died, leaving the business with certain underutilized assets that can be exploited by an acquiring company.

- Strengthen key business areas, such as research and development or marketing. Sometimes it is more efficient to fill these gaps through an acquisition rather than attempt to build the departments internally.

- Penetrate new geographic markets. It is cheaper to acquire companies already doing business in a target market than to establish market diversification from scratch.

- Acquire additional plant or production capacities, which can be utilized to achieve greater economics of scale.

- Take advantage of a bargain. The target company may be available at a distressed price, which tends to pique the interest of growing companies even if they are not necessarily looking for acquisition candidates. This situation often comes about because of a death or divorce affecting the company's founders.

- Acquire certain patents, copyrights, trade secrets, or other intangible assets that are available only by means of an acquisition.

In essence, the statement of the objectives should be a reality check, answering the key questions:

- Why are we doing this?
- Are we convinced that growth via acquisition makes sense

as compared to other forms of growth strategies, such as internal expansion, joint ventures, franchising, licensing, or capital formation?

- Are we really enhancing our shareholder value and competitive position as a result of this deal?

STEP 2: Draft the Plan

The next step is to draft the actual acquisition plan. The acquisition plan defines the objectives of the buyer, the relevant trends in the target's industry, the method for finding candidates, the criteria to be used to evaluate candidates, the targeted budgets and timetables for accomplishing the transaction, the price ranges to be considered, the past acquisition track record of the company, the amount of external capital that will be required to accomplish the transaction, and related issues.

One of the overriding goals of the acquisition plan is to narrow the field as much as possible. The field is initially narrowed by choosing acquisitions as a growth strategy over alternatives such as franchising or strategic alliances. It is narrowed again by targeting the industry from which a company will be chosen. And it is narrowed further by developing criteria to screen the possible candidates. This narrowing process, in most cases, will yield a small but viable field of attractive candidates that can be approached.

Other benefits to having a well-prepared acquisition plan are:

- It provides a road map for the company's leadership to follow.
- It is a way of informing shareholders of key company objectives.
- It reduces professional and advisory fees by clearly defining objectives and reducing the reliance on outside advisors.
- It serves a screen to filter out deals that don't meet your criteria or long-term objectives.
- It mitigates the risk of doing a transaction you'll later regret by anticipating problems and clarifying objectives.
- It identifies postclosing integration challenges well in advance.
- It informs sellers of your plans for the company after closing.

In today's marketplace and with recent trends toward rollups and consolidation strategies, it is particularly important that the seller (especially when the lion's share of its compensation will be the buyer's stock) understand, accept, and respect the buyer's acquisition strategy and growth plans for the consolidated company. The well-prepared acquisition plan can be a valuable negotiation tool in dealing with sellers naturally concerned with the value and continued growth of the buyer's stock.

The acquisition plan will also identify:

- The targeted *size* of the candidates.

- The *source* of acquisition financing, including the logistics for obtaining capital when necessary and the targeted amount and method of payment to the seller.

- The *method* for finding candidates (e.g., internal search or use of intermediaries) and how to deal with unsolicited offers.

- The *desired financial returns* and/or *operating synergies* to be achieved as a result of the acquisition.

- The minimum and maximum ranges and rates of acceptable *revenues, growth, earnings,* and *net worth* of the seller.

- The *impact* of the acquisition on existing shareholders of your company.

- The likely *competing bidders* for qualified candidates.

- The members of the *acquisition team* and each of their roles.

- The nature and types of *risks* the buyer is willing to assume (versus those that are unacceptable).

- The desired *geographic location* of the target company.

- The desired *demographics* and *buying habits* of the seller's customers.

- The plans to retain or replace the *management team* of the target company, even though this policy may vary by candidate; include a section addressing at least your preliminary plans.

- Your willingness to consider *turnaround or troubled companies.* Each buyer will have a different tolerance level; some want and prefer the cost savings of buying a fixer-upper company while others prefer the company to be pretty much intact.

- Your tax and financial preferences for *asset vs. stock transactions.*

- Your openness to *full versus partial ownership* of the seller's entity, or your willingness to consider a spinoff sale, such as purchase of the assets of an operating division or the stock of a subsidiary.

- Your interest or willingness to launch an *unfriendly takeover* of a publicly held company or buy the debt from the largest creditor of a privately held company.

Applying the Criteria: How to Narrow the Field

Once all of the pertinent issues listed above have been addressed in the acquisition plan, it should be relatively easy to define the selection criteria and screen the candidates. The more typical criteria include some of the following:

- A history of stable financial and growth performance over different market cycles and under different conditions.

- A market leader in its industry niche and in its geographic region. A company with a recognized brand name and established market share.

- Products with life cycles that are not too short term, or susceptible to obsolescence or rapid technological change.

- A strong management team with research and development capability and technological know-how.

- Stable and economically favorable relationships with customers, vendors, lenders, and lessors.

- Room for growth or excess capacity in manufacturing or production.

- A range of current or potential claims or litigation in the $_____ to $_____ range.

- Sales range in the $_____ to $_____ million level, with minimum EBIT at $_____ million and an aggregate set of postclosing obligations (e.g., liabilities, union contracts) not to exceed $_____.

- Purchase price range from $_____ to $_____, with the seller willing to accept up to _____ percent of its compensation in the buyer's stock and an additional _____ percent contingent on the performance of the seller's company on a postclosing basis (exact method, such as earn-out, to be determined).

- Geographical location in the states of _____, _____ or _____; or within _____ miles of the buyer's principal headquarters.

- An existing management team that agrees to remain in place for up to _____ years.

Naturally, unless it's your birthday, you're not likely to find all of these qualifications in every candidate; if you do, there will likely be multiple bidders. Rather, the buyer must be ready to mix and match—accept some compromise in some areas. But be careful not to overlook too many warts, lest you end up with a deal that you will regret later.

Again, the goal is to compare the acquisition objectives to the strengths and weaknesses of each seller. The acquisition team must have a clear idea as to *how* each targeted company will complement the buyer's strengths and/or mitigate its weaknesses. The qualitative and quantitative screening criteria suggested here will help the buying team ensure that the right candidates are selected. They are intended to filter out the wrong deals and mitigate the chances of postclosing regrets and problems.

Approaches for the Company That's Not for Sale

As discussed earlier in this chapter, there's a definite challenge when the ideal candidate is not currently for sale. In these cases, the owner of the company must be approached subtly by a senior member of the buying team and sold on the idea of selling. Here is how that's generally done.

1. Introduce yourself and give information about your company's business, product literature, financial highlights, and other data. Explain why you identified the company as a candidate. This will let the prospective seller know that you are a credible buyer

and that you have given serious consideration to the idea of acquiring his or her company.

2. Request a meeting in order to discuss how the proposed transaction will be advantageous to both parties.

3. Maintain contact after the meeting, even if the owner insists the company is not for sale. Send periodic newsletters and bulletins regarding the progress of your company, and reaffirm continued interest. Call and visit from time to time. Sometimes it takes years for owners to reach a decision to sell. By maintaining contact, you can develop a relationship with the seller and create an environment of mutual trust and respect.

When, and if, your candidate expresses interest, you will want to act quickly to keep the momentum going. Set up a meeting to learn the seller's objectives and pricing expectations, review the company's operating and financial performance, and identify any concerns or reservations the seller may have. Your goal is to get the information you need to determine a preliminary price and to structure a letter of intent that outlines the key points of the proposed acquisition.

Dealing With the Seller's Management Team

If you are going to want the seller's key managers to stay on and help manage the integrated company, from the outset, you will need to allay their concerns about job security and career potential. Most managers will not believe that you intend to keep them all. It's likely that the best managers will leave if they feel their jobs are in jeopardy. Be prepared to answer the following questions:

"Will I still have a job?"
"Will I continue in my present role?"
"How will my performance be evaluated?"
"Will I be better or worse off as a result of this transaction?"
"What will I be paid?"

Communicating your vision and performance expectations is key to obtaining management's commitment early on. A good way to do this is to have the seller's current management team play a role in developing the postclosing integration and communication plans. Here are other, more tangible ways of demonstrating your long-term commitment to the seller's managers, and thereby relieving any personal career anxieties:

1. Propose salary and wage adjustments, if appropriate, to bring compensation up to your company's or industry levels.
2. Establish an incentive bonus plan tied to realistic, attainable goals.
3. Provide employee contracts to key members of the management team.

Box 3-1. Buyer's Acquisition Process

The buyer's planning and implementation of an acquisition program perspective typically involves the following steps:

1. Develop acquisition objectives.
2. Analyze projected economic and financial gains to be achieved by the acquisition.
3. Assemble an acquisition team (managers, attorneys, accountants, and investment bankers) and begin the search for acquisition candidates.
4. Prepare due diligence analysis of prime candidates.
5. Begin initial negotiations and valuation of the selected target.
6. Select the structure of the transaction.
7. Identify sources of financing for the transaction.
8. Undergo detailed bidding and negotiations.
9. Obtain all shareholder and third-party consents and approvals.
10. Structure the legal documents.
11. Prepare for the closing.
12. Hold the closing.
13. Perform postclosing tasks and responsibilities.
14. Implement the integration of the two entities.

4. Review the seller's benefit plans and assure employees that the transfer will be orderly and fair.

In conclusion, the buyer and its team's primary focus is always on avoiding any surprises, from either a valuation or liability perspective. We all like to learn what we get when are buying something, particularly when there are millions of dollars at stake. Following the steps set forth in this chapter will help uncover surprises, as will the letter of intent and due diligence processes discussed in Chapters 4 and 5.

DIRECTORY OF M&A RESOURCES FOR PROSPECTIVE BUYERS (AND SELLERS)

International Business Brokers Association (IBBA)
11250 Roger Bacon Drive
Suite 8
Reston, VA 20190
(703) 437-4377
www.bizmart.com/ibba
> [The IBBA also publishes the *M&A Source Membership Directory*, which lists hundreds of mergers and acquisitions professionals and intermediaries. For more information, call 703-437-7464, or visit www.masource.org.]

Association for Corporate Growth
1926 Waukegan Road, Suite 100
Glenview, IL 60025
(800) 699-1331
www.acg.org

International Merger and Acquisition Professionals (IMAP)
3232 Cobb Parkway, Suite 437
Atlanta, GA 30339
(770) 319-7797
www.imap.com

American Society of Appraisers (ASA)
555 Herndon Parkway, Suite 125
Herndon, VA 20170
(800) 272-8258
www.appraisers.org

Directory of M&A Intermediaries
c/o The Buyout Directories
40 West 57th Street, 11th Floor
New York, NY 10019
(212) 765-5311

Mergers & Acquisitions: The Dealmaker's Journal
229 South 18th Street
Philadelphia, PA 19103
(215) 790-7000
Attn: Martin Sikora, Editor
  [Founded by M&A expert Stanley Foster Reed in 1965.]

MergerFACTS Monthly
c/o Securities Data Company
Two Gateway Center
Newark, NJ 07102
(201) 645-9608
Attn: Leah Stack
  [Securities Data offers a wide range of research and data sources
  in connection with mergers and acquisitions.]

Mergers and Acquisitions Report
c/o IDD
2 World Trade Center, 18th Floor
New York, NY 10048
(212) 432-0045
  [Weekly newsletter offering news and trends on corporate
  mergers, buyouts, and restructurings.]

World M&A Network
c/o International Executive Reports
717 D Street NW, Suite 300
Washington, D.C. 20004
(202) 628-7767
Attn: John Bailey, Editor
www.worldm_anetwork.com
  [Quarterly publication listing hundreds of companies for sale,
  merger candidates, and corporate buyers.]

There are also a wide variety of websites that facilitate the
buying and selling process, such as those maintained by the Ge-
neva Companies (geneva.com), VR Business Brokers (vrbusiness-
brokers.com), and a buying service at www.bizbuysell.com.

Chapter 4

The Letter of Intent and Other Preliminary Matters

At this stage of the transaction, both the seller and the buyer (and their respective advisors) have developed strategic plans and, it is hoped, have taken the time to understand each other's perspective and competing objectives. The field of available candidates has been narrowed, the preliminary "get to know each other" meetings have taken place, and a tentative selection has been made. After completion of the pre-sale review, the next step involves the preparation and negotiation of an interim agreement that will govern the conduct of the parties up until closing.

Although there are certain valid legal arguments to be made against the execution of any interim document, especially since some courts have interpreted them as legally binding (even if one or more parties did not initially intend to be bound), it has been my experience that a *letter of intent*, which includes a set of binding and nonbinding terms as a roadmap for the transaction, is a necessary step in virtually all mergers and acquisitions. Most parties prefer the organizational framework and psychological comfort of knowing that there is some written document in place before proceeding further and before significant expenses are incurred.

The Letter of Intent

There are many different styles of letters of intent, which vary from law firm to law firm and business lawyer to business lawyer. These styles usually fall into one of three categories: (1) binding; (2) non-

---

Box 4-1. Advantages and Disadvantages of Executing a Letter of Intent

Advantages

- Tests each party's seriousness.
- Morally commits each party to the sale.
- Sets down in writing the areas of agreement. (There may be a long delay before a sales agreement is executed.)
- Highlights the differences and any matters needing further negotiation.
- Discourages the seller from shopping around for a better deal.

Disadvantages

- May be considered a binding agreement. (State whether or not the letter of intent is meant to constitute enforceable agreement.)
- Public announcement of the prospective sale may have to be made, owing to federal securities law, if either company is publicly held.

---

binding; and (3) hybrids. Exhibit 4-1 shows a hybrid style. In general, the type to be selected depends upon the following considerations:

- The type of information to be released publicly concerning the transaction
- The degree to which negotiations have been definitive and the necessary information has been gathered
- The costs to the buyer and seller for proceeding with the transaction prior to making any binding commitment
- The rapidity with which the parties estimate a final agreement can be reached
- The degree of confidence in the good faith of each party and the absence (or presence) of competing parties

In most cases, the hybrid format is the most effective in protecting the interests of both parties and in leveling the playing field for the upcoming negotiations.

Although formally executed by the buyer and the seller, a letter of intent is often considered an agreement *in principle*. As a result, the parties should be very clear as to whether the letter of intent is a binding preliminary contract or merely a memorandum from which a more definitive legal document will be drafted upon completion of due diligence. Regardless of the legal implications involved, however, by executing a letter of intent the parties make a psychological commitment to the transaction and provide a roadmap for expediting more formal negotiations. In addition, a well-drafted letter of intent provides an overview of matters that require further discussion and consideration, such as the exact purchase price. Although a purchase price cannot realistically be established until due diligence has been completed, the seller may hesitate to proceed without a price commitment. Instead of creating a fixed

---

Box 4-2. Common Reasons Why Deals Die at an Early Stage

1. Seller has not prepared adequate financial statements (e.g., going back at least two years and reflective of the company's current condition).
2. Seller is uncooperative during the due diligence process.
3. Buyer discovers a "deal breaker" in the due diligence (e.g., large unknown or hidden actual or contingent liabilities, like an EPA cleanup matter).
4. Seller has "seller's remorse," cold feet, or has not properly thought through its after-tax consideration or compensation.
5. Seller suffers from "don't call my baby ugly" syndrome and becomes defensive when the buyer finds flaws (and then focuses on them in the negotiation) in the operations of the business, the valuation, the loyalty of the customers, the quality of the accounts receivable, the skills of the personnel.
6. There is a strategic shift (or extenuating set of circumstances) affecting the acquisition strategy or criteria of the buyer (e.g., a change in buyer's management team during the due diligence process).
7. Seller is inflexible on price and valuation when buyer discovers problems during due diligence.

price, the letter of intent incorporates a price range that is qualified by a clause or provision that sets forth all of the factors that will influence and affect the calculation of a final fixed price.

Proposed Terms

As you can see from the sample letter of intent in Exhibit 4-1, the first section addresses certain key deal terms, such as price and method of payment. These terms are usually nonbinding so that the parties have an opportunity to conduct thorough due diligence and have room for further negotiation, depending on the specific problems uncovered during the investigative process.

Binding Terms

The sample letter of intent in Exhibit 4-1 also includes certain binding terms that will *not* be subject to further negotiation. These issues that at least one side, and usually both sides, will want to ensure are binding, regardless of whether the deal is consummated. These include:

- *Legal ability of seller to consummate the transaction.* Before wasting too much time or money, the buyer will want to know that the seller has the power and authority to close the deal.

- *Protection of confidential information.* The seller in particular, and in general both parties, will want to ensure that all information provided in the initial presentation, as well as during due diligence, remains confidential.

- *Access to books and records.* The buyer will want to ensure that the seller will fully cooperate in the due diligence process.

- *Break-up or walk-away fees.* The buyer may want to include a clause providing an opportunity to recoup some of its expenses if the seller tries to walk away from the deal, owing either to a change in circumstances or to the desire to accept a more attractive offer from a different buyer. The seller may want a reciprocal clause to protect against its own expenses if the buyer walks away or defaults on a preliminary obligation or condition to closing, such as an inability to raise acquisition capital.

- *No-shop/standstill provisions.* The buyer may want a period of exclusivity during which time it has the confidence of knowing that the seller is not entertaining any other offers. The seller will want to place a limit or "outside date" on this provision in order to allow it to begin entertaining other offers if the buyer is unduly dragging its feet.

- *Good-faith deposit—refundable vs. nonrefundable.* In some cases, the seller will request a deposit or option fee, and the parties must determine to what extent, if at all, this deposit will be refundable and under what conditions. There often are timing problems with this provision, which can be difficult to resolve. For example, the buyer will want the deposit to remain 100 percent refundable if the seller is being uncooperative, or at least until the buyer completes the initial round of due diligence to ensure that there are no major problems discovered that might cause the buyer to walk away from the deal. The seller will want to set a limit on the due diligence and review period at which point the buyer forfeits all or a part of its deposit. The end result is often a progressive downward scale of refundability, as the due diligence and the deal overall reach various checkpoints toward closing. To the extent that the buyer forfeits some or all of the deposit, and the deal never closes, the buyer may want to negotiate an eventual full or partial refund if the seller finds an alternative buyer within a certain period of time, such as 180 days.

- *Impact on employees.* If an announcement is not made directly to the seller's employees, then those employees may get the unmistakable message that their jobs are unimportant, in jeopardy, or both. Supervisory personnel should be briefed first, and all of their questions answered so that they can inform their subordinates. After the closing, it is imperative that the buyer's top management assure the seller's employees of the continuation of beneficial policies and welcome them to a larger and better organization, if that is the intent. Employees who do not feel they are part of a team will have poor morale and even poorer productivity. It is essential that lines of communication be kept open during the acquisition process.

- *Key terms for the definitive documents.* Often, the letter of intent provides that it is subject to the definitive documents, such as the purchase agreement, and that those definitive documents will address certain key matters or include certain key sections, such as covenants, indemnification, representations and warranties, and key conditions for closing.

■ *Conditions to closing.* Both parties will want to articulate conditions for or circumstances under which they will not be bound to proceed with the transaction. For example, if certain contingencies are not met or events subsequently happen after the execution of the letter of intent, the parties will be released from the proceedings. Be sure to articulate these conditions clearly so that there are no surprises down the road.

■ *Conduct of the business prior to closing.* The buyer usually wants some protection that the business he or she sees today will be there tomorrow. Thus, the seller will be obligated to operate its business along the ordinary course of events and ensure that assets will not start disappearing from the premises. Also, the seller will need to be sure equipment is not left in disrepair, new customers are pursued, bonuses are not magically declared, and personal expenses are not paid the night before. These steps all deplete the value of the company prior to closing. These "negative covenants" help protect the buyer against unpleasant surprises at or after closing.

■ *Limitations on publicity and press releases.* Both parties may want to place certain restrictions on the content and timing of any press releases or public announcements of the transaction. In some cases, they may need to follow SEC guidelines.

■ *Expenses/brokers.* The letter of intent should specify, where applicable, which party shall bear responsibility for investment bankers' fees, finder fees, legal expenses, and other costs pertaining to the transaction.

Other Considerations

If either or both of the parties to the transaction are publicly traded companies, the general rule is that once the essential terms of the transaction are agreed to in principle (such as through a letter of intent), there must be a public announcement. The timing and content of this announcement must be weighed carefully by both parties. There should also be an analysis as to how the announcement will affect the price of each company's stock. The announcement should not be too early or it may be viewed by the Securities and Exchange Commission (SEC) as an attempt to influence the price of the stock.

Preparation of the Work Schedule

Following the execution of the letter of intent, the buyer's legal counsel prepares a comprehensive schedule of activities ("work schedule"), which serves as a task checklist and assignment of responsibilities. This schedule should be drawn up well before the due diligence, discussed in Chapter 5, begins. The primary purpose of the schedule is to outline all of the events that must occur and all the documents that must be prepared, both prior to the closing date and beyond. In this regard, the buyer's legal counsel acts as an orchestra leader, assigning primary areas of responsibility to the various members of the acquisition team, as well as to the seller and its counsel. The buyer's counsel must also act as a task master, ensuring that the timetable for work is met. Once all the tasks have been identified and assigned, and a realistic timetable is established for completion, then a firm closing time and date can be preliminarily determined.

Naturally, the exact list of legal documents that must be prepared and the specific tasks to be outlined in the work schedule will vary from transaction to transaction, usually depending on the specific facts and circumstances of the deal. Typically this includes:

- Whether the transaction is a stock or asset purchase
- The form and terms of the purchase price
- The nature of the business being acquired
- The nature and extent of the assets being purchased and/or liabilities being assumed
- The sophistication of the parties and their respective legal counsels

A sample work schedule for a simple asset purchase transaction is set forth on the following pages:

Timetable	Task	Responsible Parties
Six weeks before closing:	a. Letter of intent is signed; board resolutions to authorize negotiations obtained.	Seller and buyer and their counsels
	b. Due diligence request delivered to seller.	Buyer's counsel
Five weeks before closing:	a. Due diligence materials organized and delivered.	Seller's counsel
	b. Due diligence materials reviewed.	Buyer's counsel
	c. Drafts prepared of asset purchase agreement, informational schedules and exhibits to purchase agreement, employment and consulting agreements, etc.	Buyer's counsel
	d. Lien searches on seller's assets ordered to review encumbrances.	Buyer's counsel
	e. Comprehensive review made of seller's financial statements.	Buyer's accounting firm
Three to four weeks before closing:	a. Review, negotiation, and redraft of asset purchase agreement (may continue until the night before closing).	Buyer's and seller's counsel

Timetable	Task	Responsible Parties
Three to four weeks before closing (*continued*):	b. Preparation and negotiation of opinion(s) of counsel.	Buyer's and seller's counsel
	c. Complete review of all initial due diligence materials and follow-on requests, where necessary.	Buyer's counsel
	d. All board and shareholder approvals obtained (as required by state law).	Buyer's and seller's counsel
	e. Checklist prepared and process commenced for all third-party regulatory and contractual approvals (banks, landlords, insurance companies, key customers).	Buyer's and seller's counsel
Two weeks before closing:	a. Mutual review of press releases or other third-party communications regarding the deal (or sooner as required by the SEC).	Buyer's and seller's counsel
	b. Schedule prepared for closing documents (including opinions,	Buyer's counsel

Timetable	Task	Responsible Parties
Two weeks before closing (*continued*):	results of lien searches, compliance certificates).	
One week before and up to closing:	a. Any last-minute negotiations to the asset purchase agreement finalized.	Buyer's and seller's counsel
	b. Closing certificates obtained from state authorities (e.g., good standing certificates, taxes paid and current, charter and amendments).	Seller's counsel
	c. Checklist drawn up to ensure that all conditions to closing have been met or waived (e.g., third-party consents, board resolutions, intellectual property agreements).	Buyer's and seller's counsel
	d. Dry-run closing to identify open issues (highly recommended 2–3 days before closing)	Buyer and seller
	e. Closing (including payment of consideration to seller and exchange of documents of title/ stock certificates	All parties

Timetable	Task	Responsible Parties
One week before and up to closing (*continued*):	to buyer; third-party obligation assumption agreements; delivery of estimated closing accounts; third-party releases).	
	f. Resolution of post-closing matters and conditions.	All parties

In sum, the letter of intent is parallel to the engagement process, where the parties agree to get to know each other better as a precursor to a long-term relationship. The autonomy of each party must be respected, and the confidentiality of the data exchanged during the process must be preserved. The compensation to be paid for the right not to date others (as well as the penalties for violation of the covenant) must be addressed as the parties move closer to marriage. The process of getting to know each other better must be well-organized and carefully orchestrated and not haphazard. This is the process of due diligence, as discussed in Chapter 5.

Exhibit 4-1. SAMPLE LETTER OF INTENT

Ms. Prospective Seller
SellCo, Inc.
[*address*]

Re: *Letter of Intent Between BuyCo, Inc., and SellCo, Inc.*

Dear Ms. Prospective Seller:

This letter ("Letter Agreement") sets forth the terms by which BuyCo, Inc. ("BCI") agrees to purchase _____ shares of a newly authorized class of convertible preferred stock of SellCo, Inc. ("the Company") in accordance with the terms set forth below. BCI and the Company are hereinafter collectively referred to as "the Parties."

Section I of this Letter Agreement summarizes the principal terms proposed in our earlier discussions and is not an agreement binding upon either of the Parties. These principle terms are subject to the execution and delivery by the Parties of a definitive Stock Purchase Agreement, Employment Agreement and other documents related to these transactions.

Section II of this Letter Agreement contains a number of covenants by the Parties, including BCI's funding commitment and the execution and delivery of a Promissory Note in consideration therefor, which shall be legally binding upon the execution of this Letter Agreement by the Parties. The binding terms in Section II below are enforceable against the Parties, regardless of whether or not the aforementioned agreements are executed or the reasons for non-execution.

SECTION I—PROPOSED TERMS

1. Stock Purchase. The Parties will execute a Stock Purchase Agreement, pursuant to which BCI will purchase _____ shares of a newly authorized class of convertible preferred stock of the Company ("the Shares"), for a total purchase price of $_____. The Company's Board will amend its articles of incorporation (and by-laws if necessary) and take any formal corporate action necessary to create and authorize this new class of stock. The Shares will constitute _____% of the total capitalization of the Company on a fully diluted, post-transactional basis. The Shares will have no dividend or liquidation preferences to the Company's common stock ("the Common Stock") and will be identical in every other way to the Common Stock except that each of the Shares will have _____ votes compared to each share of Common Stock (which has one vote). The Shares will be automatically convertible into shares of Common Stock on a one-for-one basis upon the disposition of the Shares by BCI to any party not affiliated with BCI. Simultaneous to the issuance of the Shares to BCI, BCI will give limited revocable proxies to Prospective Seller ("the Seller"), entitling her to vote 50% of the Shares issued to BCI, respectively, on any matters on which the shareholders of the Company are entitled to vote, except mat-

(*continues*)

Exhibit 4-1. (continued)

ters relating to an initial public offering by or a sale of the Company where the holders of a majority of the Common Stock have already approved such an action. The foregoing exception will not apply, however, where all of the holders of Common Stock have unanimously approved an initial public offering by or a sale of the Company, provided, however, that all the holders of any class of stock of the Company will receive the same rights under such a transaction. Additionally, the proxies will be subject at all times to automatic revocation at the time that the proxy holder is no longer employed by the Company.

2. Employment Agreements. Prior to closing, the Company will enter into an individual employment agreement with Seller for _____-year terms at the compensation levels set forth in the Company's business plan previously presented by the Company to BCI. The employment agreement will contain such other terms and conditions as are reasonable and customary in the type of transaction contemplated hereby.

3. Board of Directors of the Company and BCI. Seller will be nominated to serve on the Board of Directors of BCI. BCI will be entitled to designate members to three of the eight seats on the Company's Board of Directors. The Company's Board (and its shareholders, if necessary) will undertake all necessary corporate action to ensure the proper size and make-up of the Company's Board. Any future borrowing by the Company will require approval by the Company's Board, and any such borrowing not related to the Company's ordinary course of business will require the approval of 70% of the Company's Board of Directors.

4. Closing and Documentation. The Parties intend that a closing of the agreements shall occur on or before _____, 19_____, at a time and place that is mutually acceptable to the Parties. BCI or its representatives will prepare and revise the initial and subsequent drafts of the necessary agreements.

SECTION II—BINDING TERMS

In consideration of the costs to be incurred by the Parties in undertaking actions towards the negotiation and consummation of the Stock Purchase Agreement and the related agreements, the Parties hereby agree to the following binding terms ("Binding Terms"):

5. Refundable Deposit. BCI will pay a refundable deposit in the amount of $_____ to the Company at the time of the execution of this Letter Agreement, and will pay an additional $_____ no later than _____ days after the execution of this Letter Agreement. All sums paid hereunder shall be deductible from the purchase price to be paid for the Shares as described in Paragraph 1. In the event that BCI does not complete the purchase of the Shares, the sums payable hereunder shall be deemed an advance and subject to repayment to BCI _____ months from the date of execution of this Letter Agreement in a lump sum with interest at the rate of 1.5% above the highest U.S. prime rate published in *The Wall Street Journal* from the date of execution of this Letter Agreement to the date of repayment. In the event that the

closing is delayed beyond _____, 19_____, BCI will advance additional funds of $_____ on _____, 19_____ and $_____ on _____, 19_____. Each additional advance shall be repaid within six months of the date of the advance at the rate of 1.5% above the highest U.S. prime rate published in *The Wall Street Journal* from the date of advance to the date of repayment. The Company shall execute and deliver a Promissory Note in consideration of the advance of funds hereunder and pursuant to the terms stated above.

6. Right of First Refusal for Additional Capital Contributions. The Company agrees to grant BCI a right of first refusal for any future equity financing (except in the case of an initial public offering). Holders of Common Stock shall have a preemptive right, however, to contribute such proportionate share of any such equity financing in order to maintain their respective interests in the Company. In the event that a valuation cannot be agreed upon by the contributing parties hereunder, an independent appraisal of the Company shall be obtained from a qualified investment banker at the Company's expense.

7. Due Diligence. The directors, officers, shareholders, employees, agents and other representatives (collectively, "the Representatives") of the Company shall (a) grant to BCI and its Representatives full access to the Company's properties, personnel, facilities, books and records, financial and operating data, contracts and other documents; and (b) furnish all such books and records, financial and operating data, contracts and other documents or information as BCI or its Representatives may reasonably request.

8. No Material Changes. The Company agrees that from and after the execution of this Letter Agreement until the earlier of the termination of the Binding Terms in accordance with Paragraph 14 below or the execution and delivery of the agreements described herein, the Company's business and operations will be conducted in the ordinary course and in substantially the same manner as such business and operations have been conducted in the past and the Company will notify BCI of any extraordinary transactions, financing or business involving the Company or its affiliates.

9. No-Shop Provision. The Company agrees that from and after the execution of this Letter Agreement until the termination of the Binding Terms in accordance with Paragraph 14 below, the Company will not initiate or conclude, through its Representatives or otherwise, any negotiations with any corporation, person or other entity regarding the establishment of a line of credit, the sale of substantially all of the assets of or the management of the Company. The Company will immediately notify the other Parties regarding any such contact described above.

10. Lock-Up Provision. The Company agrees that from and after the execution of this Letter Agreement until (a) the consummation of the transactions contemplated in Section I and the execution of definitive agreements thereby, or (b) in the event that definitive agreements are not executed, until the repayment of all amounts advanced hereunder, plus accrued interest, that without the prior written approval of BCI and

(continues)

Exhibit 4-1. (continued)

subject to any anti-dilution provisions imposed hereunder, (x) no shares of any currently issued Common Stock of the Company shall be issued, sold, transferred or assigned to any party; (y) no such shares of Common Stock shall be pledged as security, hypothecated, or in any other way encumbered; and (z) the Company shall issue no additional shares of capital stock of any class, whether now or hereafter authorized.

11. Confidentiality. Prior to Closing, neither Party nor any of their Representatives shall make any public statement or issue any press releases regarding the agreements, the proposed transactions described herein or this Letter Agreement without the prior written consent of the other Party, except as such disclosure may be required by law. If the law requires such disclosure, the disclosing party shall notify the other Party in advance and furnish to the other Party a copy of the proposed disclosure. Notwithstanding the foregoing, the Parties acknowledge that certain disclosures regarding the agreements, the proposed transactions or this Letter Agreement may be required to be made to each Party's Representatives or certain of them, and to any other party whose consent or approval may be required to complete the agreements and the transactions provided for thereunder, and that such disclosures shall not require prior written consent. BCI and its employees, affiliates and associates will (a) treat all information received from the Company confidentially, (b) not disclose such information to third parties without the prior written consent of the Company, except as such disclosure may be required by law, (c) not use such information for any purpose other than the consideration of the matters contemplated by this Letter of Intent, including related due diligence, and (d) return to the Company any such information if this Letter Agreement terminates pursuant to Paragraph 14 below.

12. Expenses; Finder's Fee. The Parties are responsible for and will bear all of their own costs and expenses incurred at any time in connection with the transactions proposed hereunder up to $_____. Any additional or extraordinary expenses above this amount shall be done by BCI; provided, however, the Company shall be responsible for any finder's fees payable in connection with the transactions contemplated hereby.

13. Break-Up Fee. The Company agrees to pay BCI a break-up fee of $_____ in the event that the sale and purchase of the shares contemplated in Section I is not accomplished by _____, 19_____, as a result of the Company's failure or refusal to close pursuant to the terms set forth above and not due to any refusal or delay on the part of BCI to close by that date.

14. Effective Date. The foregoing obligations of the Parties under Section II of this Letter Agreement shall be effective as of the date of execution by the Company, and shall terminate upon the completion of the transactions contemplated in Section I above or, if such transactions are not completed, then at such time as all of the obligations under this Section II have been satisfied, unless otherwise extended by all of the Parties or specifically extended by the terms of the foregoing provisions; provided, however, that such termination shall not relieve the Parties of liability for

the breach of any obligation occurring prior to such termination.

Please indicate your agreement to the Binding Terms set forth in Section II above by executing and returning a copy of this letter to the undersigned no later than close of business on _____, 19_____. Following receipt, we will instruct legal counsel to prepare the agreements contemplated herein. The Binding Terms shall become binding on the Company upon the advance of funds pursuant to Paragraph 5 and the execution of Promissory Note in consideration therefor.

Very truly yours,

/s/ *[Prospective Buyer]*
Prospective Buyer, President
BuyCo, Inc.

ACKNOWLEDGED AND ACCEPTED:

SellCo, Inc.

_____
By: Prospective Seller, President

Dated: _____

Chapter 5

Due Diligence

Following the preparations of both teams, the narrowing of the field, and the execution of the letter of intent, both sides must begin preparing for the due diligence process. This process involves a legal, financial, and strategic review of all of the seller's documents, contractual relationships, operating history, and organizational structure. Due diligence is not just a process, it is also a reality test—a test of whether the factors driving the deal and making it look attractive to the parties are real or illusory. Due diligence is not a quest to find the deal-breakers but a test of the value proposition underlying the transaction to make sure that the inside of the house is as attractive as the outside. Once the foundation has been dissected, it can either be rebuilt around a deal that makes sense or allow the buyer to walk away and prevent the consummation of a deal that doesn't make sense.

The seller's team must organize the documents, and the buyer's team must be prepared to ask all of the right questions, thereby conducting a detailed analysis of the documents provided. To the extent that the deal is structured as a merger, or where the seller will be taking the buyer's stock as all or part of its compensation, the process of due diligence is likely to be two-way, as the parties gather background information on each other.

The due diligence work is usually divided between two working teams: (1) financial and strategic, and to be conducted by the buyer's accountants and management team; and (2) legal, to be conducted by the buyer's counsel. Throughout the process, both teams compare notes on open issues and potential risks and problems. The legal due diligence focuses on the potential legal issues and problems that may serve as impediments to the transaction, as well as sheds light on how the transaction documents should be structured. The business due diligence focuses on the strategic and financial issues in the transaction, such as confirmation of the past financial performance of the seller; integration of the human and financial resources of the two companies; confirmation of the operating, production, and distribution synergies and economies of scale to be achieved by the acquisition; and the gathering of information necessary for financing the transaction.

Overall, the due diligence process, when done properly, can be tedious, frustrating, time-consuming, and expensive. Yet it is a necessary prerequisite to a well-planned acquisition, and it can be quite informative and revealing in its analysis of the target company and its measures of the costs and risks associated with the transaction. Buyers should expect sellers to become defensive, evasive, and impatient during the due diligence phase of the transaction. Most business managers really don't enjoy having their business policies and decisions under the microscope, especially for an extended period of time and by a party searching for skeletons in the closet. Eventually, the seller is likely to give an ultimatum to the prospective buyer: "Finish the due diligence soon or the deal is off." When negotiations have reached this point, it is best to end the examination process some time soon thereafter. Buyers should resist the temptation to conduct a hasty "once over," either to save costs or to appease the seller. Yet at the same time, they should avoid "due diligence overkill," keeping in mind that due diligence is *not* a perfect process and should not be a tedious fishing expedition.

Information will slip through the cracks, which is precisely why broad representations, warranties, liability holdbacks, and indemnification provisions should be structured into the final purchase agreement. These provisions protect the buyer, while the seller negotiates for carve-outs (e.g., a minimum "basket" of liabilities before the buyer may seek reimbursement for undisclosed or unexpected liabilities), exceptions, and limitations to liability that provide postclosing protections. The nature and scope of these provisions are likely to be hotly contested in the negotiations. Remember that the key objective of due diligence is not just to "confirm that the deal makes sense" (e.g., confirm the factual assumptions and preliminary valuations underlying the terms by which the buyer negotiates the transaction), but rather to determine whether the transaction should proceed at all. The buyer must recognize at all times that there may be a need to "jump ship" if the risks or potential liabilities in the transaction greatly exceed what is anticipated.

Effective due diligence is both an art and a science. The art is the style and experience to know which questions to ask and how and when to ask them. It's the ability to create an atmosphere of both trust and fear in the seller, which encourages full and complete disclosure. In this sense, the due diligence team is on a risk discovery and assessment mission, looking for potential problems and liabilities (the search), and finding ways to resolve these problems prior to closing and/or to ensure that risks are allocated fairly and openly after the closing.

The science of due diligence is in the preparation of comprehensive and customized checklists of the specific questions to be presented to the seller, in maintaining a methodical system for organizing and analyzing the documents and data provided by the seller, and in quantitatively assessing the risks raised by those problems discovered in the process. One of the key areas is detection of the seller's obligations, particularly those that the buyer will be expected or required to assume after closing. The due diligence process is designed first to detect the *existence* of the obligation and second to identify any *defaults or problems* in connection with these obligations that will affect the buyer after closing.

The best way for the buyer to ensure that virtually no stone remains unturned is with effective due diligence preparation and planning. The legal due diligence checklist in the following section is intended to guide the company's management team while it works closely with counsel to gather and review all legal documents that may be relevant to the structure and pricing of the transaction; to assess the potential legal risks and liabilities to the buyer following the closing; and to identify all of the consents and approvals, such as an existing contract that can't be assigned without consent, which must be obtained from third parties and government agencies.

The checklist should be a guideline, not a crutch. The buyer's management team must take the lead in developing questions that pertain to the nature of the seller's business. These questions will set the pace for the level of detail and adequacy of the review. For example, I recently worked on a deal that involved the purchase of a hockey league in the Midwest. It was easy to prepare the standard due diligence list and draw up questions regarding corporate structure and history, the status of the stadium leases, team tax returns and to question the steps that had been taken to protect the team trademarks. The more difficult task was developing a customized list. In my role as legal counsel, I asked my client the question, "If you were buying a sports league, what would you need to review?"

The key point here is that every type of business has its own issues and problems, and a standard set of questions will rarely be sufficient. The list for this client included player and coaching contracts, stadium signage and promotional leases, league-wide and local-team sponsorship contracts, the immigration status of each player, team and player performance statistics, the status of contracts with each team's star players, scouting reports and drafting procedures, ticket sales (including walkup, advance, season, group tickets, and coupons) for each team and game, promotional agreements with equipment suppliers and game-day merchandise, food and beverage concession contracts, the status of each team's franchise agreement, commitments made to cities for future teams, and unique per team advertising rates for dasher boards (the signs for advertising that surround the rink).

When done properly, due diligence is performed in multiple stages. First, all the basic data are gathered and specific topics are identified. Follow-up questions and additional data gathering can be performed in subsequent rounds of due diligence; they must be custom-tailored to the target's core business industry trends and unique challenges.

Legal Due Diligence

In analyzing the company for sale, the buyer's team carefully reviews and analyzes the following legal documents and records, where applicable.

I. *Corporate Matters*
  A. Corporate records of the seller.
    1. Certificate of incorporation and all amendments.

Box 5-1. Common Mistakes Made by the Buyer During the Due Diligence Investigation

1. *Mismatch between the documents provided by the seller and the skills of the buyer's review team.* It may be the case that the seller has particularly complex financial statements or highly technical reports that must be truly understood by the buyer's due diligence team. Make sure there is a capability fit.
2. *Poor communication and misunderstandings.* The communications should be open and clear between the buyer and the seller. The process must be well orchestrated.
3. *Lack of planning and focus in the preparation of the due diligence questionnaires and in the interviews with the seller's team.* The focus must be on asking the *right* questions, not just a lot of questions. Sellers will resent wasteful "fishing expeditions" when the buyer's team is unfocused.
4. *Inadequate time devoted to tax and financial matters.* The buyer's (and seller's) CFO and CPA must play an integral part in the due diligence process in order to gather data on past financial performance and tax reporting, unusual financial events, or disturbing trends or inefficiencies.
5. *Lack of reasonable accommodations and support for the buyer's due diligence team.* The buyer must insist that its team be treated like welcome guests, not enemies from the IRS! Many times buyer's counsel is sent to a dark room in the corner of the building to inspect documents without coffee, windows, or phones.
6. *Ignoring the real story behind the numbers.* The buyer and its team must dig deep into the financial data and test (and retest) the value proposition as to whether the deal truly makes sense. They must ask themselves, "Does the real value truly justify the price?" The economics of the deal may not hold water once a realistic look at cost allocation, inventory turnover, and capacity utilization is taken into account.

 2. Bylaws as amended.
 3. Minute books, including resolutions and minutes of all director and shareholder meetings.
 4. Current shareholders list (certified by the corporate

secretary), annual reports to shareholders, and stock transfer books.

5. List of all states, countries, and other jurisdictions in which the seller transacts business or is qualified to do business.

6. Applications or other filings in each state listed in 5, above, for qualification as foreign corporation and evidence of qualification.

7. Locations of business offices (including overseas).

B. Agreements among the seller's shareholders.

C. All contracts restricting the sale or transfer of shares of the company, such as buy/sell agreements, subscription agreements, offeree questionnaires, or contractual rights of first refusal; all agreements for the right to purchase shares, such as stock options or warrants; and any pledge agreements by an individual shareholder involving the seller's shares.

II. *Financial Matters*

A. List of and copies of management and similar reports or memoranda relating to the material aspects of the business operations or products.

B. Letters of counsel in response to auditors' requests for the preceding five years.

C. Reports of independent accountants to the board of directors for the preceding five years.

D. Revolving credit and term loan agreements, indentures, and other debt instruments, including, without limitation, all documents relating to shareholder loans.

E. Correspondence with principal lenders to the seller.

F. Personal guarantees of seller's indebtedness by its shareholders or other parties.

G. Agreements by the seller where it has served as a guarantor for the obligations of third parties.

H. Federal, state, and local tax returns and correspondence with federal, state, and local tax officials.

I. Any private placement memorandum (assuming, of course, that the seller is not a Securities Act of 1934 "Reporting Company") prepared and used by the seller (as well as any document used in lieu of a PPM, such as an investment profile or a business plan).

J. Financial statements, which should be prepared in accordance with Generally Accepted Accounting Principles (GAAP), for the past five years of the seller, including:
   1. Annual (audited) balance sheets.
   2. Monthly (or other available) balance sheets.
   3. Annual (audited) and monthly (or other available) earnings statements.
   4. Annual (audited) and monthly (or other available) statements of shareholders' equity and changes in financial position.
   5. Any recently prepared projections for the seller.
   6. Notes and material assumptions for all statements described in J 1–5, above.

K. Any information or documentation relating to tax assessments, deficiency notices, investigations, audits, or settlement proposals.

L. Informal schedule of key management compensation (listing information for at least the ten most highly compensated management employees or consultants).

M. Financial aspects of overseas operations (where applicable), including status of foreign legislations, regulatory restrictions, intellectual property protection, exchange controls, method for repatriating profits, foreign manufacturing, government controls, import/export licensing, and tariffs.

N. Projected budgets, accounts receivable reports (including detailed aging report, turnover, bad debt experience, and reserves), and related information.

III. *Management and Employment Matters*

A. All employment agreements.

B. Agreements relating to consulting, management, financial advisory services, and other professional engagements.

C. Copies of all union contracts and collective bargaining agreements.

D. Equal Employment Opportunity Commission (EEOC) and any state equivalent compliance files.

E. Occupational Safety and Health Administration (OSHA) files, including safety records and workers' compensation claims.

F. Employee benefit plans (and copies of literature issued to employees describing such plans), including the following:

1. Pension and retirement plans, including union pension or retirement plans.
2. Annual reports for pension plans, if any.
3. Profit sharing plans.
4. Stock option plans, including information concerning all options, stock appreciation rights, and other stock-related benefits granted by the company.
5. Medical and dental plans.
6. Insurance plans and policies, including the following:
   a. Errors and omissions policies.
   b. Directors' and officers' liability insurance policies.
7. Any Employee Stock Ownership Plan (ESOP) and trust agreement.
8. Severance pay plans or programs.
9. All other benefit or incentive plans or arrangements not covered by the foregoing, including welfare benefit plans.

G. All current contracts or agreements with or pertaining to the seller and to which directors, officers, or shareholders of the seller are parties, and any documents relating to any other transactions between the seller and any director, officer, or shareholder, including receivables from or payables to directors, officers, or shareholders.

H. All policy and procedures manuals of the seller concerning personnel; hiring and promotional practices; compliance with the Family Leave Act, etc.; drug and alcohol abuse policies; AIDS policies; sexual harassment policies; vacation and holiday policies; expense reimbursement policies; and so on.

I. The name, address, phone number, and personnel file of any officer or key employee who has left the seller within the past three years.

IV. *Tangible and Intangible Assets of the Seller*

A. List of all commitments for rented or leased real and personal property, including location and address, description, terms, options, termination and renewal rights, policies regarding ownership of improvements, and annual costs.

B. List of all real property owned, including location and address, description of general character, easements, rights of way, encumbrances, zoning restrictions, surveys, mineral rights, title insurance, pending and threatened condemnation, hazardous waste pollution.

C. List of all tangible assets.

D. List of all liens on all real properties and material tangible assets.

E. Mortgages, deeds, title insurance policies, leases, and other agreements relating to the properties of the seller.

F. Real estate tax bills for the real estate of the seller.

G. List of patents, patents pending, trademarks, trade names, copyrights, registered and proprietary Internet addresses, franchises, licenses, and all other intangible assets, including registration numbers, expiration dates, employee invention agreements and policies, actual or threatened infringement actions, licensing agreements, and copies of all correspondence relating to this intellectual property.

H. Copies of any survey, appraisal, engineering, or other reports as to the properties of the seller.

I. List of assets that may be on a consignment basis (or that may be the property of a given customer, such as machine dyes, molds).

V. Material Contracts and Obligations of the Seller

A. Material purchase, supply, and sale agreements currently outstanding or projected to come to fruition within twelve months, including the following:
1. List of all contracts relating to the purchase of products, equipment, fixtures, tools, dies, supplies, industrial supplies, or other materials having a price under any such contract in excess of $5,000.
2. List of all unperformed sales contracts.

B. Documents incidental to any planned expansion of the seller's facilities.

C. Consignment agreements.

D. Research agreements.

E. Franchise, licensing, distribution, and agency agreements.

F. Joint venture agreements.

G. Agreements for the payment of receipt of license fees or royalties and royalty-free licenses.

H. Documentation relating to all property, liability, and casualty insurance policies owned by the seller, including for each policy a summary description of:
1. Coverage.
2. Policy type and number.
3. Insurer/carrier and broker.
4. Premium.
5. Expiration date.
6. Deductible.
7. Any material changes in any of the foregoing since the inception of the seller.
8. Claims made under such policies.

I. Agreements restricting the seller's right to compete in any business.

J. Agreements for the seller's current purchase of services, including, without limitation, consulting and management.

K. Contracts for the purchase, sale, or removal of electricity, gas, water, telephone, sewage, power, or any other utility service.

L. List of waste dumps, disposal, treatment, and storage sites.

M. Agreements with any railroad, trucking, or any other transportation company or courier service.

N. Letters of credit.

O. Copies of any special benefits under contracts or government programs that might be in jeopardy as a result of the proposed transaction (e.g., small-business or minority set-asides, intrafamily transactions or favored pricing, internal leases or allocations).

P. Copies of licenses, permits, and governmental approvals applied for or issued to the seller that are required in order to operate the businesses of the seller, such as zoning, energy requirements (natural gas, fuel, oil, electricity, etc.), operating permits, or health and safety certificates.

Note: This section is critical and will be a key area in the negotiations, as discussed in Chapter 10. Therefore, it is suggested that the buyer's team request copies of *all* of the seller's material contracts and obligations and then organize them as follows:

Schedule of All Contracts and Obligations of Seller That Are to Be Assumed by Buyer After Closing*	*Status of Each Contract or Obligation*	*To What Extent Third-Party Consents Will Be Required for Assignment or Assumption of These Contracts or Obligations*
	Sample Responses:	*Sample Responses:*
A. _____	Current	Not required
B. _____	Received notice of default on _____, 19____; cured on _____, 19____	Consent to assignment requested _____, 19____ and obtained _____, 19____

Schedule of All Contracts and Obligations of Seller That Are to Be Assumed by Buyer After Closing*	Status of Each Contract or Obligation	To What Extent Third-Party Consents Will Be Required for Assignment or Assumption of These Contracts or Obligations
C. _____	Notice of default received; Default not yet cured!	Consent to assumption required but not yet requested

*For example, contracts that have a remaining term in excess of six months.

VI. Litigation and Claims—Actual and Contingent

A. Opinion letter from each lawyer or law firm prosecuting or defending significant litigation to which the seller is a party describing such litigation.

B. List of material litigation or claims for more than $5,000 against the seller asserted or threatened with respect to the quality of the products or services sold to customers, warranty claims, disgruntled employees, product liability, government actions, tort claims, and breaches of contract, including pending or threatened claims.

C. List of settlement agreements, releases, decrees, orders, or arbitration awards affecting the seller.

D. Description of labor relations history.

E. Documentation regarding correspondence or proceedings with federal, state or local regulatory agencies.

Note: Be sure to obtain specific representations and warranties from the seller and its advisors regarding any knowledge pertaining to potential or contingent claims or litigation!

VII. Miscellaneous

A. Press releases (past two years).

B. Resumes of all key management team members.

C. Press clippings (past two years).

D. Financial analyst reports, industry, surveys, etc.

E. Text of speeches by the seller's management team, especially if reprinted and distributed to the industry or the media.

F. Schedule of all outside advisors, consultants, etc. used by the seller over the past five years (domestic and international).

G. Schedule of long-term investments made by the seller.

H. Standard forms (purchase orders, sales orders, service agreements, etc.).

The buyer's acquisition team and its legal counsel gather data to answer the following ten legal questions during the legal phase of due diligence:

1. What legal steps will need to be taken to effectuate the transaction (e.g., director and stockholder approval, share transfer restrictions, restrictive covenants in loan documentation)? Has the appropriate corporate authority been obtained to proceed with the agreement? What key (e.g., FCC, DOJ) third-party consents (e.g., lenders, venture capitalists, landlords, key customers) are required?

2. What antitrust problems, if any, are raised by the transaction? Will filing with the FTC be necessary under the pre-merger notification provisions of the Hart-Scott-Rodino Act?

3. Will the transaction be exempt from registration under applicable federal and state securities loans under the "sale of business" doctrine?

4. What are the significant legal problems or issues now affecting the seller or that are likely to affect the seller in the foreseeable future? What potential adverse tax consequences to the buyer, seller, and their respective shareholders may be triggered by the transaction?

5. What are the potential postclosing risks and obligations of the buyer? To what extent should the seller be held liable for such potential liability? What steps, if any, can be taken to reduce these

potential risks or liabilities? What will it cost to implement these steps?

6. What are the impediments to the assignability of key tangible and intangible assets of the seller company that are desired by the buyer, such as real estate, intellectual property, favorable contracts or leases, human resources, or plant and equipment?

7. What are the obligations and responsibilities of the buyer and seller under applicable environmental and hazardous waste laws, such as the Comprehensive Environmental Response Compensation and Liability Act (CERCLA)?

8. What are the obligations and responsibilities of the buyer and seller to the creditors of the seller (e.g., bulk transfer laws under Article 6 of the applicable state's commercial code)?

9. What are the obligations and responsibilities of the buyer and seller under applicable federal and state labor and employment laws (e.g., will the buyer be subject to successor liability under federal labor laws and as a result be obligated to recognize the presence of organized labor and therefore be obligated to negotiate existing collective bargaining agreements)?

10. To what extent will employment, consulting, confidentiality, or noncompetition agreements need to be created or modified in connection with the proposed transaction?

Business and Strategic Due Diligence

At the same time as legal counsel is performing its legal investigation of the seller's company, the buyer assembles a management team to conduct business and strategic due diligence. The level and extent of this general business and strategic due diligence will vary, depending on the experience of the buyer in the seller's industry and its familiarity with the seller company. For example, a financial buyer entering into a new industry, and with no prior experience with the seller, should conduct an exhaustive due diligence—not only on the seller's company but also on any relevant trends within the industry that might directly or indirectly affect the deal. In contrast, a management buyout by a group of industry veterans who have been with the seller over an extended period of time will probably need to conduct only a minimum amount of business or strategic due diligence; in this case, the focus will be on legal due diligence and assessment and assumption of risk.

In conducting the due diligence from a business perspective, the buyer's team is likely to encounter a wide variety of financial problems and risk areas when analyzing the seller. These typically include an undervaluation of inventory, overdue tax liabilities, inadequate management information systems, related-party transactions (especially in small, closely held companies), an unhealthy reliance on a few key customers or suppliers, aging accounts receivable, unrecorded liabilities (e.g., warranty claims, vacation pay, claims, sales returns, and allowances), or an immediate need for significant expenditures as a result of obsolete equipment, inventory, or computer systems. Each of these problems poses different risks and costs for the acquiring company, and these risks must be weighed against the benefits to be gained from the transaction.

For the buyer just getting to know the seller's industry, the following two basic questions should be asked:

1. How would you define the market or markets in which the seller operates? What steps will you take to expedite your learning curve of trends within these markets? What third-party advisors are qualified to advise you on key trends affecting this industry?

2. What are the factors that determine success or failure within this industry? How does the seller stack up? What are the image and reputation of the seller within the industry? Does it have a niche? Is the seller's market share increasing or decreasing? Why? What steps can be taken to enhance or reverse these trends?

The following checklist is designed to provide the acquisition team with a starting point for analysis of the seller. It helps to level the playing field in the negotiations, since the seller usually starts with greater expertise regarding its industry and its business. Here are some examples (this checklist is not intended to be exhaustive) of the topic areas and specific questions that should be addressed in due diligence on a given seller:

The Seller's Management Team

1. Has the seller's organization chart been carefully reviewed? How are management functions and responsibilities delegated and implemented? Are job descriptions and employment manuals, among other things, current and available?

2. What is the general assessment of employee morale at the lower echelons of the corporate ladder? To what extent are these rank-and-file employees critical to the seller's long-term health?

3. What are the future growth prospects of the principal labor markets from which the seller depends on attracting key employees? Are employees with the necessary skills generally available? How are the seller's employees recruited, evaluated, trained, and rewarded?

4. What are the background and experience of the seller's key management team? What is the reputation of this management team within the industry? Has there been high turnover among the seller's top management? Why or why not? Who are the seller's key professional advisors and outside consultants?

5. What are the basic management styles, practices, and strategies of the seller's current team? What are the strengths and weaknesses of the management team? To what extent has the seller's current management engaged in long-term strategic planning, developed internal controls, or structured management and marketing information systems?

Operations of the Seller

1. What are the seller's production and distribution methods? To what extent are these methods protected either by contract or proprietary rights? Have copies of the seller's brochures and reports describing the seller and its products and services been obtained?

2. To what extent is the seller operating at its maximum capacity? Why? What are the significant risk factors (e.g., dependence on raw materials or key suppliers or customers) affecting the seller's production capacity and ability to expand? What are the significant costs of producing the seller's goods and services? To what extent are the production and output of the seller dependent on economic

cycles or seasonal factors? *Note:* Obtain a breakdown of major sales by specific product and specific customer categories in order to fully assess the seller's financial performance, dependence on key customers, or product line susceptibility to risk.

3. Are the seller's plant, equipment, supplies, and machinery in good working order? When will these assets need to be replaced? What are the annual maintenance and service costs for these key assets? At what levels are the seller's inventories? What are the breakeven production efficiency and inventory turnover rates for the seller company and how do these compare with industry norms?

4. Does the seller maintain production plans, schedules, and reports? Have copies been obtained and analyzed by the buyer? What are the seller's manufacturing and production obligations pursuant to long-term contracts or other arrangements? What long-term (postclosing) obligations or commitments have been made on the purchase of raw materials or other supplies or resources?

5. What is the status of the seller's inventories (e.g., amount and balance in raw materials and finished goods in relation to production cycles and sales requirements)? What is the condition of the inventory? To what extent is it obsolete? *Note:* Be sure to get a breakdown and an analysis of all expenses (e.g., amounts, trends, categories) in order to assess the profitability of the seller's business, as well as to determine where postclosing expense savings can be obtained or economies of scale achieved.

Sales and Marketing Strategies of the Seller

1. What are the seller's primary and secondary markets? What is the size of these markets and what is the seller's market share within each market? What strategies are in place to expand this market share? What are the current trends affecting either the growth or the shrinkage of these particular markets? How are these markets segmented and reached by the seller?

2. Who are the seller's direct and indirect competitors? What are the respective strengths and weaknesses of each competitor? In what principle ways do companies within the seller's industry compete (e.g., price, quality, or service)? For each material compet-

itor, the buyer should seek to obtain data on the competitor's products and services, geographic location, channel of distribution, market share, financial health, pricing, policies, and reputation within the industry.

Box 5-2. Common Due Diligence Problems and Exposure Areas

There are virtually an infinite number of potential problems and exposure areas for the buyer, which may be uncovered in the review and analysis of the seller's documents and operations. The specific issues and problems will vary based on the size of the seller, and nature of its business, and the number of years that the seller (or its predecessors) have been in business.

1. "Clouds" in the title to critical tangible (real estate, equipment, inventory) and intangible (patents, trademarks) assets. Be sure the seller has clear title to these assets and that they are conveyed without claims, liens, and encumbrances.
2. A wide variety of employment or labor law issues or liabilities that may be lurking just below the surface, which will not be uncovered unless the right questions are asked. Questions designed to uncover wage and hour law violations, discrimination claims, OSHA compliance, or even liability for unfunded persons under the Multi-Employer Pension Plan Act should be developed. If the seller has recently made a substantial workforce reduction (or if you as the buyer are planning postclosing layoffs), then the requirements of the Worker Adjustment and Refraining Notification Act (WARN) must have been met. The requirements of WARN include minimum notice requirements of sixty days prior to wide-scale terminations.
3. The possibility of environmental liability under CERCLA or related environmental regulations.
4. Unresolved existing or potential litigation. These cases should be reviewed carefully by counsel.
5. A seller's attempt to "dress up" the financial statements prior to sale, often to hide inventory problems, research and development expenditures, excessive overhead and administrative costs, uncollected or uncollectible accounts receivable, unnecessary or inappropriate personal expenses, unrecorded liabilities, and tax contingencies.

3. Who are the seller's typical customers? What demographic data have been assembled and analyzed? What are the customers' purchasing capabilities and patterns? Where are these customers principally located? What political, economic, social, or technological trends or changes are likely to affect the demographic makeup of the seller's customer base over the next three to five years? What are the key factors that influence the demand for the seller's goods and services?

4. What are the seller's primary and secondary distribution channels? What contracts are in place in relation to these channels? How could these channels or contracts be modified or improved? How will these channels overlap or conflict with the existing distribution channels of the buyer?

5. What sales, advertising, public relations, and promotional campaigns and programs are currently in place at the seller's company? To what extent have these programs been effectively monitored and evaluated?

Financial Management of the Seller

1. Based on the financial statements and reports collected in connection with the legal due diligence, what key sales, income, and earnings trends have been identified? What effect will the proposed transaction have on these aspects of the seller's financial performance? What are the various costs incurred in connection with bringing the seller's products and services to the marketplace? In what ways can these costs be reduced or eliminated?

2. What are the seller's billing and collection procedures? How current are the seller's accounts receivables? What steps have been (or can be) taken to expedite the collection procedures and systems? How credible is the seller's existing accounting and financial control system?

3. What is the seller's capital structure? What are the key financial liabilities and debt obligations of the seller? How do the seller's leverage ratios compare to industry norms? What are the seller's monthly debt-service payments? How strong is the seller's relationship with creditors, lenders, and investors?

A way for the buyer to ensure that the seller has been forth-right in disclosing all material obligations and liabilities (whether actual or contingent) is to prepare an affidavit. An affidavit like the one in Exhibit 5-1 (see next page) provides additional protection against misrepresentation or material omissions by the seller, its lawyers, and its auditors. The affidavit can be customized to a particular transaction and include the specific concerns that may arise during the transaction and afterwards.

Conclusion

Due diligence must be a cooperative and patient process between the buyer's and seller's teams. Any attempts to hide or manipulate key data will only lead to problems down the road. Material mis-representations or omissions can (and often do) lead to postclosing litigation, which is expensive and time-consuming for both parties. Another mistake in due diligence often made by the seller is to forget the human element. I have worked on deals where the law-yers were sent into a dark room in the corner of the building, with-out any support or even coffee; on other deals, we were treated like royalty, with full access to support staff, computers, telephones, food, and beverages. It is only human, as buyer's counsel, to be a bit more cooperative in the negotiations when the seller's team is supportive and allows counsel to do his job.

Exhibit 5-1. Affidavit Regarding Liabilities

State of _____ ⎞
                          ⎬ ss.:
County of _____ ⎠

Prospective Seller, being of lawful age and being first duly sworn upon her oath, states:

1. I am the sole shareholder of the S Corporation which trades under the name "SellerCo," and I have full right to sell its assets as described in the Bill of Sale dated _____, 19_____. Those assets are free and clear of all security interests, liabilities, obligations, and encumbrances of any sort.

2. There are no creditors of SellerCo, or me, or persons known to me who are asserting claims against me for the assets being sold, which in any way affect the transfer to Prospective Buyer of the trade name SellerCo, its goodwill, and its assets, including the equipment as set forth in the Bill of Sale dated _____, 19_____. I agree to pay all gross receipt and sales taxes and all employment taxes of any sort due through closing. I am current in regard to these taxes and all other taxes, and there are no pending disputes as to any of my taxes or the taxes of SellerCo.

3. There are no judgments against SellerCo or me in any federal or state court in the United States of America. There are also no replevins, attachments, executions, or other writs or processes issued against SellerCo or me. I have never sought protection under any bankruptcy law nor has any petition in bankruptcy been filed against me. There are no pending administrative or regulatory proceedings, arbitrations, or mediations involving SellerCo or me, and I do not know and have no reasonable ground to know of any proposed ones or any basis for any such actions.

4. There are no known outstanding claims by any employees of SellerCo or me, and I expressly recognize that no claims of, by, or on behalf of any employees arising prior to closing are being transferred to Prospective Buyer.

5. There are no and have been no unions that have been or are involved in any business that I own, and particularly, SellerCo. Furthermore, there currently is no union organizational activity underway in any business that I own, and particularly, SellerCo.

6. There are and have been no multi-employer pension plans or other pension or profit-sharing plans involved in any business that I own, and particularly, SellerCo.

7. I have always conducted SellerCo according to applicable laws and regulations.

8. From the time when the purchase agreement was executed through closing, I have conducted the business called SellerCo only in the usual and customary manner. I have entered into no new contracts and have assumed no new obligations during that time period.

9. I shall remain fully liable for payment of all bills, accounts payable, or other claims against SellerCo or me created prior to closing. None of them are being transferred to Prospective Buyer.

10. I hereby warrant and represent to Prospective Buyer that all statements in paragraphs one through nine of this Affidavit are true and correct.

11. a. I agree to indemnify and hold harmless Prospective Buyer in respect to any and all claims, losses, damages, liabilities, and expenses, including, without limitation, settlement costs and any legal, accounting, and other expenses for investigating or defending any actions or threatened actions, reasonably incurred by Prospective Buyer in connection with:

i. Any claims or liabilities made against Prospective Buyer because of any act or failure to act of myself arising prior to closing in regard to SellerCo; or

ii. Any breach of warranty or misrepresentation involved in my sale of SellerCo to Prospective Buyer.

b. As to claims or liabilities against Prospective Buyer arising prior to closing in connection with SellerCo, or any claims arising at anytime in regard to any profit-sharing or pension plan started prior to closing involving SellerCo, or any breach of warranty or other material misrepresentation made by me, I agree that Prospective Buyer has the option to pay the claim or liability and deduct the amount of it from any money owed to me, after giving me reasonable notice of the claim and reasonable opportunity to resolve it. This right of setoff expressly applies to any damages Prospective Buyer suffers as a result of any breach of any warranty I have given to Prospective Buyer. Prospective Buyer's right of setoff against any money owed me shall not be deemed his exclusive remedy for any breach by me of any representations, warranties, or agreements involved in the sale of SellerCo to him, all of which shall survive the closing and any setoff made by Prospective Buyer.

12. I agree to execute any further documents to complete this sale.

Prospective Seller

Subscribed and Sworn to before me this _____ day of _____, 19_____.

Notary Public

My Commission Expires:

_____, 19_____

Note: Proper use of this affidavit depends on the purchase agreement used.

Chapter 6

An Overview of Regulatory Considerations

There are a wide variety of regulatory considerations in a merger or acquisition, usually falling into one of two categories: (1) *general* regulatory issues, which affect all types of transactions; and (2) *industry-specific* regulatory issues, which affect only certain types of transactions in certain industries. The general regulatory considerations include issues such as antitrust, environmental, securities, and employee benefits matters, which are discussed below. Some industry-specific regulatory issues involve federal and state regulators, who may exercise rights of approval over those transactions that involve a change in ownership or control or that may have an anticompetitive effect on a given industry. Any transaction in the broadcasting, health care, insurance, public utilities, transportation, telecommunications, financial services, and even the defense contracting industries should be analyzed carefully by legal counsel to determine what level of governmental approval may be necessary to close the transaction. Regulatory agencies such as the Federal Communications Commission (FCC) and the Pension Benefit Guaranty Corporation (PBGC) have broad powers to determine whether the proposed franchiser will be in the best interests of the consuming general public or, in the case of the PBGC, of the employees and retirees of a given seller.

In addition to the federal laws described above, there are a wide variety of state laws that should be carefully considered by the parties. These involve state "anti-takeover" statutes, which may place certain restrictions on how and when a hostile takeover may be launched and the laws affecting bulk transfers that appear in

Article 6 of the Uniform Commercial Code of each state. These bulk transfer laws are designed to protect the seller's creditors by ensuring that they receive proper notice in advance of any proposed transfer of a significant portion of the seller's assets (e.g., outside the ordinary course of business).

In certain regulated industries, government approvals are needed to effectuate the transfer of government-granted licenses, permits, or franchises. These may range from the local liquor board's approving the transfer of a liquor license in a small restaurant acquisition to FCC approval for the transfer of a multibillion dollar communication license, such as in one recently approved transaction between Bell Atlantic and NYNEX. Bell Atlantic had agreed to purchase NYNEX for $25.6 billion, subject to, among other things, the Department of Justice's approval from an antitrust perspective and the FCC's approval of the transfer of NYNEX's communications licenses to Bell Atlantic. In the Bell Atlantic-NYNEX deal, the Justice Department approved the deal as *not* having an anticompetitive effect from a consumer perspective *well before* the FCC finished its analysis of the proposed deal on the industry and subsequently gave its approval to the transfer of the licenses. Let's take a look at one critical area of regulatory consideration—the federal and state environmental laws.

Environmental Laws

Prior to the 1970s, sellers normally had little or no legal obligation to disclose information concerning the presence or use of potentially dangerous substances on their premises, nor to report the release of such substances into the environment to the potential buyers of their businesses. What obligations did exist were imposed by state or local governments regulating public nuisances or engaging in emergency planning.

In the 1970s and early 1980s, however, as the federal government passed new laws concerning health and the environment, it created new obligations to report on the presence, use, and release of dangerous substances under certain circumstances. The Clean Water Act, the Toxic Substances Control Act (TSCA), the Resource Conservation and Recovery Act (RCRA), and the Comprehensive Environmental Response, Compensation, and Liability Act (CERCLA or Superfund) all contain provisions requiring notification of government authorities in the event of chemical spills and other emergencies. In addition, TSCA and regulations promulgated pursuant to the Occupational Safety and Health Act (OSHA) require chemical manufacturers and others to compile and report information on the presence and use of hazardous chemicals on their premises. Each of these laws has a unique, limited scope—for example, covering some substances but not others—and the result is a patchwork of different but sometimes overlapping reporting requirements.

In 1986, Congress enacted the Emergency Planning and Community Right-To-Know Act (EPCRA), found in Title III of the Superfund Amendments and Reauthorization Act of 1986 (SARA). Subchapter I of EPCRA creates a framework for state and local emergency response planning, and in that setting imposes on companies two types of reporting obligations: (1) to provide information about the presence of extremely hazardous substances so as to facilitate emergency planning; and (2) to immediately notify authorities in the event of a release. Subchapter II of EPCRA requires companies to file additional reports on the presence of hazardous substances at their facilities, and also to report on the periodic release of toxic chemicals. Unlike the other federal laws, much of the information that is reported under EPCRA is available to the public.

Not only did EPCRA not completely supersede other federal reporting provisions, it also did not preempt state law. Several states have passed "right-to-know" or other reporting laws, the most aggressive being California's Proposition 65. However, because EPCRA's reporting requirements are fairly extensive, and because they are implemented largely by the states themselves, in general the importance of state reporting laws has been diminished.

Any company that makes, uses, or otherwise is involved with potentially dangerous substances may be required under federal law to notify authorities of a release of a dangerous substance into the environment. In many cases, a company's obligations will be satisfied by reporting under EPCRA and CERCLA, but in some cases the Clean Water Act, TSCA, or RCRA might be applicable.

This complex web of federal and state environmental laws creates legal issues for both buyer and seller in a proposed merger or acquisition, usually surrounding the problem of allocating liability for environmental problems under federal laws such as RCRA and CERCLA and state laws that address hazardous waste discharge and disposal. The seller should obtain an environmental audit from a qualified consulting firm prior to the active recruitment of potential buyers in order to assess its own liability under the federal and state laws, even though it is very likely that the buyer will want to do its own independent review and assessment of the seller's sites, insurance policies, and possible areas of exposure.

The potential liability under federal and state environmental laws is typically one of the broadest areas requested by buyers in the areas of representations and warranties, such as described below.

Assume for the balance of this chapter that Growth Co. Corp (GCC) has identified Target Co., Inc. (TCI), a closely held manufacturer, as an acquisition candidate.

> *Hazardous Material.* Other than as set forth on Schedule 11, (1) no amount of substance that has been designated under any law, rule, regulation, treaty, or statute promulgated by any governmental entity to be radioactive, toxic, hazardous, or otherwise a danger to health or the environment, including, without limitation, PBS, asbestos, petroleum, urea-formaldehyde, and all substances listed as hazardous substances pursuant to the Comprehensive Environmental Response, Compensation, and Liability Act of 1980, as amended, or defined as hazardous waste pursuant to the United States Resource Conservation and Recovery Act of 1976, as amended, and the regulations promulgated pursuant to said laws (a "hazardous material"); and (2) no underground or above-ground storage tanks containing hazardous material, are present in, on, or under any property, including the land and the improvements, ground water and surface water thereof, that either seller has at any time owned, operated, occupied, or leased. Schedule 00 identifies all underground and above-ground storage tanks, and the capacity, age,

and contents of such tanks, located on property owned, operated, occupied, or leased by TCI.

Hazardous Materials Activities. TCI has not transported, stored, used, manufactured, disposed of, released or sold, or exposed its employees or others to hazardous materials or any product containing a hazardous material (collectively, "seller's hazardous materials activities") in violation of any rule, regulation, treaty, or statute promulgated by any governmental entity.

Environmental Permits and Compliance. TCI currently holds all environmental approvals, permits, licenses, clearances, and consents (the "environmental permits") necessary for the conduct of seller's hazardous material activities and the business of TCI as such activities and business are currently being conducted. All environmental permits are in full force and effect. TCI is in compliance in all material respects with all terms and conditions of the environmental permits and is in compliance in all material respects with all other limitations, restrictions, conditions, standards, prohibitions, requirements, obligations, schedules, and timetables contained in the laws, rules, regulations, treaties, or statutes of all governmental entities relating to pollution or protection of the environment or contained in any regulation, code, plan, order, decree, judgment, notice, or demand letter issued, entered, promulgated, or approved thereunder. To the best of TCI's knowledge after due inquiry, there are no circumstances that may prevent or interfere with such compliance in the future. Schedule 11 includes a listing and description of all environmental permits currently held by TCI. For purposes of this agreement, knowledge of TCI includes the knowledge of the persons who, as of the closing date, were its officers, directors, and stockholders (including the trustees, officers, partners, and directors of stockholders that are not natural persons).

Environmental Liabilities. No action, proceeding, revocation proceeding, amendment procedure, writ, injunction, or claim is pending, or to the best knowledge of TCI, threatened against TCI or the business of TCI concerning any environmental permit, hazardous material or the seller's hazardous materials activity or pursuant to the laws, rules, regulations, treaties, or statutes of any governmental entity relating to pollution or protection of the environment. There are no past or present actions, activities, circumstances, conditions, events, or incidents that could involve either TCI (or any person or entity whose liability TCI has retained or assumed, either by contract or operation of law) in any environmental litigation, or impose upon TCI (or any person or entity whose liability either seller has retained or assumed, either by contract or operation of law) any material environmental liability including, without limitation, common law tort liability.

Federal Securities Laws

Mergers and acquisitions among small and growing privately held companies do not generally raise many issues or trigger filing requirements under the federal securities laws. Where one or both of the companies is publicly traded, and hence has registered its securities under the Securities Act of 1933, however, a host of reporting obligations are triggered, as follows:

- *10-Q and 10-K reports.* A discussion of the proposed transaction may need to be included in either or both of the acquiring company's and the target's quarterly and annual filing with the SEC. The acquiring company will usually be obligated to include the information in its scheduled SEC reports if the acquisition is deemed to be significant. A *significant* acquisition is typically defined as one where the target's assets or pre-tax income exceeds 10 percent of the acquiring company's assets or pre-tax income.

- *Registration statements.* If the acquiring company plans to issue new securities as part of the consideration to be given to shareholders of the target, then a registration statement should be filed with the SEC.

- *Proxy information.* If the proposed transaction must be approved by the shareholders of either the acquiring company or the target, then the SEC's special proxy rules and regulations must be carefully followed.

- *Tender offers.* When a buyer of a publicly held company elects to make a tender offer directly to the shareholders of the target, rather than negotiating through management, then the filing requirements in the Williams Act apply. This includes the filing of the SEC's Schedule 13D whenever the purchaser becomes the beneficial owner of more than 5 percent of the target's equity securities, which gives notice to the SEC, as well as the target company's officers and directors, of the buyer's intentions.

Federal Antitrust Laws

The central concern of federal government policy is with those acquisitions that increase the danger that companies in a particular market will have *market power*—the power to raise prices or limit production free from the constraints of competition. This danger increases when a market is dominated by a few large companies with substantial market shares. Federal antitrust laws prohibit any acquisition of stock or assets that tends to substantially lessen competition. Acquisition of the stock or assets of a competitor (horizontal acquisition) is most likely to raise antitrust concerns, especially if it occurs in a market that is already dominated by a few companies. An acquisition involving companies in a supplier-purchaser relationship (vertical acquisition), or companies that may be potential competitors, also could raise antitrust concerns, but in general vertical transactions are of less concern from an antitrust perspective.

The Department of Justice (DOJ) and the Federal Trade Commission (FTC) may seek to stop acquisitions that they consider likely to significantly lessen competition. Furthermore, the Hart-Scott-Rodino Act requires that the FTC and DOJ be given advance notification of all mergers and acquisitions involving companies and transactions above a specified minimum size, the details of which are discussed below.

Horizontal Acquisitions

The principal responsibility for enforcing antitrust laws with respect to business combinations continues to be exercised by the DOJ and the FTC. Both have issued merger guidelines to help businesses assess the likelihood that a particular business transaction may be challenged under the federal antitrust laws. These federal agencies consider a number of factors in assessing the legality of an acquisition involving companies competing in the same market, or horizontal acquisition. However, the respective market shares of the combining companies, as well as the degree of market concentration (i.e., the number of companies competing in the market), continue to be the starting point for every analysis. Combinations of market shares not considered significant in less concentrated markets may raise serious problems when market concentration is high.

Because of the importance of market share and market concentration, the definition of *market* is critical. Among other things, the guidelines take into account reasonable product substitutes, production facilities that may be easily converted to making a particular product, and foreign imports. Once the market is defined, the federal agencies seek to measure the significance of particular combinations in terms of the extent to which they increase market concentration. While various tests are available, the agencies use a measure known as the Herfindahl-Hirschmann Index (HHI). The competitive significance of particular acquisitions is then examined in terms of both the level of the market's HHI following the acquisition and the extent to which the acquisition increases the HHI.

In addition to market shares and market concentration, federal enforcement agencies consider ease of entry into the market. Where barriers to entry—such as patents, proprietary technology, know-how, and high "sunk" capital investments—do not exist and other companies could enter the market with relative ease and within a relatively short time if prices rose to noncompetitive levels, an acquisition may not be considered anticompetitive, even though it produces a high postacquisition HHI. Other factors given varying degrees of weight under the guidelines are changing market conditions that might undermine the significance of market shares, such as rapidly changing technology; the financial condition of a company, which might affect its future competitive significance; characteristics of a product, which make price collusion difficult or unlikely; and efficiencies resulting from the combination.

Vertical Acquisitions

Acquisitions involving suppliers and their customers could raise questions under the antitrust laws. Courts, as well as earlier federal enforcement policies, have expressed concerns that such acquisitions could foreclose access by competitors to necessary suppliers or distribution outlets. The foreclosure effect has been measured by reference to the share of the market held by the supplier company and share of purchases of the product made by the customer company. Current federal enforcement policy is somewhat skeptical about claims that vertical acquisitions produce anticompetitive effects. It limits the inquiry primarily to the question of whether such an acquisition is likely to create an unacceptable barrier to entry. This would make it necessary for any new entrant to enter at both the supplier and purchaser levels in circumstances where it is difficult to do so, and thus insulates concentrated markets at either level from new competition.

Hart-Scott-Rodino Act

The premerger notification requirements of the Hart-Scott-Rodino Act (H-S-R) can have an important impact on an acquisition timetable. Under H-S-R, and the regulations issued under it by the FTC, acquisitions involving companies and transactions of a certain size cannot be consummated until certain information is supplied to the federal enforcement agencies and until specified waiting periods elapse.

The premerger notification program was established to avoid some of the difficulties that antitrust enforcement agencies encounter when they challenge anticompetitive acquisitions after they occur. The enforcement agencies have found that it is often impossible to restore competition fully because circumstances have changed once a merger has taken place; furthermore, any attempt to reestablish competition is usually costly for the parties and the public. But prior review under the premerger notification program has created an opportunity to avoid these problems by enabling the enforcement agencies to challenge anticompetitive acquisitions before they are consummated.

The Hart-Scott-Rodino Antitrust Improvements Act requires that persons contemplating proposed business transactions of a certain size report their intentions to the antitrust enforcement agencies before consummating the transactions. If a proposed transaction is reportable, then both the acquiring business and the business being acquired must submit information about their respective business operations. They report to the Federal Trade Commission and to the Department of Justice, and wait a specified period of time before consummating the proposed transaction. During that waiting period, the enforcement agencies review the antitrust implications of the proposed transaction. Whether a particular transaction is reportable is determined by application of the act and the premerger notification rules.

As a general matter, the act and the rules require both parties to file notifications under the premerger notification program if all of the following conditions are met:

1. One person has sales or assets of at least $100 million.
2. The other person has sales or assets of at least $10 million.
3. As a result of the transaction, the acquiring person will hold a total amount of stock or assets of the acquired person valued at more than $15 million, or, in some stock transactions, even if the stock held is valued at $15 million or less, if it represents 50 percent or more of the outstanding stock of the issuer being acquired and the issuer is of a certain size.

The first step in determining reportability is to determine who the "acquiring person" is and who the "acquired person" is. These technical terms are defined in the rules and must be applied carefully. In an assets acquisition, the acquiring person is the buyer and the acquired person is the seller. In an acquisition of the seller's voting stock, the acquiring person is the voting securities to be acquired. Thus, in many acquisitions of voting stock, the sellers are shareholders of the seller, yet the applicable regulations impose a reporting obligation on that acquired person despite the fact that, in such voting securities transactions, the acquired person may have no direct dealings with the acquiring person. The rules require that a person proposing to acquire voting securities directly from shareholders, rather than from the issuer itself, serve notice on the issuer of those shares to make sure that the acquired person knows about its reporting obligation.

Once you have determined who the acquiring and acquired persons are, you must determine whether the size of each person meets the act's minimum size criteria. This test generally measures a company's size based on the company's last regularly prepared balance sheet. The size of a person includes not only the business entity that is making the acquisition or the business entity whose assets are being acquired or which issued the voting securities being acquired but also the parent of that business entity and any other entities that the parent controls.

The next step is to determine what voting securities, assets, or combination of voting securities and assets are being transferred in the proposed transaction. Then you must determine the value of the voting securities and/or assets or the percentage of voting securities that will be held as a result of the transaction. Calculating what will be held as a transaction is complicated and requires application of several complex rules. The securities held as a result of the transaction include those that will be transferred in the proposed transaction and certain assets of the acquired person that the acquiring person has purchased within certain time limits.

In some instances, a transaction may not be reportable, even if the size of person and the size of transaction tests have been satisfied. The act and rules set forth a number of exemptions, describing particular transactions or classes of transactions that need not be reported despite the fact that the threshold criteria have been satisfied. For example, the acquisition of voting securities of an issuer is exempt if the acquiring person owns 50 percent or more of that issuer prior to the proposed acquisition. The acquisition of voting securities of a foreign issuer may be exempt if the foreign company did no business in the United States and holds no assets in the United States.

Once it has been determined that a particular transaction is reportable, each party must submit its notification to the Premerger Notification Office of the Federal Trade Commission and to the director of operations of the Antitrust Division of the Department of Justice. In addition, each acquiring person must pay a $20,000 filing fee to the Premerger Notification Office for each transaction that it reports.

Labor and Employment Law

There are a wide variety of federal and state labor and employment law issues that must be addressed by the buyer as part of its overall due diligence on the seller's business. This includes a comprehensive review of the seller's employment practices and manuals to ensure historical compliance with the laws governing such areas as employment discrimination, immigration law compliance (e.g., that all I-9 forms have been properly completed), sexual harassment, age discrimination (e.g., compliance with the Older Workers Benefit Protection Act, which should also be carefully examined before any older workers are dismissed on a postclosing basis, and the Age Discrimination in Employment Act), drug testing, and wage and hour laws, as well as its compliance with the Family and Medical Leave Act (FMLA), the Americans with Disabilities Act (ADA), and the Worker Adjustment and Retraining Notification Act (WARN), which governs plant closings and retraining requirements.

Where applicable, it will be necessary to review collective bargaining agreements, with a particular focus on the buyer's duty to bargain with the union as a successor employer.

The buyer must also be aware of the wide range of potential Employee Retirement Income Security Act (ERISA) liability issues that it may confront if the employee benefit plans established by the seller are not properly structured or funded. The buyer must also develop a strategy for the integration of the seller's plans into its own, which may involve transferring plan assets in whole or in part, or the utilization of surplus plan assets. There are many different types of employee benefit plans, including qualified or *defined contribution plans*, which include profit-sharing plans, thrift plans, many purchase pension plans, stock bonus plans, and employee stock-ownership plans, as well as defined benefit plans and executive compensation plans.

Employee benefit plans can represent one of the largest potential liabilities of a business enterprise. The employee benefit plans involving the greatest potential liabilities are defined benefit pension plans, postretirement medical and life insurance benefits, and deferred compensation programs for executives. In many cases, the liability for an employee benefit plan shown on the financial statements may not adequately portray the true liability. A buyer is well advised to have an actuary compute the value of the employee benefits—both retirement plans and retiree medical plans—in order to be sure that the balance sheet provision is adequate.

The treatment of employee benefit plans in corporate acquisition, merger, and disposition situations has taken on greater and greater importance since the passage of ERISA in 1974. The importance of employee benefits plans grows with each new development in the benefits arena, including the Multiemployer Pension Plan Amendments Act of 1980 (MEPPAA), Retirement Equity Act of 1984 (REA), the Single Employer Pension Plan Amendments Act of 1986 (SEPPAA), the Tax Reform Act of 1986 (TRA 86), the Omnibus Budget Reconciliation Acts (OBRA) of 1987, 1989, 1990, and 1993, the Unemployment Compensation Act of 1992 (UCA), the Retirement Protection Act of 1994 (RPA), and Statements 87, 88, and 106 of the Financial Accounting Board (F.A.S. 87, 88, and 106). Employee benefit plans can be the source of major off-balance sheet liabilities that have to be dealt with by the parties to the transactions. In some cases, employee benefit plans will dictate whether the transaction is structured as a sale of stock or a sale of assets. In a few cases, employee benefit plans may result in the deal's falling through. In still other situations, employee benefit plans can be utilized to accomplish the transaction.

Generally, employee benefit plan considerations do not dictate the structure of a corporate acquisition. There are, however, a few exceptions. A seller that faces a potentially large withdrawal liability with respect to a multiemployer pension plan may insist on a sale of stock rather than a sale of assets. On the other hand, a buyer that does not want to inherit a burdensome plan from the seller may insist on a sale of assets. In the case of a sale of assets, the buyer is not generally obligated to assume the plans of the seller. This decision depends on the nature of the plans, their funding status, their past history of compliance with the laws, and the nature of the adjustment in the purchase price with respect to the plans.

The biggest difficulty related to employee benefit liabilities in a merger or acquisition is in determining the appropriate adjustment of the purchase price. Since the liabilities involve actuarial calculations, they are totally dependent upon assumptions as to interest rates, life expectancies, and other factors that will impact on the ultimate liability under the plan. The parties have to agree to these assumptions or to a method of arriving at these assumptions in order to calculate whether the plan is overfunded or underfunded. One such method for a pension plan would be to value the plan's liabilities using the PBGC's assumptions for terminated pension plans. While the PBGC rates are not the most favorable rates in the marketplace, they do represent the rates that will be utilized to determine whether the plan is underfunded in the event the plan should terminate. Another approach is to value the liability on an ongoing basis rather than on a termination basis.

The most important aspect of the acquisition process for the buyer is to start its investigation of the employee benefit plans early and to do as thorough a job as possible. The buyer should be especially concerned with identifying items that are hidden liabilities. Obviously, a buyer should review the plans and their summary plan descriptions. To the extent that there are actuarial reports for the plans, the buyer should examine copies of them, and make sure they reflect any recent plan amendments that increase benefits. Collective bargaining agreements should also be checked to determine if they call for benefit increases that were not contemplated in the most recent actuarial report. If a union negotiated plan bases benefits on the compensation of the employees, the buyer should check to see if large wage increases have been negotiated. Finally, the buyer should review any postretirement medical or life insurance benefits provided by the seller.

The purchase agreement should contain detailed and explicit provisions with respect to handling employee benefits. If responsibility for a benefit program has to be divided between the buyer and the seller, it is easier to have a fair division of the responsibility if it is negotiated in advance. Buyers rarely get significant concessions from sellers after the deal has closed. A set of sample representations and warranties to cover these issues is set forth below.

Definitions.

1. "Benefit arrangement" means any benefit arrangement, obligation, custom, or practice, whether or not legally enforceable, to provide benefits, other than salary, as compensation for services rendered, to present or former directors, employees, agents, or independent contractors, other than any obligation, arrangement, custom, or practice that is an employee benefit plan, including, without limitation, employment agreements, severance agreements, executive compensation arrangements, incentive programs or arrangements, sick leave, vacation pay, severance pay policies, plant closing benefits, salary continuation for disability, consulting, or other compensation arrangements, workers' compensation, retirement, deferred compensation, bonus, stock option or purchase, hospitalization, medical insurance, life insurance, tuition reimbursement or scholarship programs, employee discount arrangements, employee advances or loans, any plans subject to Section 125 of the Code, and any plans providing benefits or payments in the event of a change of control, change in ownership, or sale of a substantial portion (including all or substantially all) of the assets of any business or portion thereof, in each case with respect to any present or former employees, directors, or agents.

2. "Seller benefit arrangement" means any benefit arrangement sponsored or maintained by TCI or with respect to which TCI has or may have any liability (whether actual, contingent, with respect to any of its assets or otherwise), in each case with respect to any present or former directors, employees, or agents of TCI as of the closing date.

3. "Seller plan" means any employee benefit plan for which TCI is the "plan sponsor" (as defined in Sec-

tion 3(16)(B) of ERISA) or any employee benefit plan maintained by TCI or to which TCI is obligated to make payments, in each case with respect to any present or former employees of TCI as of the closing date.

4. "Employee benefit plan" has the meaning given in Section3(3) of ERISA.

5. "ERISA" means the Employee Retirement Income Security Act of 1974, as amended, and all regulations and rules issued thereunder, or any successor law.

6. "ERISA affiliate" means any person that, together with TCI, would be or was at any time treated as a single employer under Section 414 of the Code or Section 4001 of ERISA and any general partnership of which either seller is or has been a general partner.

7. "Multiemployer plan" means any employee benefit plan described in Section 3(37) of ERISA.

8. "Qualified plan" means any employee benefit plan that meets, purports to meet, or is intended to meet the requirements of Section 401(a) of the code.

9. "Welfare plan" means any employee benefit plan described in Section 3(1) of ERISA.

Schedule 11. This schedule contains a complete and accurate list of all seller plans and seller benefit arrangements. With respect, as applicable to seller plans and seller benefit arrangements, true, correct, and complete copies of all the following documents have been delivered to GCC and its counsel:

1. All documents constituting the seller plans and seller benefit arrangements, including but not limited to, insurance policies, service agreements, and formal and informal amendments thereto, employment agreements, consulting arrangements, and commission arrangements.

2. The most recent Forms 5500 or 5500 C/R and any financial statements attached thereto and those for the prior three years.

3. The most recent summary plan description for the seller plans.

Contributions to a Qualified or Multiemployer Plan. Neither TCI nor any ERISA affiliate maintains, contributes to, or is obligated to contribute to, nor has either TCI or any ERISA affiliate ever maintained, contributed to, or been obligated to contribute to, any qualified plan or multiemployer plan. Neither TCI nor any ERISA affiliate has any liability (whether actual or conditional, with respect to its assets or otherwise) to or resulting from any employee benefit plan sponsored or maintained by a person that is not a seller or any ERISA affiliate. Neither seller nor any ERISA affiliate has or has ever had any obligations under any collective bargaining agreement. The seller plans and seller benefit arrangements are not presently under audit or examination (nor has notice been received of a potential audit or examination) by the IRS, the Department of Labor, or any other governmental agency or entity. All group health plans of each seller and their ERISA affiliates have been operated in compliance with the requirements of Sections 4980B (and its predecessors) and 5000 of the code, and each seller has provided, or will have provided before the closing date, to individuals entitled thereto all required notices and coverage under Section 4980B with respect to any qualifying event (as defined therein) occurring before or on the closing date.

It is critical to understand how certain regulatory considerations affect the structure and even the viability of a given merger or acquisition. The growth and consideration in a variety of regulated industries such as telecommunications, financial services, and electrical/gas utilities have made an understanding of these regulations a precursor to getting a deal to the closing table. Work with your transactional counsel to make sure that attorneys well-versed in obtaining these necessary regulatory approvals are part of the acquisition team.

Chapter 7

Structuring the Deal

There are virtually an infinite number of ways in which a corporate merger or acquisition may be structured. Indeed, there are probably as many potential deal structures as there are qualified and creative transactional lawyers and investment bankers. The goal is not to create the most complex structure but rather one that fairly reflects the goals and objectives of the buyer and seller. Naturally, not all of the objectives of each party will be met each time; there will almost always be a degree of negotiation and compromise. But virtually all structures, even the most complex, are at their roots basically either mergers or acquisitions, including the purchase or consolidation of either stock or assets. The creativity often comes in structuring the deal to achieve a particular tax advantage or strategic result or to accommodate a multistep or multiparty transaction. This chapter looks at some of the typical structures, as well as a few alternative types of transaction, such as spinoffs, shell mergers, and employee stock ownership plans.

Some Core Questions

At the heart of each transaction are the following key issues that will affect the structure of the deal:

- How will tangible and intangible assets be transferred to the purchaser from the seller?
- At what price and according to what terms?
- What issues discovered during due diligence may affect the structure of the deal?

- What liabilities will be assumed by the buyer? How will risks be allocated among the parties?
- What are the tax implications to the buyer and seller?
- What are the long-term objectives of the buyer?
- What role will the seller have in the management and growth of the underlying business after closing?
- To what extent will third-party consents or governmental filings or approvals be necessary?
- What arrangements will be made for the seller's key management team, whose members may not necessarily be among the selling owners of the company?
- Does the buyer currently have access to all of the compensation to be paid to the seller or will some of these funds need to be raised from debt or equity markets?

There are also a wide variety of corporate, tax, and securities law issues that help decide the structure of a given transaction. These issues must be carefully considered from a legal and accounting perspective, however at the heart of each structural alternative are the following basic questions:

- Will the buyer be acquiring stock or assets of the target company?
- In what form will the compensation from the buyer to the seller be made (e.g., cash, notes, securities)?
- Will the purchase price be fixed, contingent, or payable over time on an installment basis?
- What are the tax consequences of the proposed structure for the acquisition? (See Chapter 6.)

Stock vs. Asset Purchases

Perhaps the most fundamental issue in structuring the acquisition of a target company is whether the transaction will take the form of an asset or a stock purchase. Each form has its respective advantages and disadvantages, depending on the facts and circumstances surrounding the transaction. The buyer and seller should consider the following factors in determining the ultimate form of the transaction.

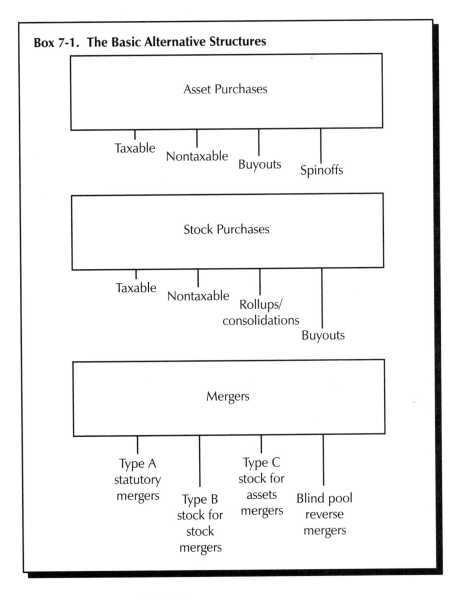

Box 7-1. The Basic Alternative Structures

STOCK PURCHASES

The Buyer's Perspective—Advantages

1. Tax attributes carry over to buyer (e.g., net operating loss and credit carryforwards).

2. Avoids many of the restrictions imposed on sales of assets in loan agreements and potential sales tax.

3. Preserves the right of the buyer to use the seller's name, licenses, and permits.

4. No changes in the corporation's liability, unemployment, or workers' compensation insurance ratings.

5. Nontransferable rights or assets (e.g., license, franchise, patent) can usually be retained by the buyer.

6. Continuity of the corporate identity, contracts, and structure.

The Seller's Perspectives—Advantages

1. Taxes are only on the sale of stock.

2. All obligations (i.e., disclosed, not disclosed, unknown, and contingent) and nontransferable rights can be transferred to the buyer.

3. Gain or loss is usually capital in nature.

4. If stock held by individuals is IRC Section 1244 stock and is sold at a loss, the loss is generally treated as ordinary.

5. May permit seller to report gains from the sale of stock on an installment basis.

6. Does not leave the seller with the problem of disposing assets that are not bought by the purchaser.

The Buyer's Perspective—Disadvantages

1. There is less flexibility to cherry-pick key assets of the seller.

2. The buyer may be liable for unknown, undisclosed, or contingent liabilities (unless adequately protected in the purchase agreement).

3. No step-up in basis (i.e., seller's basis is carried over to the buyer at historical tax basis).

4. Normally does not terminate existing labor union collective bargaining agreements and generally results in the continuation of employee benefit plans.

5. Dissenting shareholders have a right of appraisal for the value of their shares, with the right to be paid the appraised value, or else remain minority shareholders.

The Seller's Perspective—Disadvantages

1. Offer and sale of the company's securities may need to be registered under certain circumstances.

2. Seller cannot pick and choose assets to be retained.

3. May not use the corporation's net operating loss and credit carryforwards to offset gain on sale.

4. Loss on sale of stock may not be recognized by corporate shareholder who included the company in his consolidated income tax return.

ASSET PURCHASES

The Buyer's Perspective—Advantages

1. The buyer can be selective as to which assets of the target company will be purchased.

2. The buyer is generally not liable for the seller's liabilities unless specifically assumed under the contract.

3. Stepup in basis of assets acquired is equal to the purchase price, allowing higher depreciation and amortization deductions.

4. Buyers are generally free of any undisclosed or contingent liabilities.

5. Normally results in termination of labor union collective bargaining agreements; employee benefit plans may be maintained or terminated.

6. Buyers may elect new accounting methods.

The Seller's Perspective—Advantages

1. Sellers maintain corporate existence.

2. Ownership of nontransferable assets or rights (e.g., licenses, franchises, patents) are usually retained.

3. Corporate name and goodwill can generally be maintained.

4. Corporation's tax attributes (e.g., net operating loss and credit carryforwards) are retained.

The Buyer's Perspective—Disadvantages

1. No carry over of the seller corporation's tax attributes (e.g., net operating loss and credit carryforwards).

2. If it is a bargain purchase, there's a step down in the basis of assets.

3. Nontransferable rights or assets (e.g., license, franchise, patent) cannot be transferred to buyers.

4. Transaction more complex and costly in terms of transferring specific assets or liabilities (i.e., title to each asset transferred and new title recorded); state sales tax may apply.

5. Lender's consent may be required to assume liabilities.

6. Loss of the corporation's liability, unemployment, or workers' compensation insurance ratings.

The Seller's Perspective—Disadvantages

1. Double taxation if the corporation also liquidates.

2. Generates various kinds of gain or loss to the seller based on the classification of each asset as capital or ordinary.

3. Transaction more complex and costly in terms of transferring specific assets or liabilities (i.e., title to each asset transferred and new title recorded); state sales tax may apply.

4. Bill of sale must be comprehensive, with exhibits attached in order to ensure that no key assets are overlooked and as a result not transferred to the buyer.

5. A variety of third-party consents will typically be required to transfer key tangible and intangible assets to the buyer.

6. Seller will be responsible for liquidation of the remaining corporate "shell" and for distributing the proceeds of the assets sale to its shareholders, which may result in a double taxation unless a Section 338 election is made.

7. Asset acquisition requires compliance with applicable state bulk sales statutes, as well as state and local sales and transfer taxes.

Tax Issues Affecting the Structure of the Transaction

In a given merger or acquisition, there are a wide variety of tax issues that must be considered and understood as part of the negotiation and structuring of the transaction. These issues affect the valuation and pricing, as well as the structure, of the deal and may be a condition precedent to closing. This section provides an overview of the basic tax issues to be addressed in a merger or acquisition; however, it will be limited to a summary because the tax laws are very complex and constantly changing. You should discuss these issues with the certified public accountant (CPA) who serves as a part of the acquisition team.

Tax Strategies

Mergers and acquisitions may be completely tax free, partially tax free, or entirely taxable to the seller. Each party and its advisors will have its own, often differing views on how the transaction should be structured from a tax perspective, depending on the nontax strategic objectives of both parties and their respective tax and financial positions. In some cases, the tax consequences will be the primary driving force in the transaction; in other cases, the tax issues are secondary or even a nonissue. In addition to the taxable aspects of the transaction, there will be a wide variety of other tax issues to be considered, such as the tax basis of the assets acquired, the impact of the imputed interest rules on the transaction, and the tax aspects of any deferred consideration and/or incentive compensation to the seller.

The general tax-related goals of the seller usually include:

- *Deferring the taxation* of the gain realized on the sale of the business to a future date, such as if the seller acquires the buyer's securities, which may appreciate in value, but the seller need not generally pay taxes on these gains until these securities are sold.

- Classifying the income that is recognized as *capital gain* rather than as ordinary income. The changes to the tax laws in 1997 provide preferential treatment for capital gains.

▪ Ensuring that *cash is available* to pay for taxes as they become due and avoiding the double tax at both corporate and shareholder levels.

Again, the strategic objectives must be balanced against the tax consequences. If the seller has an immediate need for liquidity or has no desire to receive the buyer's securities (the seller may not accept the buyer's postclosing vision and plans for the combined entities), then it will be difficult to achieve nontaxable status.

Over the years, the changes to the federal tax laws have chipped away at a buyer's motivations for having a transaction characterized as tax free. The buyer's ability to carry over favorable tax attributes of the seller has been diminished, such that the buyer's use of its own securities as consideration to pay the seller often have to do more with preservation of cash than with applicable tax laws.

If the transaction is taxable, then the stepped-up basis will be increased to equal to the fair market value of the consideration paid to the seller. If the transaction is nontaxable, the buyer is able to carry over the seller's tax basis to its own financial statements. If the buyer would prefer to carry these assets on the balance sheet at the stepped-up tax basis (such as if the buyer is paying much more than the seller's tax basis), or if the buyer would prefer not to issue securities to the seller to prevent dilution of ownership, then the buyer should opt for a taxable transaction. The buyer should be ready for the seller to raise its price to meet the additional costs of the taxes in negotiating the final terms of the deal.

Most corporate acquisitions will be deemed to be taxable transactions if structured as a purchase of either stock or assets in exchange for cash, promissory notes, or other forms of consideration. Nontaxable transactions usually fall into the category of mergers, in that they involve an exchange of the target company's stock or assets for the purchaser's equity securities or of a subsidiary created by the purchaser, coupled with some direct or indirect continuing relationship between the buyer and the seller and their respective shareholders. These nontaxable transactions must fall within one of the several reorganization categories contained in IRS Code Section 368.

Box 7-2. Taxable vs. Nontaxable Deals

Taxable	*Nontaxable*
• Purchase of stock for cash, promissory notes, or other nonequity consideration • Purchase of assets for cash, promissory notes, or other nonequity consideration	• Exchange of the buyer's stock for the seller's stock • An exchange of the buyer's stock for all or substantially all of the seller's assets
Note: Taxable transactions generally anticipate that the seller will have little or no continuing equity participation in the acquired company.	*Note:* Nontaxable transactions generally anticipate a continuing, direct, or indirect equity participation in the acquired company by the seller or its shareholders.

Tax-Free Reorganizations

The three principal forms of tax-free reorganizations under the Internal Revenue Code are the Type A Statutory Merger, the Type B Stock-for-Stock Merger, and the Type C Stock-for-Assets Merger. If the parties choose to structure the transaction as a tax-free reorganization, then the requirements set forth below must be followed.

- *"A" reorganization.* A Type A reorganization is a statutory merger or consolidation under state law. No express limitations are imposed on the type of consideration that can be used in the transaction or on the disposition of assets prior to the merger. This is a very flexible acquisition device that permits shareholders to receive property, including cash, in addition to stock of the acquiring corporation.
- *"B" reorganization.* A Type B reorganization is an acquisition by one corporation, in exchange solely for all or part of its voting stock or that of its controlling company. If, immediately after the acquisition, the acquiring corporation has control (at least 80 percent of the total combined with power of all classes of stock and at

least 80 percent of the total number of shares of all other classes of stock) of such other corporation, whether or not the acquiring corporation had control immediately before the acquisition. Counsel to the buyer, however, must be particularly sensitive to any cash payments, such as a finder's fee or the payment of appraisal rights to dissenting shareholders.

- *"C" reorganization.* A Type C reorganization is an acquisition by one corporation, in exchange solely for all or part of its voting stock (or that of its parent) and of substantially all of the properties of another corporation. The transferor corporation must distribute the stock, securities, and other properties it receives from the acquiring corporation, as well as any retained assets, as part of the plan of reorganization.

The tax aspects of the proposed transaction are among the most important issues to be addressed by the acquisition team. These laws are complex and are constantly changing. Therefore, knowledgeable advisors should be carefully consulted.

Accounting Issues Affecting the Structure of the Transaction

The accounting advisors of the buyer and seller must determine which method of accounting will be used to characterize the transaction and how the accounting method selected will be applied. For each merger or acquisition, the accounting team must determine whether the transaction is a *pooling of interests* or a *purchase* for accounting purposes. Other accounting issues that must be addressed include the allocation of the consideration to the various assets or other rights being purchased, as well as the special challenges of accounting for goodwill.

The Challenge of Meeting the Pooling-of-Interests Conditions

Frequently the buyer will want pooling-of-interests accounting treatment in order to combine historical financial information

---

Box 7-3. Purchase vs. Pooling of Interests

Purchase	*Pooling of Interests*
▪ Transaction treated as a classic acquisition and the accounting methods parallel those used in the ordinary purchase of assets (e.g., historical cost accounting).	▪ Transaction treated as classic merger and the buyer and seller's ownership interests are "pooled" into a single entity as if that entity and its respective shareholders had always existed on a combined basis.
▪ The purchase price of the seller's company paid by the buyer is allocated to the net assets obtained, and the difference between the cost and the fair market value is recorded as the residual or goodwill.	▪ The net effect of this method of accounting being applied to the transaction is that the assets and liabilities of the combined companies are not stepped up, both before and after the transaction closes.
▪ The net effect of this method of accounting being applied to the transaction is that the financial performance of the buyer and seller are consolidated only for postclosing reporting periods.	▪ Only applies if specific conditions are met.
▪ This accounting applies to all deals <u>unless</u> the pool-of-interests conditions are met.	

---

and avoid possible amortization of goodwill and increased depreciation charges. For pooling of interests, with limited exceptions, only voting common stock may be issued. In an assets acquisition, pooling of interests may be used only if the acquiring corporation acquires *all* of the net assets of the acquired corporation at the date the transaction is consummated. Additionally, the transaction must meet a complex set of criteria established by the IRS to qualify as a pooling-of-interests transaction.

Box 7-4. The Five Basic Alternative Structures

1. Asset Purchase

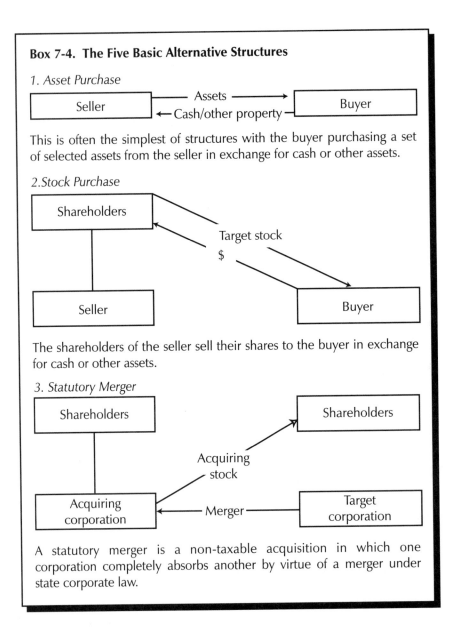

This is often the simplest of structures with the buyer purchasing a set of selected assets from the seller in exchange for cash or other assets.

2.Stock Purchase

The shareholders of the seller sell their shares to the buyer in exchange for cash or other assets.

3. Statutory Merger

A statutory merger is a non-taxable acquisition in which one corporation completely absorbs another by virtue of a merger under state corporate law.

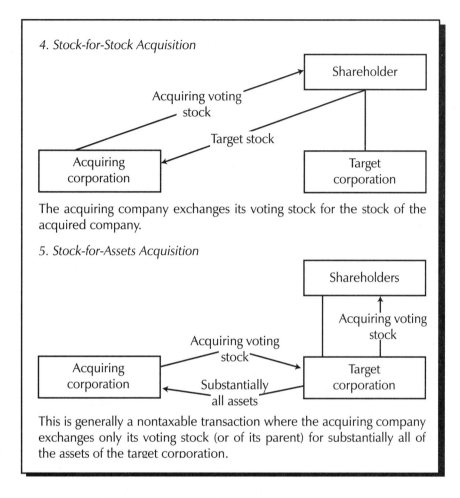

4. Stock-for-Stock Acquisition

The acquiring company exchanges its voting stock for the stock of the acquired company.

5. Stock-for-Assets Acquisition

This is generally a nontaxable transaction where the acquiring company exchanges only its voting stock (or of its parent) for substantially all of the assets of the target corporation.

One-Step vs. Staged Transactions

A key issue regarding the structure of the deal is whether the entire transaction will be completed in one fell swoop or whether it will occur over a series of steps. The parties may want to get to know each other better before considering a full-blown merger, or there may be some contingencies affecting the value of the company that are driving the buyer, or even the seller, to want to slow things down and consider a preliminary transaction as the first step.

For example, from the buyer's perspective, there may be certain governmental approvals needed that affect the seller's valuation, such as the approval of the Food and Drug Administration (FDA) for a new line of pharmaceutical or medical devices. These approvals may be two years away; if they are not obtained, that would significantly affect the value of the seller's business. In such a case, the buyer may want to consider an alternative and more preliminary initial structure, such as a strategic alliance (as a first step toward a merger) or a technology licensing agreement (as a first step toward an acquisition). There may even be certain shares exchanged to allow cross-ownership, or the buyer may want to purchase a minority interest in the seller with an option to purchase the balance within six months after obtaining FDA approval.

Even the seller may have certain reservations about the buyer or want to see certain contingencies met before it commits to selling 100 percent of its business. The buyer may be waiting for some key third-party approval or event to take place and before which the seller is reluctant to commit, such as the buyer's being in the process of filing for approval of an initial public offering (IPO) of its securities. If these securities are to serve as part of the seller's compensation, then it may be wise to wait, thereby ensuring that there will be a secondary market (and hence liquidity) for the shares before moving forward. In such cases, the parties would enter into a letter of intent, but there would typically be a clause that allows the seller to walk away from the deal if the offering is unsuccessful.

Some transactions are multistaged for strategic reasons, and some may be structured to be one stage with the possibility of being multistaged if certain postclosing contingencies are not met. A very interesting example of such a hybrid deal was the transaction between PSINet of Herndon, Virginia, and IXC Communications of Austin, Texas, in July 1997. PSINet, an Internet access service provider, agreed to sell to IXC a 20 percent stake in the company (which represented about 10 million shares at a then-current valuation of $93 million) in exchange for much-needed rights to use IXC's coast-to-coast network of high-speed data cables. This enabled PSINet to remain competitive (from a data-carrying capacity perspective) in the Internet access provider industry.

But there's more to this story. In a very risky step that puts tremendous pressure on PSINet to perform, the deal structure also had a stipulation under which PSINet pledged that if the $93 million worth of stock given to IXC in exchange for the cable access rights was not worth at least $240 million by the year 2001, then PSINet would be forced to make up the difference in stock or cash, which could easily result in IXC's eventually owning all or most of PSINet's shares. It is interesting to note that many of PSINet's competitors, such as UUNet Technologies and BBN Corp., had already been acquired by major telephone companies (which also had access to the high-speed fiber-optic cable lines). But PSINet, in an attempt to remain independent, had missed the window of higher valuations that buyers were paying in 1996 and early 1997 and was reluctant to sell out entirely in mid-1997 owing to fears that it would not obtain a high enough selling price. This deal structure would seem to indicate that the company is confident that the high valuations in its industry will in fact return before the year 2001.

Method of Payment

The way in which the seller will be paid is quite clearly one of the most important aspects of structuring the deal. The method of payment for the acquisition of stock or assets ordinarily involves balancing both business and tax considerations. Often a particular fact or set of circumstances will outweigh the others and determine the method of payment. Although the personal, strategic, and tax needs of all parties must be considered, there are a wide variety of forms of payment that should be considered before a final decision is determined. These forms of payment include cash, marketable securities, parcels of real estate, the rights to intangible assets (licenses, franchises), secured and unsecured promissory notes, the common and preferred securities of the purchaser (or its affiliates)—(and often with the promise that these securities will one day be publicly traded), earn-outs, consulting and employment agreements, royalty and license agreements, or even the exchange of another business. All of these tools should be considered in structuring the elements of the purchase price.

For example, a seller concerned about the financial and/or business viability or the creditworthiness of a buyer will demand payment in cash for assets or stock being sold. Alternatively, a seller reluctant to completely dispose of its interest in a business, or that wishes to defer tax to a later taxable year, may be willing to take the buyer's stock and/or take back a promissory note as part of the compensation. Tax considerations may dictate the form of payment. From a buyer's perspective, debt is often preferable to stock, since interest may be tax deductible. For example, in a leveraged acquisition the business assets acquired are expected to generate sufficient cash flow to pay off the debt incurred to acquire the assets.

Cash

In the 1996 film, *Jerry Maguire*, Cuba Gooding, who portrays the football player who is represented by Tom Cruise's character as an agent, says "Show me the money!" Although at first blush most sellers envision that an all-cash deal is the preferred route (with small, unmarked bills being best), they must consider a wide variety of payment methods that, in the long run, may result in a much greater total price.

There are certain circumstances when an all-cash transaction makes sense, such as when the seller suspects that the buyer will be unable to honor the types of consideration that rely on the buyer's long-term viability and credibility. From a buyer's perspective, an all-cash transaction can be internally financed, or financed through the cash flow of the combined companies and/or the acquired company, or even financed through asset-based lending, to be collateralized by the business assets or stock acquired.

Debt

If the creditworthiness of the buyer is high, then the seller may be willing to accept promissory notes from the buyer as part of the consideration. These promissory notes may be secured by the assets of the buyer, or by the seller's assets, or not at all. It is also possible that the notes will be subordinated to a senior commercial lender if the buyer borrows money from a bank as part of its capital to acquire the seller's business.

Stock

The securities of the buyer may constitute all or part of the payment to the seller for the business assets or stock. In some situations, common stock of the buyer or the newly formed subsidiary (or even a new class of preferred stock) will be issued to encourage a seller to maintain an economic interest in the ongoing viability of the business assets or stock being sold. Under this type of payment structure, a seller can participate as a shareholder in any future growth in value or profits derived from the combined entities and is motivated to ensure the success of the business.

Convertible Securities

Convertible debt securities often enable buyers and sellers to obtain the benefits of both the stock and debt form of payment. From a seller's perspective, convertible debt securities provide downside protection and a fixed return while allowing the opportunity to reap the benefits of growth in value or profits derived from the combined entities. From a buyer's perspective, they provide the tax advantages of interest deductions while enabling buyers to avoid payments of principal at maturity, should such instrument be converted into equity.

Contingent Payments

Often buyers and sellers are unable to agree on the determination of the value of the assets or stock being sold or may want to reserve the right to adjust the terms of the transaction in light of changes in circumstances or expectations. Such *contingent consideration acquisitions* provide for additional payments based on periodic recalculations of the value of the assets or stock sold or related income, typically based on the performance of the seller's business (or even the consolidated entities) on a postclosing basis. These are commonly referred to as *earn-outs*.

Similarly, the parties to an acquisition may provide for the

repayment of cash or other considerations, through the use of es-
crows or other security arrangements, upon the occurrence of specified contingencies.

Nontraditional Structures and Strategies

There are many types of nontraditional deal structures and acquisitions strategies that are not as straightforward as a stock or asset
purchase, such as spinoffs, rollups, leveraged buyouts, and employee stock ownership plans. These deal structures are often a
smaller slice of an overall corporate restructuring, but nevertheless
they have become an increasingly larger part of the annual merger
and acquisition activity.

An Introduction to Spinoffs

The early to mid-1990s saw a wave of spinoff activity on Wall
Street that was unprecedented. Large and mid-size companies
were breaking apart as fast as they were merging, with spinoffs,
spinouts, and related transactions surging in number and size from
1991 to 1996. There were $100 billion in spinoffs from 1991 to 1995,
with another $121 billion from 1995 to 1997, according to Securities
Data Corp. The demand continues to grow, as Wall Street seems to
greet nearly every castoff business unit as a budding superstar. For
the companies doing the spinning, the allure is to divest noncore,
often mediocre business units as they untangle the conglomeratiz-
ation of two decades and enjoy the benefits of a tax-free reorganization.[1] For the spunoff concern and its managers, the appeal lies

1. In spring of 1997, legislation was introduced to remove the tax-free treatment
of these transactions. The legislation, sponsored by Senate Finance Committee
Chairman William V. Roth, Jr. (R-Del.) and ranking minority member Sen. Daniel
Patrick Moynihan (D-N.Y.) and House Ways & Means Committee Chairman Bill
Archer (R-Tex.), would eliminate tax-free treatment of what are called "intra-
group distributions." Most large companies hold their assets in a complex web of
subsidiaries, and before they are able to spin off assets to the shareholders, they
often have to shuffle them around to corral them into one direct subsidiary of the
parent, using such "intra-group distributions." Under the bill, these distributions
would now be taxable, but under other provisions of current law, most big companies could defer paying the federal tax until they actually spin off a subsidiary
to shareholders. State and local taxes, however, would be due immediately.

in the prospect of moving to a more entrepreneurial organization. Well-known spinoffs that were welcomed by shareholders include General Motors' shedding of Electronic Data Systems; Sears, Roebuck's spinoffs of both Dean Witter, Discover & Co., and Allstate Insurance Co.; AT&T's spinoff of Lucent Technologies; and Sprint's spinoff of Sprint Cellular.

Although some respectable companies have been created as a result of spinoffs, it has also been said that "you don't spinoff your crown jewels for no reason." Many spinoffs have been criticized by the IRS as attempts to dump liabilities onto spinoff entities, which then have balance sheets laden with debt and a core focus with limited potential.

The spinoff deal must meet the rigorous Internal Revenue Service business-purpose test designed to ensure that the spinoff has a valid business reason. Among the purposes that are acceptable to the IRS are that the deal will help with access to capital markets, debt-financing prospects, competitive position, management direction, or retention of key employees.

The Taxpayer Relief Act of 1997 ('97 Act) curtailed the tax benefits of spinoffs. Under the '97 Act, a spinoff coupled with a related acquisition will be taxable to the distributing company if new shareholders acquire a 50 percent or greater interest (by vote or value) in the distributing or distributed corporation. Acquisitions within the four-year period beginning two years before the spinoff are rebuttably presumed part of a tainted overall plan or series of related transactions. In a significant change from earlier-considered versions, the '97 Act provides that the taxable gain occurs with respect to the *distributed* stock, whether it is the distributing or distributed company that is acquired.

In a related change, the '97 Act taxes spinoffs within an affiliated group of corporations if they are part of a "Morris Trust" transaction in which control shifts. Other intragroup spinoffs may be subject to new regulations preventing basis shifts that, under current rules, could generate distortions.

The major planning areas for dealing with the new Morris Trust rules are:

1. Avoiding characterization of the acquisition as part of a plan (or series of related transactions) encompassing the spin-

off—a more promising prospect when two or more years pass after the spinoff and before the acquisition or when there is a clear change of circumstances, such as a "surprise" post-spinoff or hostile tender offer

2. Structuring around the 50 percent vote or value standard through the use of leverage and multiple classes of stock

Leveraged Buyouts

A leveraged buyout (LBO) is a transaction in which capital borrowed from a commercial lender is used to fund all or a large portion of the purchase price paid to be paid to the seller. Generally, the loans are arranged with the expectation that the earnings of the business will easily repay the principal and interest. The LBO potentially has great rewards for the buyers, who although they frequently make little or no investment own the target company free and clear after the acquisition loans are repaid. LBOs are often arranged to enable the managers of subsidiaries or divisions of large corporations to purchase those subsidiaries or divisions that the corporation wants to divest—known as an MBO, or management buyout.

The LBO transaction will generally take one of two basic forms: the sale of assets or a cash merger. Under the cash merger format, the acquired company disappears upon merger into the acquiring company and its shareholders receive cash for their shares. Under the sale-of-assets format, the operating assets become part of the buying company, but the selling company is generally given the option of either receiving cash or continuing to hold its shares in the selling company.

At the heart of the LBO transaction is the dynamic of financing the acquisition by employing the assets of the acquired company. Large unused borrowing capacity is the characteristic that typically enables a purchaser to use the seller's assets to borrow the purchase price. Specific factors that enhance borrowing capacity are:

1. Large amounts of excess cash and cash equivalents, such as certificates of deposit and other short-term paper
2. A limited amount of current debt

3. Demonstrated ability over a number of years to achieve substantial earnings
4. Substantial undervalued assets, which when taken individually have a market value in excess of the depreciated value at which they are carried on the seller's balance sheets, sometimes called "hidden equity"
5. Subsidiaries with operations in unrelated industries that possess large amounts of excess properties that can be readily liquidated for cash without detriment to ongoing operations
6. The potential for hidden cash flow for the purchaser arising from income sheltered by depreciable property, the basis of which is readjusted upward as a consequence of the sale

Because of the complexities and uncertainties associated with arranging financing of this nature, the purchase agreement should provide that the buyer's obtaining the financing is a condition precedent to the purchaser's obligations under the agreement.

Consolidations/Rollups

A major structural trend or strategy that became popular in the mid to late 1990s was the consolidation, or *rollup*. Under such a strategy, the buyer is a holding company that has targeted an industry that may be ripe for consolidation within a given region or in a market niche. The rollup strategy may be horizontal or vertical in nature, but it typically involves the aggressive acquisition of competitors in a given market to achieve operating efficiencies, synergies, and market dominance. The buyer is usually looking to leverage the strength of its balance sheet or market capitalization to drive sales jointed and eliminate competition where possible. Obviously, antitrust laws are an issue (see Chapter 6) and some acquisitions will be friendly and some hostile.

The consideration paid to the seller is usually the securities of the buyer. It is best to devise a consolidation plan and compensation strategy that provides an incentive for the current management to stay in place and build up the value of their equity in the consolidated entity. The rollup buyer, or "consolidator," must look at each deal to see how the target fits into the overall strategy and to examine the impact of the given acquisition on the earnings, valuation, and taxes of the consolidated entities. If the consolidator (the buyer in a rollup strategy) is public or close to an initial public offering, it must also consider the reaction of Wall Street, the business media, and the investment bankers to each transaction.

Some rollup companies are the result of venture capital firms picking target industries, hiring management teams to manage the consolidation process, and then financing the deals with their own capital resources. The well-managed rollup companies have a specific strategic focus and rigid criteria for evaluating deals. They are not just haphazardly accumulating companies to build an asset base or a revenue stream through consolidation. These better-managed companies are constantly searching for cross-marketing opportunities by and among their operating divisions to their customers, as well as ancillary yet related products and services that can be added to the menu.

We see such a situation in the case of U.S. Office Products, which has acquired over 200 companies in 2 years to amass nearly $3 billion in aggregate revenues in the areas of office products, office services, travel services, and related industries. In fact, the USOP strategy has been so successful that its founder, Jonathan Ledecky, created Consolidated Capital Corp. (CCC) in late 1997 and filed with the SEC to raise $500 million for a public offering to do a new string of acquisitions. Even though CCC had not yet identified *which* industry it would be targeting, as of the date of this writing investors were already lining up to buy stock, and the offering is likely to be oversold.

An alternative approach was the rollup strategy completed by HFS, which targeted a few industries such as retail, real estate brokerage, and hotel services and then made a series of focused acquisitions. Other successful rollups include Corestaff (temporary services), Cable Design Technologies (cable wire manufacturing), JACOR Communications (a consolidator in the small- to mid-size radio station markets), Fortress Group (a consolidator in the homebuilding industry), American Medserve (institutional prescription services), and Lason Holdings (paperwork management services).

If a seller is approached by a consolidator that offers primarily its own securities in order to "join the team," the seller should realize that most of its upside in the deal is tied to the ability of the buyer to successfully execute its business and consolidation plan. Sellers should make sure they understand and agree with a buyer's strategy and vision, and that they are clear as to their role post-closing.

ESOPs as an Acquisition or Exit Strategy for Sellers

An employee stock ownership plan (ESOP) is an alternative available to sellers for disposing of their businesses. This option comes with certain tax advantages for both seller and buyer. There are a wide range of small and middle-market companies that cannot find suitable buyers (or that choose to "sell" their companies to their employees). These sellers often create an ESOP to buy all or substantially all of the company, using deferred compensation. Two general categories of ESOPs are:

1. *Leveraged ESOP.* Uses borrowed funds (either directly from the company or from a third-party lender based on the guaranty of the company, with the securities of the employer as collateral) to acquire the employer's securities. The loan will be repaid by the ESOP from employer and employee contributions, as well as from any dividends that may be paid on the employer's securities.

2. *Nonleveraged ESOP.* A stock bonus plan (or contribution stock bonus plan with a money purchase pension plan) that purchases the employer's securities with funds from the employer that would have been paid as some other form of compensation (that *were not* provided by a third-party lender).

General Legal Considerations in Structuring an ESOP

ESOPs, as with all types of deferred compensation plans, *must* meet certain requirements set forth by the IRS. Failure to meet these requirements will result in the contributions by the sponsoring employer *not* being tax deductible. To ensure that the seller is in compliance with IRS regulations, the ESOP must be created with the following considerations:

- Establish a trust in order to make contributions. The trust must be for the exclusive benefit of the participants and their beneficiaries.

- Not discriminate in favor of officers, major shareholders, or highly compensated employees, particularly regarding the allocation of assets and income distribution. A good rule of thumb is that at least 70 percent of all nonhighly compensated employees must be covered by the plan.

- Benefit no fewer than the lesser of fifty employees or 40 percent or more of the employees of the plan sponsor.

- Invest primarily in the securities of the sponsoring employer. Although there are no strict guidelines, it is assumed that the ESOP portfolio will include at least 50 to 60 percent of the employer's securities at any given time.

- Vest in compliance with one of the minimum vesting schedules set forth by the IRS. The plan must either adopt the five-year "cliff" vesting (employee is vested after five years of service) or the seven-year "scheduled" vesting (20 percent fully vested after three years, increasing 20 percent per year until 100 percent vesting is reached after seven years).

- Establish voting requirements that conform to those of the IRS. Under the code, voting rights may be vested in the trust's fiduciary, except under certain circumstances where rights must be passed through to the plan's participants. Generally, passing through becomes an issue when the vote will involve mergers, consolidations, reorganizations, recapitalizations, liquidations, major asset sales, and the like. Voting rights "in toto" may be passed through to employees, however, at the discretion of the employer in structuring the plan. Failure to fully "pass through" these rights may raise personnel and productivity problems. If the employees do not feel like true owners and, as a result, they are cynical about the ESOP, they may defeat a major incentive for adopting the ESOP.

- Comply with IRS rules regarding the distribution of ESOP benefits and assets. The plan must provide for a prompt (within one year) distribution of benefits to the participant following retirement, disability, or death. The nature and specific timing of the distribution will depend in part on the cause for separation from service with the company, as well as whether the sponsoring employer is closely held as opposed to publicly traded.

- The employer's contributions should be based on a specific percentage of payroll, such as a money-purchase pension plan, or based on some other formula, such as a percentage of profits, as is the case with some profit-sharing plans. This form provides for maximum flexibility in that contributions are in the complete discretion of the employer. Each year the employer simply makes a determination of the appropriate amount of contribution. It should be noted that the plan provides for a minimum contribution sufficient to permit the plan to pay any principal and interest due with respect to a loan used to acquire employer securities. The employers' contribution may be made in cash or other property, including employer's securities. In the event that the employer contributes its own securities, it may obtain a so-called cashless deduction. The employer is entitled to deduct the fair market value of the securities so contributed, and the contribution involves no cash outlay by the employer.

- Provide adequate consideration in connection with the purchase of employer stock in an ESOP. This requires some method for valuation of the shares. For publicly traded companies, this requirement is generally not a problem, since the prevailing market price is a sufficient indication of value. For privately held companies, however, value must be determined by the fiduciaries of the plan acting in good faith. This will generally require an independent appraisal by a qualified third-party appraisal firm, initially upon the establishment of the ESOP and at least annually thereafter. The cost and impact of such an appraisal of a closely held company should be considered before adopting an ESOP plan.

Key Legal Documents for the Establishment of an ESOP

There are many legal documents that must be prepared in connection with the organization and implementation of an ESOP. These documents must be prepared by counsel, however, only after input has been received by all key members of the company's ESOP team (e.g., financial and human resources staff, accountants, investment bankers, commercial lenders, the designated trustee, the designated appraisal firm). The preliminary analysis that should be conducted *prior to* the preparation of the documents should include:

- Impact on dilution, ownership, control, and earnings of the company
- Type of securities to be issued (common vs. preferred)
- Tax deductibility of contributions and related tax issues
- Registration of the securities, where required, under federal and state securities laws
- Employee motivation and productivity improvement analysis
- Current and future capital requirements and growth plans of the company
- Interplay of the ESOP with other current or planned employee benefit plans within the company
- Timetable for planning, organization, and implementation of the ESOP

ESOP Documentation

Once these and other factors have been considered, and the strategic decisions made, counsel may be instructed to prepare the necessary documentation. In a leveraged ESOP, the documents may include:

- ESOP plan
- ESOP trust agreement (which may be combined with the plan)
- ESOP loan documentation (e.g., loan agreement, note guaranty); the initial set of documents may be from the commercial lender to the sponsoring employer, with a mirror-image loan being made by the employer to the ESOP
- ESOP stock purchase agreement, where stock is purchased from the employer or its principal shareholders
- Corporate charter amendments and related board resolutions
- Legal opinion and valuation reports

The primary issues to be addressed by each of these documents are as follows:

The ESOP Plan (where trust agreement is self-contained)

1. Designation of a name for the ESOP
2. Definition of key terms (e.g., "participant," "year of service," "trustee")
3. Eligibility to participate (standards and requirements)
4. Contributions by employer (designated amount or formula; discretionary)
5. Investment of trust assets (primarily in employer securities, plans for diversification of the portfolio; purchase price for the stock; rules for borrowing by the ESOP)
6. Procedures for release of the shares from encumbrances (formula as ESOP obligations are paid down)
7. Voting rights (rights vested in trustee; special matters triggering employee voting rights)
8. Duties of the trustee(s) (accounting, administrative, appraisal, asset management, recordkeeping, voting obligations, preparation of annual reports, allocation and distribution of dividends)
9. Removal of trustee(s)
10. Effect of retirement, disability, death, and severance of employment
11. Terms of the put option (for closely held companies)
12. Rights of first refusal upon transfer
13. Vesting schedules

ESOP Stock Purchase Agreement

1. Appropriate recitals
2. Purchase terms for the securities
3. Conditions to closing
4. Representations and warranties of the seller
5. Representations and warranties of the buyer
6. Obligations prior to and following the closing
7. Termination
8. Opinion of counsel
9. Exhibits, attachments, and schedules

Box 7-5. Structuring the Offer to Meet the Needs of Both Parties

Seller's Needs

1. Price
2. Form of consideration (e.g., cash, stock, notes)
3. Continuing employment or involvement
4. Important qualitative concerns
5. Hidden agenda

Buyer's Needs

1. Control
2. Return on investment
3. Minimal cash equity
4. Retention of key managers
5. Structured to meet lenders' needs

Tools to Bridge the Gap

1. Cash is king (try to limit net worth)
2. Unsecured, subordinated long-term notes with low fixed interest rates
3. Employment and consulting contracts
4. Noncompete agreement
5. Earn-outs

As you can see, there are as many potential ways to structure a deal as there are motivations and objectives of each party, and this chapter only touches the tip of the iceberg. Remember, it's not a contest among the lawyers to come up with the most complex structure; rather, they should use creativity and experience to design a structure (or multiple structures) that best serves the needs not only of buyer and seller but also of any third parties that are critical to the transaction—e.g., the source(s) of capital or key vendors and customers. And even the best structures will not adequately serve the parties if the price is not right, as we will see in Chapter 8.

Chapter 8

Valuation and Pricing of the Seller's Company

Although a formal valuation of the seller's business is a vital component of the buyer's analysis of the proposed transaction, it is important to realize that valuation is not an exact science nor will pure valuation issues typically drive the terms and pricing of the transaction. There are numerous acceptable valuation methods and, in most situations, each yields a different result. In fact, the formal mathematical valuation should play only one part in the overall pricing of the deal and in determining the true value of the transaction to the parties. While all methods should, in theory, yield the same results, they rarely do, owing to factors including, but not limited to, market conditions, the industry in which the target company operates, and the type and nature of the business.

Certain traditional approaches to valuation also come under attack when our economy is largely driven by the value of brand management and leveraging, the ability to train and retain highly skilled knowledge workers, the ability to get and keep loyal customers, and a company's inventory of strategic relationships and efficient distribution channels. None of these intangible assets will appear on a traditional balance sheet, nor will lumping them together under an archaic concept known as goodwill really give them justice. Today's industrial giants include companies such as Microsoft and America On-Line, which have been built almost solely from leveraging and replication of intangible assets. This

I gratefully acknowledge and thank Ray and Donna Fanning for their significant contributions to this chapter.

new category of *power asset* raises challenges both for the accounting profession and for qualified business appraisers, as set forth below.

Of the three main methods of valuation, no one method provides a price that cannot be questioned. But the methods are useful in that they provide points from which to start. They supply a range of reasonable values backed by various valid methods of justification. In the end, it is vital to remember that the value or price of a company is dependent on the particular time of the valuation and on the true motivations and goals of the key players involved.

The valuation of a business in the context of an acquisition, as opposed to estate planning or other purposes, often involves consideration of investment or strategic value beyond a street analysis of *fair market value*. The valuation may be done by the seller prior to entertaining prospective buyers, by the buyer who identifies a specific target, or by both parties during negotiations to resolve a dispute over price. *Fair market value* is commonly defined as the amount at which property would change hands between a willing seller and a willing buyer when neither is under compulsion and both have reasonable knowledge of the relevant facts.

The Challenges in the Valuation of a Smaller Company

As discussed in Chapter 1, the transactional focus of this book is for deals ranging in the $1 million to $250 million range; as a result, smaller, nonpublic companies are the targeted businesses. These smaller, closely held businesses are more difficult to value, owing to the following informational challenges and to risks that result in lower valuations.

Smaller companies, in general, present certain information risks (e.g., a lack of access to reliable and substantiated data leading to more hypothetical projections than would be the norm with larger companies,) which makes valuation more difficult. This is because, in smaller firms, there is a:

- Lack of externally generated information, including analyst coverage, resulting in a lack of forecasts

- Lack of adequate press coverage and other avenues to disseminate company-generated information
- Lack of internal controls
- Possible lack of internal reporting

In addition, there are numerous firm-specific reasons why small companies are difficult to analyze from a valuation perspective:

- There is an inability to obtain any financing or reasonably priced financing.
- The company may lack product, industry, and geographic diversification.
- There is no ability to expand into new markets.
- The company lacks management expertise.
- There is sensitivity to macro- and microeconomic movements.
- There is no dividend history.
- The company is more sensitive to business risks, supply squeezes, and demand lulls.
- There is an inability to control or influence regulatory activity and union activity.
- The business lacks economies of scale or large-scale operational synergies.
- The company lacks access to distribution channels.
- There are poor relationships with suppliers and customers.
- The business lacks product differentiation or brand-name recognition.
- The deep pockets necessary for staying power are not there.

Investors in the private markets, in general, require higher rates of return than does the public. As a result, private company valuations tend to be lower, as illustrated in Box 8-1.

Use of a Professional Business Appraiser

There are several different ways to arrive at a valuation of the seller's company. For example, sellers could use a self-evaluation and

Box 8-1. Median P/E Paid-In Acquisitions

	Acquisitions of Public Companies	*Acquisitions of Private Companies*	*Percentage Difference*
1987	21.7	15.2	
1988	18.3	12.8	
1989	18.4	12.7	
1990	17.1	13.2	
1991	15.9	8.5	
1992	18.1	17.6	
1993	19.7	22.0	
1994	19.8	22.0	
1995	19.4	15.5	
1996	21.7	17.7	
Mean	19.0	15.7	−17.8%
Median	18.9	16.4	−13.2%

Source: Mergerstat Review January 1997.

buyers and sellers could both study comparable companies and transactions. But the most widely accepted method by both buyers and sellers in a merger or acquisition is to use a professional business appraiser. A professional business appraiser is able to ensure that the starting point for negotiations is a valid one and that there is a strong and clear justification for the valuation.

An appraiser is trained to look at a company and its assets, management, employees, financials, future projections, and the like as objectively as possible, then turn this assessment into a range of values that are valid for determining the selling price of the company. The target company will have to be cooperative with the appraiser in order for the appraiser to arrive at a reasonable range of prices. Often the target company can feel threatened by an appraiser's detailed look at every aspect of the company's operations and management, but this access is important for the appraiser to arrive at a fair valuation. An appraiser probably will request access to various offices and/or work sites run by the company, as well as approval to interview key personnel from both management and employee ranks. And, of course, the appraiser will request to see complete financial records from recent years.

Determining Strategic Value

It is essential to clearly define the terms under which a professional business appraiser will be working in order to avoid problems down the road. First, the expected *time frame* for completion of the appraisal must be set forth in advance and must be reasonable. Do not expect to hire an appraiser on Monday and receive a complete report on Wednesday. A proper appraisal will take a minimum of several weeks to be completed. Also, be sure to clearly explain *how* the finished product should be delivered, that is, via oral or written report. Be careful to lay out exactly the amount of the *appraiser's fee* and *when* that fee will be paid. Beware of fee structures that could be subject to a conflict of interest. For example, do not hire an appraiser who pushes for his or her fee to be a percentage of the end value stated for the company or an appraiser who offers to accept payment only upon completion of the merger or acquisition transaction. In both cases, the appraiser has an apparent incentive to alter the value of the company to fit his or her best interests, and the appraisal may lack credibility as a negotiating tool.

In the context of a proposed acquisition, a veteran appraiser creates a strategic model of a pro forma showing what the seller's business would look like under the umbrella of the prospective buyer's company. The first step is to normalize current operating results to establish *net free cash flow*. Next, the appraiser examines several "what-if" scenarios to determine how specific line items would change under various circumstances. This exercise allows the appraiser to identify a range of *strategic values* based on the projected earnings stream of the seller's company under its proposed new ownership. The higher this earnings stream, the higher the purchase price.

To arrive at these strategic values, the appraiser obtains large amounts of financial data and general information on many aspects of the seller's business, such as the quality of management or the company's reputation in the marketplace. The appraiser must be alert throughout this process to capture bits of information that will be useful in the final evaluation of the company's strategic values. In addition, the appraiser considers other elements that may not be apparent without further probing. The appraiser attempts to assess how the value of the target company will be affected by any changes to the operations or foundation of the company as a result of the proposed transaction, such as a loss of key customers or key managers.

The professional business appraiser should also examine the seller's intangible assets when determining strategic values. The list of intangible assets should include items such as customer lists, intellectual property, patents, license and distributorship agreements, regulatory approvals, leasehold interests, and employment contracts. To the extent that the seller can supply specifics on its intangibles, since certain intangibles may not be readily apparent, they will enhance the valuation.

Finally, the appraiser conducts an analysis of the seller's financial procedures and accounting practices, and performs an evaluation as to the appropriateness and accuracy of these procedures. The appraiser evaluates the expected effect that credit ratings have on the value of the company. The company's reputation in the business community, while difficult to precisely define, also has an effect on the future value of the firm. The appraiser is able to learn much about the company's potential based on the company's own future plans and projections.

The Basic Methods of Valuation

Whether you use a professional business appraiser or attempt a self-evaluation, it is helpful to understand the basic methods of valuation used to arrive at a value for the seller's company. Although a comprehensive discussion of valuation methods and techniques is beyond the scope of this book, set forth here is an overview of three approaches. A professional business appraiser typically applies a few different methods of valuation that fit into these categories and uses the knowledge gained from these exercises to pick one or two methods that stand out as the most sensible for providing a range of values for the company.

The Comparable Worth Method

The notion of *comparable worth* uses the performance and potential selling prices of comparable publicly and privately held companies to arrive at a value. The appraiser examines those companies where sufficient data are available that operate in the same or similar industry and that provide the same or similar products and/or services. The justification for this method lies in the premise that potential buyers will not pay more for the target company than what they would spend for a similar company that trades publicly. The appraiser must carefully choose the most parallel public and private companies with which to compare the seller's company. Obviously, the companies should be as similar to the target company as possible, particularly in regard to geographical location and relationship to suppliers.

Because it will not be possible to find companies that are identical in all respects to the target company, it is important for the appraiser to use the available data as creatively as possible. For example, owing to differences in the companies' sales volumes, it is more useful to compare the ratio of sales to costs than to compare absolute amounts of sales to each other. Comparisons of this type provide a clearer picture of the relative strengths and weaknesses of the target company in comparison to other companies in the industry.

Once the appraiser has some preliminary range of valuations derived from this method of comparison, he or she must adjust the prices for situations particular to the target company. If, for example, the target company has profits that are consistently above industry averages owing to an unusually low cost structure, then the value of that target company must be adjusted upward from the comparables to account for that competitive advantage. As with all methods of valuation, the prices and subsequent adjustments must be substantiated, and must evolve as data becomes available. In the example just mentioned, the buyer must be able to see and understand the justification for the target company's being valued higher than apparent comparables, or it will not be willing to pay the premium.

As discussed earlier in this chapter, if the target company is a closely held company, the comparable worth method can present some difficulties. The goals of financial reporting for a publicly held company can be quite different from those of a closely held company. A publicly held company's management strives to show high earnings on its financial reports in order to attract people to buy its stock and therefore to improve its price-earnings ratio. On the other hand, a closely held company's management may be a sole entrepreneur or a small group that wishes to minimize the earnings shown on its financial reports in order to minimize its tax burden. Both goals are legitimate, but clearly the difference in objectives can cause some confusion for an appraiser trying to compare the key financial ratios of a closely held target company to publicly held similar companies in the industry.

The Asset Valuation Method

If the seller's company has a large portion of its value wrapped up in fixed assets, an appraiser may lean toward some type of *asset valuation* when attempting to price the company. The justification for asset valuation lies in the proposition that the buyer will pay no more for the target company than it would pay to obtain a comparable set of substitute assets. Within these guidelines, the appraiser can choose how to value the substitute assets. The *cost of reproduction* takes into account the cost to construct a substitute asset using the same materials as the original at current prices, while the *cost of replacement* utilizes the cost to replace the original asset at current prices, adhering to modern standards and using modern materials. The appraiser will consider the time that would be required to reach the point at which replacement or new assets could be put in place and in a usable state.

When using the asset valuation method, the appraiser examines each asset held by the company, both tangible and intangible. It is easy to understand the degree of detail required in this method to arrive at a fair valuation. The appraiser must assess all machinery and equipment, real estate, vehicles, office furniture and fixtures, land, and inventory. However, the appraiser should also include in his or her assessment the value of intangibles like patents and customer lists. These intangibles often are referred to as the company's goodwill—the difference in value between the company's hard assets and the true value of the company. While intangibles do have legitimate value, it generally is more difficult to convince a buyer of the value of an intangible item than of a tangible asset. This is because the buyer usually wants to be able to see and verify the assets in order to feel comfortable with the price he or she will pay. It generally will be in the seller's best interest to supply the business appraiser with as much concrete detail about the company's intangibles as possible. The greater value of goodwill that can be attributed to specific, well-defined intangibles, the higher the price at which the company is likely to be valued. For example, rather than lumping patents that the company holds under the intangible goodwill category, list the patents as separate assets and include specifics pertaining to the patents, such as dates of expiration and their effects on the company's operations.

The Financial Performance Method

The third and perhaps the most commonly used valuation method in the context of small to medium acquisitions is the financial performance method. Actually a set of valuation methods, this approach attempts to measure historical performance, as well as predict future performance, in determining the value of the seller's business to the buyer at postclosing.

1. *Net present value (NPV) analysis.* NPV is perhaps the most common method of financial performance analysis used by appraisers in a preacquisition valuation. It is a capital budgeting model that compares the present value of the proposed transaction's benefits with the present value of the proposed transaction's costs. The difference between benefits and costs is the net present value of the proposed deal. A positive NPV means that the proposed transaction's benefits exceed its costs, and the decision to undertake the proposed deal increases the value of the buyer and its shareholder wealth. A negative NPV means that the proposed transaction's costs exceed its benefits, and the decision to undertake the proposed transaction would decrease the value of the buyer and its shareholder wealth. An NPV of zero means that the proposed transaction's benefits are equal to its costs, and the deci-

sion to undertake a proposed transaction does not increase or decrease the value of the buyer or the wealth of its shareholders.

To conduct an accurate NPV analysis, the appraiser gathers
financial data and evaluates future projections of cash flow based
on the perceived level of risk and length of time considered. It is
the appraiser's job to review all financial documents and search for
mistakes, inconsistencies, and areas of disagreement, such as future earnings claims. This type of painstaking examination is not
easy for a company to endure, but it is vital to the successful completion of the appraisal.

The net present value calculation takes into account the time
value of money, meaning that one dollar today has more purchasing power than one dollar will five years from now. A quick calculation can be performed using the following formula:

$$NPV = C_o + \Sigma\ (C_t\ /\ (1 + r_t)^t),$$

where:

NPV equals the net present value,

C_o equals the initial cash flow or value (equal to the price paid
for the target),

C_t equals the cash flow at each subsequent year in consideration (expected profit or loss),
r_t equals the discount rate for each subsequent year in consideration,
^{t} equals each subsequent year in consideration.

The discount rate is a very important element in this calculation and can be defined as the expected rate of return for the investment. For example, assume that the president of the company
AQUIRECO is looking into the possibility of acquiring the BUYME
Company. She decides to make a conservative evaluation of the
transaction. She knows that the most that AQUIRECO is willing to
pay for the BUYME Company is $1 million, and that $100,000 annual profit is a safe estimate for BUYME Company's future operations, according to currently available financial data. Additionally,
after taking into account both the time value of money and the risk

involved in the acquisition of BUYME Company, she arrives at a discount rate of 10 percent. AQUIRECO feels that the value of the acquisition of the BUYME Company must be realized within five years in order to be an attractive investment. Therefore, AQUIRECO's president is able to perform the following calculation to gauge the attractiveness of the conservative view.

$$NPV = -1,000,000 + [(100,000 / (1 + .1)) + (100,000 / (1 + .1)^2) + (100,000 / (1 + .1)^3) + (100,000 / (1 + .1)^4) + (100,000 / (1 + .1)^5)],$$

or $NPV = -\$620,921.$

Since the NPV is less than zero, AQUIRECO's president would choose not to acquire BUYME Company, given all assumptions described previously.

2. *Internal rate of return (IRR) analysis.* The IRR is a capital budgeting model represented by the discount rate that equates the price with the anticipated profits from the proposed transaction. Computing the IRR is tantamount to answering the following question: If the proposed transaction were similar to a bank account, what interest rate would the bank have to offer in order to produce the same benefits as the proposed deal?

There are two steps for the professional business to evaluate the seller's business based on the IRR methods: (1) calculating the IRR, and (2) comparing the IRR to the required rate of return. Acceptable proposed transactions are those whose IRR is greater than the required return. Proposed transactions should be rejected if the IRR is less than the required rate of return. Shareholders are indifferent when the IRR is equal to the required rate of return.

3. *Return on investment (ROI) ratio.* In certain cases, the professional business appraiser may concentrate on the ROI ratio in evaluating a target company. Taken as an average of the recent years earnings to equity and long-term debt, the ROI can be useful in providing an important benchmark for the buyer. It is important to remember, however, that the decision to purchase a company must be made based on the interaction of numerous factors; the whole picture, not just fragments, must be studied in order to

make a sound decision. The process of evaluating a company's financial health and future growth prospects is a very involved process through which the professional business appraiser must be trained to lead the potential buyer.

Selecting a Method

The professional business appraiser (or whoever is conducting the analysis) should not use any one method of valuation without considering other methods or other factors. One method may overlook key aspects of the business that will be uncovered only after the further investigation required for another method is completed. For example, if the appraiser utilizes a number of methods and consistently arrives at a range of $2.2 million to $2.6 million, then an asset valuation that yields a result of only $1.5 million can be explored and eliminated if the appraiser finds that the value of its assets is not a fair approximation of the entire company's value, owing to intangibles or other market or competitive trackers. However, if the only method utilized were the asset valuation method, then the company would be underpriced dramatically.

Proper valuation of a company is never simple. A valuation method that appears to be too simple probably is. For purposes other than merger and acquisition transactions, simple methods are commonly used, and are actually prescribed by law in some cases. However, for a merger or acquisition, it is wise to invest a bit more time and effort initially than to experience remorse after the deal has been consummated.

The simple methods mentioned above include many commonly heard in the business world, such as *industry multipliers*. Multipliers are set by unknown entities based on unknown factors that most likely were valid at one time in a particular market, but may no longer hold true. For example, it may be heard that in Industry X, the price to pay for business is five times the company's annual earnings or amount of goodwill. It will, however, be quite difficult to convince a well-informed potential buyer to purchase a company for a price defined only by such a formula. From the seller's perspective, there is no guarantee that its company is not worth more than the amount arrived at by using a simple formula without basis. In fairness to both parties, the appraiser should not take the easy way out of this task.

The Final Valuation Report

At the end of the appraiser's analysis , he or she will produce a final report detailing the range of values for the seller's business. Ironically, just when it would seem as if the formal valuation process has ended, the acquisition team must evaluate the impact the report will have on the actual price and structure of the transaction.

If the buyer perceives that it will benefit from the economics of scale that will be created by the acquisition, it may be willing to pay more than would otherwise be expected. This is known as the *acquisition premium,* an added cost to the buyer's shareholders and a windfall to the seller's shareholders. On the other hand, if the buyer is really just looking to buy only certain assets or views the acquisition as a short-term tactic, then the price it is willing to pay may not even approach the price given by the appraiser. From the seller's point of view, if it really is not anxious to give up the business just yet, the negotiated price may be driven higher. However, if the seller has motivation to sell quickly, the negotiated price could plummet.

It is an essential facet of the valuation process that while the detailed methods of valuation can provide a solid starting point, that often remains all that they provide. The final negotiated price can vary widely and is dependent on diverse factors, including: the market conditions, the timing of the negotiations and the valuation date, the internal motivation and goals of both the buyer and seller, the operating synergies that will result from the transaction, the structure of the transaction, and other factors that may not even be defined explicitly.

Buyers and sellers and their advisory teams must understand the strategic and financial benefits of these valuation methods. These techniques, however, do have their limitations and should certainly not be the only data or circumstances considered when arriving at a final price or structure.

Chapter 9

Financing the Acquisition

Let's assume that the buyer's team has followed all of the steps in the process thus far: It has identified its strategic objectives, prepared the acquisition plan, identified the qualified candidates, narrowed the field, negotiated and signed the letter of intent, conducted the valuation and negotiated the purchase price, conducted the due diligence, and instructed counsel to start working on the definitive documents. The team breathes a sigh of relief until it realizes: *How are we going to pay for all of this at closing?*

The range of options available to a buyer to finance an acquisition range from the very simple to the very complex, and the structure of the deal will vary with each transaction. Each deal presents its own challenges, its own set of seller's needs, its own financial market conditions, and so forth. Overall, the size and complexity of the transaction, the cash available to the buyer, the market for the buyer's securities, the terms of the purchase price, and the financial market conditions at the time of purchase determine the range of options available to the buyer.

This chapter looks at some common sources of debt and equity financing used by buyers in connection with acquisition financing. I refer to the "borrower" as the buyer that is trying to raise debt capital to pay for the acquisition, and the "offeror" as the buyer that is trying to raise equity capital.

The Seller as a Source of Financing

Sellers will in many cases be willing to provide some or a significant portion of the purchase price in *take-back financing,* particularly if they don't have an immediate need for the cash or if they believe that the company is worth more than the buyer is able (or willing) to pay. Similarly, the buyer may use seller financing to either keep the seller motivated in the company's future success or force the seller to prove that the business truly has the upside potential that has been represented. In other words, the seller absorbs some of the risk. Seller financing may also be a necessary option if the buyer is having difficulty obtaining a commitment from third-party lenders or investors.

Seller financing can be *fixed*, such as a simple installment sale or unsecured promissory note; *equity*, such as taking some of the buyer's common or preferred stock (or convertible debt) as payment; *contingent*, such as warrants (options to purchase the shares at a fixed price at a later point in time); or other types of conditional payments such as earn-outs. With earn-outs, the seller receives additional payments only if the acquired business performs above a specified level in the future, or in the event that a specific postclosing condition is met, or if a certain event occurs (or does not occur), such as FDA approval or the issuance of a patent. Sellers that agree to accept a portion of their consideration in this manner must recognize the economic risks, such as the possibility that the buyer will default on its obligations or that one of the sellers will buy back the company it previously sold (which is often not performing at the levels when it was originally conveyed).

Debt Financing Alternatives

Although all available sources of debt financing should be considered, traditional commercial bank loans are the most common source of acquisition capital for small and growing buyers. Typically the buyer needs only one asset-based lender, and the loan is secured by the inventory and accounts receivables of the acquired business. The buyer/borrower is responsible for obtaining the balance of the purchase price. The buyer/borrower is also responsible for ensuring that there is sufficient working capital after making loan payments to continue operations and execute the business plan. If the buyer needs additional funding and the seller is unwill-

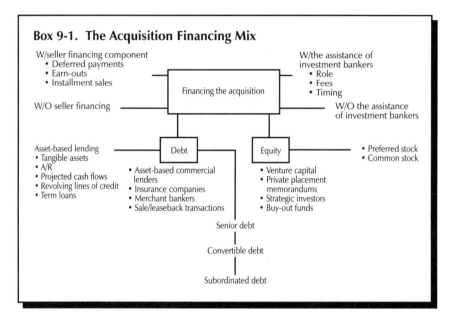

ing to provide financing, then the buyer/borrower may need to convince a second lender to provide funds based on project cash flows (rather than purely hard assets). In this case, the secondary lender will usually insist on an equity participation and/or more aggressive lending terms.

Understanding the Lender's Perspective

In recent years, commercial lending banks have changed the way in which they make loans for merger and acquisition deals. The local approval of loans is a steadily fading practice, while the loan-approval process has come to resemble the due diligence review of a securities offering. Lenders now behave like investors, conducting competitive analyses, examining market share trends, and so forth. These stricter loan standards mean that buyers must have more equity than before. In most instances, sellers' take-back notes must be entirely subordinated to the institutional financing. The classic leveraged buyout of the 1980s is a rarity for banks, primarily because collateral alone is no longer sufficient; cash flow and balance sheet strength have become equally important.

These stricter loan standards mean fewer debt-driven deals are getting done, but the deals that are being done are at lower interest rates and have generally lower default rates. In addition, virtually all institutional lenders have taken a harder line on collateralized financing. Inventories, once a building block of many merger and acquisition loans, are becoming extremely difficult to finance. Rapidly changing technology can make high-tech goods obsolete almost overnight, while the steady increase in retail chain store failures threatens the worth of surviving stores' merchandise.

The real estate component may also be difficult to finance. Money is available, but underwriting requirements are increasingly onerous. Whereas once the loan-to-market-value ratio was 60 or 65 percent, now lenders will advance only 50 or 60 percent of the appraised value. For loans to manufacturers and distributors, lenders usually restrict their loans to high-ceiling, general-purpose buildings—a criterion that can sink many potential LBOs. All would-be borrowers are subject to often daunting scrutiny regarding soil contamination and other environmental hazards. Finally, real estate lenders, like institutional lenders in general, now place great emphasis on cash flow, both historical and projected.

In all this, the role of lending officers has changed considerably. Despite often impressive titles, their only major responsibility is to get prospective deals into the pipeline. Once the loan application has been completed and turned over to the first screening level, the lending officer's primary role is to monitor the approval process. This has changed institutional lending from a relationship business to a transaction business. It also places more responsibility on the lending officer. Because he or she does not have the authority to approve a loan, or in many cases to even call a meeting of the loan approval committee, it is more important than ever that the lending officer know in detail the lender's underwriting criteria. It is altogether too easy for a loan application to wend its way from level to level over several weeks, only to be rejected by the final authority because of something that was apparent at the outset.

Before attempting to understand the types of loans available from commercial banks, it is important to understand the perspective of the average commercial bank when it analyzes the buyer's loan proposal. Banks are in the business of selling money, and capital is the principal product in their inventory. Bankers, however, are both statutorily and personally averse to risk. The bank's shareholders and board of directors expect that loan officers will take all necessary steps to minimize the risk to the institution in each transaction and obtain the maximum protection in the event of default. Therefore, the types of loans available to the buyer/borrower, the terms and conditions of loan agreements, and the steps taken by the bank to protect its interest all have a direct relationship to the level of risk that is perceived by the lending officer and the loan committee. The management team that has been assigned to obtain the acquisition financing from a commercial bank must be in a position to show how the typical risks in an acquisition will be mitigated in preparation for the negotiation of the loan documentation.

Steps in the Loan Process

There are three key steps in obtaining acquisition financing from typical commercial lenders.

STEP 1: Preparing the Loan Proposal

The loan proposal should focus on the history of the buyer, the performance of the seller, and the reasons why the proposed deal makes sense. The loan proposal should also contain a copy of the signed letter of intent, as well as the financial statements of both parties. From the buyer/borrower's perspective, this will mean a loan proposal package that demonstrates the presence of a strong management team; an accounts receivable management program; the ability of the combined entity to service the debt, shown in financial statements and projections; the stability of the company through its longstanding and synergistic relationships with suppliers, distributors, and employees; and an understanding of the trends in the marketplace. The loan proposal should also explain the structure of the proposed transaction and give the underlying rationale for selecting this structure. All of these factors will be assessed by a loan officer in determining the merits of the proposed deal and the relative risk to the bank in making a loan in connection with the proposed acquisition.

Although the exact elements of a buyer/borrower's loan proposal will vary depending on the size of the company, its industry, and the terms of the proposed transaction, most lenders want the following fundamental questions answered:

- Who is the borrower?
- How much capital is needed and when?
- How will the capital be allocated and for what specific purposes?
- Why does the proposed transaction make sense from a financial, strategic, and operational perspective?
- What additional market share, cost savings, or other efficiencies will be achieved as a result of this transaction?
- How will the combined entity service its debt obligations (e.g., application and processing fees, interest, principal, or balloon payments)?
- What protection (e.g., tangible and intangible assets to serve as collateral) can the borrower provide the bank in the event that the company is unable to meet its obligations?

Although the answers to these questions are all designed to assist the banker in an assessment of the risk factors in the proposed transaction, they are also intended to provide the commercial loan officer with the information necessary to persuade the loan committee to approve the transaction. You must understand that the loan officer, once convinced of the merits of the deal, will then serve as an advocate on behalf of the buyer/borrower in presenting the loan proposal to the bank's loan committee. The loan documentation, terms, rates, and covenants that the loan committee will specify as a condition for making the loan will be directly related to the ways in which the buyer/borrower is able to demonstrate its ability to mitigate and manage the risk to the lender in connection with financing the proposed transaction.

The loan proposal should include the following categories of information, many of which can be borrowed or modified from the acquisition plan:

- *Summary of the request.* An overview of the history of the buyer and the seller, the amount of capital needed, the proposed repayment terms, the intended use of the capital, and the collateral available to secure the loan.

- *History of the borrower.* A brief background of the buyer and/or the seller; its capital structure; the key founders; the stage of development and plans for growth; a list of key customers, suppliers, and service providers; management structure and philosophy; plant and facility; the key products and services offered; and an overview of any intellectual property owned or developed.

- *Market data.* An overview of trends in the industry; the size of the market; the buyer's and/or seller's market share; an assessment of the competition (direct and indirect); proprietary advantages; marketing, public relations, and advertising strategies; market research studies; and future industry prospects.

- *Financial information.* Pro forma postacquisition balance sheets and projected income statements, federal and state tax returns, appraisals of key assets or company valuations, current balance sheet, credit references, and a two-year income statement. The role of the capital requested (with respect to the buyer's and/or seller's plans for growth), an allocation of the loan proceeds, and the buyer's and/or seller's ability to repay must be carefully explained, and a discussion of its ability to service the debt must be supported by a three-year projected cash flow statement on a monthly basis.

- *Schedules and exhibits.* A schedule of supporting documents (such as a letter of intent between buyer and seller) and background information on the seller's performance. Resumes of the buyer's principals, recent articles about the buyer or seller, a schedule of patents and trademarks, a picture of the seller's products or site, and an organization chart of the proposed management structure for the postclosing business should also be appended as exhibits to the loan proposal.

STEP 2: Understanding the Types of Commercial Bank Loans

During the process of planning the capital structure and in preparing the loan proposal, it is important for the buyer/borrower to understand the various types of loans that are available from a commercial bank (one or more of which could be tailored to meet specific requirements) in the context of a proposed acquisition. Loans are usually categorized by the term of the loan, the expected use of the proceeds, and the amount of money to be borrowed. The availability of these various loans depends on both the nature of the industry and the bank's assessment of the company's creditworthiness.

The following are typical loan categories.

- *Short-term loans.* Ordinarily used for a specified purpose, with the expectation by the lender that the loan will be repaid at the end of the project. For example, a seasonal business may borrow capital in order to build up its inventory in preparation for the peak season. When the season comes to a close, the lender expects to be repaid immediately. Similarly, a short-term loan could be used to cover a period when the company's customers or clients are in arrears; when the accounts receivable are collected, the loan is repaid. Short-term loans are usually made in the form of a promissory note (see discussion of loan documentation below) payable on demand, and may be secured by the inventory or accounts receivable that the loan is designed to cover; or it may be unsecured, under which no collateral will be required. Unless the company is a startup or operates in a highly volatile industry (thereby increasing the risk in the eyes of the lender), most short-term loans will be unsecured, thereby keeping the loan documentation and the bank's processing time and costs to a minimum. Lenders generally view short-term loans as self-liquidating in that they can be repaid by foreclosing on the current assets that the loan has financed. The fact that the bank's transactional costs are low, along with its perception of the lower risk during this short period of time, makes short-term borrowing somewhat easier for a growing business to obtain and serves as an excellent means for establishing a relationship with a bank and demonstrating creditworthiness.

- *Operating lines of credit.* Consist of a specific amount of capital that is made available to the company on an "as needed" basis over a specified period of time. A line of credit may be short term

(60–120 days) or intermediate term (one to three years), renewable or nonrenewable, and at a fixed or fluctuating rate of interest. Borrowers should be especially careful to negotiate ceilings on interest rates; to avoid excessive commitment, processing, application, and related upfront fees; and to ensure that repayment schedules will not be an undue strain for the company. The company should also ensure that its obligations to make payments against the line of credit are consistent with its own anticipated cash-flow projections.

▪ *Intermediate-term loans.* Usually provided over a three- to five-year period for the purposes of acquiring equipment, fixtures, furniture, and supplies; expanding existing facilities; acquiring another business; or for working capital. The loan is almost always secured, not only by the assets being purchased with the loan proceeds but also by the other assets of the company, such as inventory, accounts receivable, equipment, and real estate. The loan usually calls for a loan agreement, which typically includes restrictive covenants that govern the operation and management of the company during the term of the loan. The restrictive covenants (discussed in greater detail below) are designed to protect the interests of the lender and ensure that all payments are made on a timely basis, before any dividends, employee bonuses, or noncritical expenses are paid.

▪ *Long-term loans.* Generally extended for specific, highly secured transactions, such as the purchase of real estate or a multiuse business facility, in which case a lender will consider extending a long-term loan to a small company for 65 to 80 percent of the appraised value of the land or building. As a general rule, commercial banks do not provide long-term financing to small businesses. The risk of market fluctuations and business failure over a ten- or twenty-year term is simply too high for the commercial lender to feel comfortable.

STEP 3: Negotiating the Loan Document

Negotiating the financing documents requires finding the delicate balance between the requirements of the commercial lender and the needs of the buyer/borrower. The lender will want to have all rights, remedies, and protection available to mitigate the risk of loan default; on the other hand, the borrower will want to minimize the level of control exercised by the lender (generally through the affirmative and negative covenants of the loan agreement) and achieve a return on investment that greatly exceeds its loan payments and cost of capital. Before the borrower examines the documents, it is important to understand what will be negotiated.

Interest rates will generally be calculated in accordance with prevailing market rates, the degree of risk inherent in the proposed transaction, the extent of any preexisting relationship with the lender, and the cost of administering the loan.

Collateral may be pledged that has a value equal or greater to the proceeds of the loan. Under such circumstances, the borrower should attempt to keep certain assets of the business of the seller (and in some cases its own as well) outside of the pledge agreement so that they are available to serve as security in the event that additional capital is needed at a later time. Beyond the traditional forms of tangible assets that may be offered to the lender, buyer/borrowers should also consider intangibles (such as assignment of lease rights, key-man insurance, intellectual property, and goodwill) as candidates for serving as collateral. Naturally these assets could be very costly to a firm in the event of default and should be pledged only when the ability to repay is readily available.

Restrictive covenants are designed to protect the interests of the lender. The typical loan agreement will contain a variety, as follows.

1. *Affirmative covenants* detail activities that must be undertaken by the borrower, including:

- Furnishing audited financial statements (income and expenses and balance sheets) at regular intervals (usually quarterly and annually with the annual statement to be prepared and certified by an independent certified public accountant).
- Furnishing copies of all financial statements, reports, and returns that are sent to shareholders or to governmental agencies.
- Giving access to its properties and to its books of accounts and records.

- Keeping and maintaining proper books of account.
- *Complying with all applicable laws, rules, and regulations.*
- Maintaining all property in good order and repair.
- Maintaining an agreed dollar amount of net worth (or an agreed ratio of current assets to current liabilities).
- Keeping and maintaining proper and adequate levels of insurance on all assets, based on industry norms.
- Paying debts and taxes as due.
- Purchasing and paying premiums on key-man insurance that names the company as beneficiary.

2. *Negative covenants* are actions that may not be taken unless and until the borrower obtains the lender's consent, such as:

- Engaging in any business not related to the present business.
- Creating any mortgage, lien, or other security other than the pending security on the property securing the loan.
- Creating any mortgage, lien, or other encumbrance, including conditional sales agreements, other title-retention agreements, or lease-purchase agreements on any property of the company or its subsidiaries (unless excepted).
- Incurring any new indebtedness except for trade credit or renewals, extensions, or refunding of any current indebtedness. The company's right to incur indebtedness may be conditioned upon compliance with a specified ratio (actual or pro forma) of pretax income to interest expense for a designated period.
- Entering into leases of real or personal property (as lessee) in excess of a specified aggregate amount. The company's right to make leases may be conditioned upon compliance with a specified ratio (actual or pro forma) of pretax income to fixed charges for a designated period.
- Purchasing, redeeming, or otherwise acquiring or retiring for cash any of the company's capital stock (with stated exceptions), such as from posttax earnings in excess of a specified amount or for regular sinking fund requirements on preferred stock.
- Paying any cash dividends (with stated exceptions), such as from posttax earnings earned subsequent to a specified date or in excess of a specified amount.

- Becoming a guarantor, except as to negotiable instruments endorsed for collection in ordinary course.
- Making loans or advances to or investments in any person or entity other than its subsidiaries.
- Merging or consolidating with any other corporation or selling or leasing substantially all or the entirety of its assets. There may be exceptions where the company is the surviving corporation.
- Permitting net worth or current assets to fall below a specified level.
- Permitting capital expenditures to exceed a specified amount, which may be on an annual basis, with or without right to cumulate.
- Permitting officers' and directors' remuneration to exceed a specified level.
- Selling or disposing of all of the stock of a subsidiary (subject to permitted exceptions) or permitting subsidiaries to incur debt (other than trade debt).

These covenants should be carefully reviewed for consistency in relation to other corporate documents, such as the company's by-laws and shareholders' agreements.

Prepayment rights negotiate for the right to prepay the principal of the loan without penalty charges. Many commercial lenders seek to attach prepayment charges that have a fixed rate of interest in order to ensure that a minimum rate of return is earned over the projected life of the loan.

Hidden costs and fees include closing costs, processing fees, filing fees, late charges, attorney fees, out-of-pocket expense reimbursement (e.g., courier, travel, photocopying), court costs, and auditing or inspection fees in connection with the debt financing. Commercial lenders also earn revenue by requiring that the borrower maintain a minimum balance or deposit in the bank as a condition for closing on the loan.

Understanding the Legal Documents

When the buyer will be using debt as a component of the overall acquisition financing process, there is a parallel transaction in the form of a loan closing, which must be accomplished prior to the purchase transaction. The following sections discuss some of the documents a buyer will be expected to sign in connection with the closing of the loan.

The Loan Agreement

The loan agreement sets forth all of the terms and conditions of the transaction between the lender and the buyer/borrower. The key provisions include the amount, term, repayment schedules and procedures, special fees, insurance requirements, conditions precedent, restrictive covenants, the company's representations and warranties (with respect to status, capacity, ability to repay, title to properties, litigation), events of default, and remedies of the lender in the event of default. The provisions of the loan agreement and the implications of the covenants should be reviewed carefully by an experienced attorney and a knowledgeable accountant. The long-term legal and financial impact of the restrictive covenants should also be analyzed. The buyer/borrower should negotiate to establish a timetable under which certain covenants will be removed or modified as the company's ability to repay is clearly demonstrated. Do not rely on any verbal assurances by the loan officer that a waiver of a default on a payment or a covenant will subsequently be available.

The Security Agreement

The security agreement identifies the collateral to be pledged in order to secure the loan (which may be the assets of the seller and/or the buyer/borrower), usually referencing terms of the loan agreement, as well as the promissory note (especially with respect to the restrictions on the use of the collateral and the procedures upon default of the debt obligation). The remedies available to the lender in the event of default range anywhere from selling the collateral at a public auction to taking possession of the collateral and using it for an income-producing activity. The proceeds of any alternative chosen by the lender will be principally for repaying the outstanding balance of the loan. If any proceeds are left, then they can be distributed to the shareholders of the borrower unless there are unsecured lenders next in line.

The Financing Statement

The financing statement records the interests of the lender in the collateral and is filed with the state and local corporate and land records management authorities. It is designed to give notice to other potential creditors of the company that a senior security interest has been granted in the collateral specified in the financing statement. Specific rules regarding this document and the priority of competing creditors can be found in the applicable state's version of the Uniform Commercial Code (UCC).

The Promissory Note

The promissory note serves as evidence of the obligation of the buyer/borrower to the lender, with many of its terms included in the more comprehensive loan agreement (such as the interest rate, the length of the term, the repayment schedule, the ability of the company to prepay without penalty, the conditions under which the lender may declare an event of default, and the rights and remedies available to the lender upon such default).

The Personal Guaranty

The personal guaranty serves as further security to mitigate the risk of the transaction to the lender and is personally executed by the buyer/borrower. The terms of the guaranty should be carefully reviewed and negotiated, especially with respect to its term, scope, rights of the lender in the event of default, and type of guaranty provided. For example, if negotiated properly, the lender can be forced to exhaust all possible remedies against the company before being able to proceed against the guarantor or may be limited to proceed against certain assets of the guarantor. Similarly, the extent of the guaranty could be negotiated so that it is reduced each year as the company grows stronger and its ability to independently service the debt becomes more evident.

Box 9-2. Tips for Managing Tripartite Transactions

The buyer/borrower faces the challenge of trying to keep its transactions for raising debt or equity capital on track along with its deal with the seller. These tripartite transactions can be difficult to manage, but the following tips should keep everything in harmony for a synchronized closing.

- Timing is everything. Like an orchestra leader, the buyer must ensure that the lender is in the loop at all appropriate times on due diligence, deal negotiations, preclosing conditions, and the coordination of the closing. It is incumbent on the buyer to make sure that the financing transaction closes prior to the closing of the acquisition itself.

- The lender will be doing due diligence on the buyer as well as its own independent due diligence on the seller. The lender's due diligence will not only be on the two companies but also on the viability of the postclosing integration plan and the documentation of the transaction. The lender will want to see the executed confidentiality agreements, executed letters of intent, responses to due diligence requests, and all other documents that may directly or indirectly affect its rights as a lender.

- The lender will want to review the buyer's acquisition plan, with a particular focus on the value of the collateral securing the loans (where applicable), the historical earnings and cash flows of the seller, the track record and experience of the buyer, trends within the seller's industry, and the pro forma financial projections for a postclosing consolidated company.

- The buyer must pay careful attention to *cost-of-capital* issues and *debt-to-equity ratios*, which will vary from transaction to transaction. The sources of capital and their expected return on investment will also vary. For example, a senior lender, who will insist on a preferred position over other creditors, such as the subordinated lender, will often lend up to 70 percent of the purchase price, depending on the amount of assets available for collateral and the strength of the projected (as well as the historical) cash flows. If the senior lenders are properly secured, then they may not be as difficult in the negotiation of loan covenants and minimum interest rates. The subordinated lenders, on the other hand, are typically willing to provide 10 to 30 percent of the purchase price, but will generally demand a 15 to 30 percent annual return over a five- to ten-year investment horizon. Both the senior lender and the subordinated lender will usually look to the buyer to provide between 15 and 30 percent of the total capital required for the transaction. The general rule is, the larger the lender's portion of the acquisition financing puzzle, the higher its expected return on investment. If the buyer turns to the equity markets, it should be aware that most buyout funds, venture capitalists, and private investors will be looking for 20 to 30 percent returns on their investments.

Equity Financing

Equity financing involves the offer and sale of the buyer's securities for the purposes of raising the capital to pay the seller, as well as to provide working capital for the new combined company. Securities are sold via private placements, negotiations with buyout or venture capitalists, and strategic investors. There are a wide variety of resources available to identify sources of equity capital, including the following:

Regional Investment Bankers Association (RIBA)
171 Church Street, Suite 260
Charleston, SC 29401
(803) 557-2000
Jeff Adduci, President

National Venture Capital Association (NVCA)
1655 Fort Myer Drive
Suite 700
Arlington, VA 22209
(703) 351-5269

National Association of Small Business Investment Companies
  (NASBIC)
1199 N. Fairfax Drive
Suite 200
Alexandria, VA 22314
(703) 683-1601

Pratt's Guide to Venture Capital Firms
Published by Venture Economics (a subsidiary of Securities Data
  Publishing)
40 West 57th Street, 11th Floor
New York, NY 10019
(800) 455-5844

Directory of Buyout Financing Sources
Published by The Buyout Directories
40 West 57th Street, 11th Floor
New York, NY 10019
(212) 765-5311

In addition to these associations and directories, buyers should consider contacting national underwriters and even insurance companies that have participated in the equity financing of larger acquisitions.

Types of Equity Securities

Before turning to a few of these strategies in more detail, let's take a look at the types of equity securities that may be offered and sold by the buyer/offeror to acquisition financing sources. Each type of equity security carries with it a different set of rights, preferences, and potential rates of return in exchange for the capital contributed to the company. For example, the typical growing company, whose value to an investor is usually greatly dependent on intangible assets such as patents, trade secrets or goodwill, and projected earnings, will tend to issue equity securities before incurring additional debt. Typically, its balance sheet lacks the assets necessary to secure the debt, while additional debt is likely to increase the risk of company failure to unacceptably dangerous levels.

The three types of equity securities are as follows:

1. *Common stock.* An offering of common stock and the related dilution of interest is often a traumatic experience for owners of growing companies that are used to operating closely held corporations. The need for growth capital beyond what is available through personal savings or corporate retained earnings results in a realignment of the capital structure and a redistribution of ownership and control. Although the offering of additional common stock is generally costly and entails a surrender of some ownership and control, it does offer the company an increased equity base and a more secure foundation upon which to build a company, while the likelihood of obtaining future debt financing is greatly increased.

2. *Preferred stock.* In exchange for their capital, purchasers of preferred stock receive dividends at a fixed or adjustable rate of return (similar to a debt instrument), with priority over dividends distributed to the holders of the common stock, as well as a preference on the distribution of assets in the event of liquidation. The preferred stock may or may not have certain rights with respect

to voting, convertibility to common stock, antidilution rights, or redemption privileges that may be exercised either by the company or the holder.

Although the fixed dividends payments are not tax deductible and ownership of the company is still diluted, the balance between risk and reward is still achieved because the principal invested need not be returned (unless there are provisions for redemption). In addition, the preferred stockholders' return on investment is limited to a fixed rate of return (unless there are provisions for conversion of the preferred stock to the common), and the claims of the preferred stockholders are subordinated to the claims of creditors and bondholders in the event of a failure to pay dividends upon the liquidation of the company. The use of convertible preferred stock is especially popular with venture capitalists.

3. *Convertible securities.* Convertible securities provide the holder with an option to convert the underlying security, such as a note or preferred stock (based on specified terms and conditions), into common stock. The incentive for conversion is usually the same as for the exercise of a warrant—namely, that the price of the common stock be higher than the current rate of return provided by the convertible security. Convertible securities offer several distinct advantages to a company.

- They are an opportunity to obtain growth capital at lower interest rates and with less restrictive covenants in exchange for a chance to participate in the company's success if it meets its projections and objectives.
- They generate proceeds that are 10 to 30 percent above the sale price of common stock at the time the convertible security is issued. There are greater earnings per share because the company can obtain the same capital by selling fewer shares of convertible securities than by selling common stock.
- They represent a general broadening of the market of prospective purchasers for the securities, since certain buyers may wish to avoid a direct purchase of common stock but would consider an investment in convertible securities.

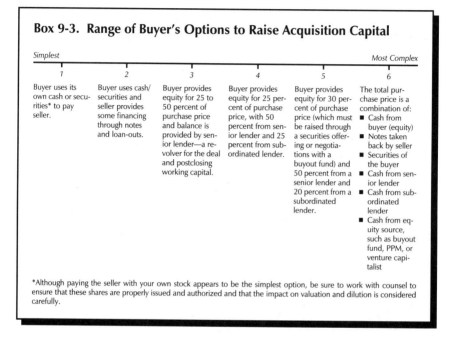

Box 9-3. Range of Buyer's Options to Raise Acquisition Capital

Simplest   *Most Complex*

1	2	3	4	5	6
Buyer uses its own cash or securities* to pay seller.	Buyer uses cash/securities and seller provides some financing through notes and loan-outs.	Buyer provides equity for 25 to 50 percent of purchase price and balance is provided by senior lender—a revolver for the deal and postclosing working capital.	Buyer provides equity for 25 percent of purchase price, with 50 percent from senior lender and 25 percent from subordinated lender.	Buyer provides equity for 30 percent of purchase price (which must be raised through a securities offering or negotiations with a buyout fund) and 50 percent from a senior lender and 20 percent from a subordinated lender.	The total purchase price is a combination of: ■ Cash from buyer (equity) ■ Notes taken back by seller ■ Securities of the buyer ■ Cash from senior lender ■ Cash from subordinated lender ■ Cash from equity source, such as buyout fund, PPM, or venture capitalist

*Although paying the seller with your own stock appears to be the simplest option, be sure to work with counsel to ensure that these shares are properly issued and authorized and that the impact on valuation and dilution is considered carefully.

Private Placement Offerings

The private placement offering is any type of offering of securities by a small or growing company that does *not* need to be registered with the Securities and Exchange Commission (SEC). In order to determine whether a private placement is a sensible strategy for raising acquisition capital, the buyer/offeror must have a fundamental understanding of federal and state securities laws affecting private placements (which follow here in an overview), be familiar with the preparation requirements, and have a team of qualified legal and accounting professionals to assist with the preparation of the offering documents or private placement memorandum (PPM).

The private placement generally offers reduced transaction and ongoing costs for the offeror because of its exemption from many of the extensive registration and reporting requirements imposed by federal and state securities laws. The private placement alternative usually also offers the ability to structure a more complex and confidential transaction, since the offerees will typically be a small number of sophisticated investors. In addition, a private placement permits a more rapid penetration into the capital markets than would a public offering.

Federal Securities Law

As a general rule, the Securities Act of 1933 requires a filing of a registration statement with the SEC prior to the offer to sell any security in interstate commerce unless an exemption is available, of which private placement is the most commonly recognized. The penalties for failing to register or for disclosing inaccurate or misleading information are quite stringent. Registration is also an expensive and time-consuming process, and a network of underwriters and brokers or dealers must be assembled to make a market for the security. In addition, a registrant is also subject to strict periodic reporting requirements.

To qualify for a private placement, the buyer/offerer must work with legal counsel to structure the transaction within the various categories of exemptions available. They include Section 4(2) (the broad private offering exemption designed for "transaction(s) not involving any public offering"); Section 3(a)(11) (an intrastate exemption); and the most common, Regulation D (which encompasses three specific transactional exemptions from the Sections 3(b) and 4(2)).

Section 4(2) allows an exemption from registration for transactions by an issuer not involving a public offering. The vague language of the act has been a source of much controversy and confusion in the legal and financial communities. Over the years, court cases have established that to qualify for this exemption, targeted investors in a 4(2) offering must have access to the same kind of information that would be available if the issuer were required to register. However, terms like "access to" and "same kind" generally leave discretion to the company and its attorney of the exact method of presenting the necessary information. In relying on an exemption under Section 4(2), the offering should be structured in accordance with the following guidelines:

1. The offering should be made directly to prospective investors without the use of any general advertising or solicitation.

2. The number of offerees should be limited.

3. The offering should be limited to either insiders (such as officers of the company or family members) or sophisticated investors who have a preexisting relationship with the buyer/offeror or the company.

4. The prospective investor should be provided (at a minimum) with recent financial statements, a list of critical risk factors that influence the investment, and an open invitation to inspect the company's facilities and records.

5. If in doubt as to whether Section 4(2) applies to a particular offering, *do not rely on it;* rather, attempt to structure the transaction within one of the Regulation D exemptions.

Section 3(a)(11) allows for an exemption for "any security which is part of an issue offered and sold only to persons resident within a single state by an issuer which is a resident and doing business within such state." The key issue in relying on this exemption is to ensure that the offering is truly an intrastate offering. This test is deceptive; however, the SEC has adopted Rule 147 to assist in determining whether the requirements of Section 3(a)(11) have been met. Precautionary steps must be taken to ensure that all offerees are residents of the particular state because even one nonresidential offeree will jeopardize the availability of the exemption.

Rule 504 under Regulation D permits offers and sales of not more than $1 million during any twelve-month period by an issuer that is not subject to the reporting requirements of the Securities Exchange Act of 1934 and that is not an investment company. Rule 504 places virtually no limit on the number or the nature of the investors that participate in the offering. The SEC also requires that its Form D be filed for all offerings under Regulation D within 15 days of the first sale. But even if accreditation is not required, it is *strongly recommended* that certain baseline criteria be developed and disclosed in order to avoid unqualified or unsophisticated investors.

Even though no formal disclosure document or prospectus needs to be registered and delivered to offerees under Rule 504, there are many procedures that still must be understood and followed, and a disclosure document is nevertheless strongly recommended. An offering under Rule 504 is still subject to the general antifraud provisions of the Exchange Act; thus, every document or other information that is actually provided to the prospective investor must be accurate and not misleading by virtue of its content or its omissions. Finally, a buyer/offeror seeking to raise capital under Rule 504 should examine applicable state laws very carefully. Although many states have adopted overall securities laws similar to Regulation D, many of these laws do not include an exemption similar to 504 and, as a result, a formal memorandum (which is discussed later in this chapter) may need to be prepared.

Rule 505 under Regulation D is often selected over Rule 504 by companies as a result of its requirements being consistent with many state securities laws. Rule 505 allows for the sale of up to $5 million of the issuer's securities in a twelve-month period to an unlimited number of accredited investors and up to thirty-five nonaccredited investors (regardless of their net worth, income, or sophistication). An *accredited investor* is any person in at least one of the eight categories set out in Rule 501(a) of Regulation D. Included in these categories are officers and directors of the company who have "policy-making" functions, as well as outside investors who meet certain income or net worth criteria. Rule 505 has many of the same filing requirements and restrictions imposed by Rule 504 (such as the need to file a Form D), in addition to an absolute prohibition on advertising and general solicitation for offerings and restrictions on which companies may be an issuer. Any company that is subject to the "bad boy" provisions of Regulation A is disqualified from being a 505 offeror; this applies to persons who have been subject to certain disciplinary, administrative, civil, or criminal proceedings, or to sanctions which involve the company or its predecessors.

Rule 506 is similar to Rule 505; however, the issuer may sell its securities to an unlimited number of accredited investors and up to thirty-five nonaccredited investors. For buyer/borrowers needing over $5 million to complete the proposed acquisition, this exemption is the most attractive because it has no maximum dollar limitation. The key difference under Rule 506 is that any nonaccredited investor must be sophisticated. A *sophisticated investor* is one who does not fall within any of the eight categories specified by Rule

501(a) and is believed by the issuer to "have knowledge and experience in financial and business matters that render him capable of evaluating the merits and understanding the risks posed by the transaction (either acting alone or in conjunction with his "purchaser representative"). The best way to remove any uncertainty over the sophistication or accreditation of a prospective investor is to request that a comprehensive Confidential Offeree Questionnaire be completed before the securities are sold. Rule 506 does eliminate the need to prepare and deliver disclosure documents in any specified format if exclusively accredited investors participate in the transaction. As with Rule 505, an absolute prohibition on advertising and general solicitation exists.

State Securities Laws

Regulation D was designed to provide a foundation for uniformity between federal and state securities laws. This objective has been met in some states, but it still has a long way to go on a national level. Full compliance with the federal securities laws is only one level of regulation that must be taken into account when developing plans and strategies to raise capital through an offering of securities. Whether or not the offering is exempt under federal laws, registration may still be required in the states where the securities are to be sold under "blue sky" laws.

The level of review varies widely among the states, ranging from very tough "merit" reviews designed to ensure that all offerings of securities are fair and equitable to very lenient "notice only" filings designed to promote full disclosure. The securities laws and requirements of each state where an offer or sale will be made should be checked very carefully prior to the distribution of the offering documents. Every state in the nation does, in fact, have some type of statute governing securities transactions and securities dealers. When drafting the offering, these laws should be reviewed to determine the following:

- If the particular limited offering exemption selected under federal law will also apply in the state
- Which pre-sale or postsale registration with the applicable states or mandatory state legends are required

- The remedies available to an investor who has purchased securities from a company that has failed to comply with applicable state laws

  - Who may offer securities for sale on behalf of the company

Small Corporate Offering Registration

Most states have now adopted the Small Corporate Offering Registration (SCOR), which simplifies Regulation D as a source of acquisition financing for small businesses. SCOR allows for a question-and-answer format disclosure document that you can fill in with the assistance of your accountant or attorney. This new format significantly reduces the cost of compliance without sacrificing the quality of information available to prospective investors to reach an informed decision. There are restrictions on the structure of offerings that can be made under the U-7, the details of which should be discussed carefully with your attorney.

Preparing the Private Placement Memorandum

The offeror should work with legal counsel to prepare the document and exhibits that constitute the private placement memorandum (PPM). The PPM describes the background of the company, details of the proposed transaction, historical performance of the seller, risks to the investor, and terms of the securities being sold. In determining the exact degree of disclosure that should be included in the document, there are several factors that affect the type of information that must be provided and the format in which the data are to be presented.

- The minimum level of disclosure that must be made under federal securities laws, which depends, in part, on the exemption from registration being relied upon.

- The minimum level of disclosure that must be made under an applicable state's securities laws, which naturally depends on the state or states in which an offer or sale of the securities is to be made.

- The expectations of the targeted investors; some investors will expect a certain amount of information presented in a specified format regardless of what the law may require.

- The complexity or the nature of the company and the terms of the offering

Many buyer/offerors should prepare detailed disclosure documents, regardless of whether or not they are required to do so, in order to avoid liability for misstatements, fraud, or confusion, especially if the nature of the company and/or the terms of its offering are very complex.

First, each transaction or proposed offering of securities must be carefully reviewed by legal counsel to determine the minimum level of disclosure that must be provided to prospective investors under applicable federal and state laws. Once this is established, the costs of preparing a more detailed document than may be required should be weighed against the benefits of the additional protection provided to the company by a more comprehensive prospectus. The key question will always be, What is the most cost-effective vehicle for providing the targeted investors with the information that they require and that both applicable law and prudence dictate they must have? There are no easy answers.

The specific disclosure items to be included in the PPM will vary depending on the size of the offering and the nature of the investors under federal securities laws and any applicable state laws. The text should be descriptive, not persuasive, and allow the reader to reach his or her own conclusions as to the merits of the securities being offered by the company. At the minimum every good PPM must include the following material.

- *Introductory materials.* These introduce the prospective investor to the basic terms of the offering. A cover page should include a brief statement about the buyer and seller, the core business of each company, the terms of the offering (often in table form), and all required "legends" required by federal and state laws. The cover page should be followed by a summary of the offering, which serves as an integral part of the introductory materials and cross-reference point for the reader. The third and final parts of the introductory materials are usually a statement of the investor suitability standards, which includes a discussion of the federal and state securities laws applicable to the offering, and the definitions of an accredited investor as applied to the offering.

- *Description of the company.* This is obviously a statement of the buyer's and seller's history and should include a discussion of each company's history; principal officers and directors; products and services; management and operating policies; performance history and goals; competition; trends in the industry; advertising and marketing strategy; suppliers and distributors; intellectual property rights; key real and personal property; customer demographics; and any other material information that would be relevant to the investor.

- *Risk factors.* This is usually the most difficult section to write, yet it is viewed by many as clearly one of the most important to the prospective investor. Its purpose is to outline all of the factors that make the offering or the projected acquisition plans risky or speculative. Naturally, the exact risks to the investors posed by the offering will depend on the nature of the company and the trends within that industry.

- *Capitalization of the issuer.* This issue should be discussed, providing the capital structure of the buyer/offeror both before and after the offering and before and after the proposed acquisition. For the purposes of this section in the PPM, all authorized and outstanding securities must be disclosed, including all long-term debt.

- *Management of the company.* This section should include a list of names, ages, special skills, or characteristics and biographical information on each officer, director, or key consultant; compensation and stock option arrangements; bonus plans; special contracts or arrangements; and any transactions between the company and individual officers and directors, including loans, self-dealing, and related types of transactions. The role and identity of the buyer/offeror's legal and accounting firms should also be disclosed, as well as any other experts retained in connection with the offering.

- *Terms of the offering.* This should describe the terms and conditions, the number of shares, and the price. If the securities are to be offered through underwriters, brokers, or dealers, then the names of each distributor, the terms of the relationship, the commissions to be paid, the obligations of the distributor (e.g., guaranteed or best efforts offering), and any special rights, such as the right of a particular underwriter to serve on the board of directors, any indemnification provisions, or other material terms of the offering, should be given.

- *Allocation of proceeds.* This section must state the principle purposes for which the net proceeds will be used and the approximate amount intended to be used for each purpose. The buyer/offeror should give careful thought to this section because any deviation from the use of funds as described in the PPM could trigger liability.

- *Dilution.* This section should include a discussion of the number of shares outstanding prior to the offering, the price paid, the net book value, the effect on existing shareholders of the proposed offering, and dilutive effects on new purchasers at the completion of the offering. Often the founding shareholders, and sometimes their key advisors or the people who will help promote the PPM, will have acquired their securities at prices substantially below those in the prospective offering.

- *Description of securities.* This should explain the rights, restrictions, and special features of the securities being offered. Also, this section should explain provisions of the articles of incorporation or bylaws that affect capitalization, such as preemptive rights, total authorized stock, different classes of shares, or restrictions on declaration and distribution of dividends.

- *Financial statements.* To be provided by the issuer, these will vary depending on the amount of money to be raised, applicable federal and state regulations, and the company's nature and stage of growth. The PPM should provide a discussion and explanation of these financial statements and an analysis of current and projected financial conditions.

- *Exhibits.* Items such as the articles of incorporation and bylaws, key contracts or leases, brochures, news articles, marketing reports, and resumes of the principals, may be appended as exhibits to the PPM.

Subscription Materials

Once the prospective investors and their advisors have made their decisions to provide capital to the buyer/offeror in accordance with the terms of the PPM, there are documents that must be signed to evidence the investors' desires to subscribe to purchase the securities offered by the PPM. The various subscription materials that should accompany the PPM serve several purposes, such as to protect the company against a claim of noncompliance and to screen out potentially difficult investors. Two key documents are as follows:

- *Subscriber questionnaire.* This is developed in order to obtain certain information from prospective offerees and then serves as evidence of the required sophistication level and the ability of offerees to fend for themselves as required in a PPM. The buyer/offeror should obtain information regarding the prospective purchaser's background, citizenship, education, employment, investment, and/or business experience.
- *Subscription agreement.* This is the contract between the purchaser (investor) and the issuer of the securities. It should contain acknowledgement of:

1. The receipt and review by the subscriber of the PPM
2. The restricted nature of the securities to be acquired and knowledge of the fact that the securities were acquired under an exemption from registration
3. Any particularly significant suitability requirements, such as amount of investment or passive income or tax bracket, that the issuer feels may be crucial to the purchaser's ability to obtain the benefits of the proposed investment
4. An awareness of specific risks disclosed in the information furnished
5. The existence of the purchaser representative (if one is used)

The subscription agreement should also require a signature to confirm the accuracy and completeness of the information contained in the offeree or purchaser questionnaire and the number and price of the securities to be purchased and the manner of payment.

The subscription agreement often contains an agreement on the part of the purchaser to indemnify the issuer against losses or liabilities resulting from any misrepresentations on the part of the prospective purchaser that would void or destroy the exemption from registration that the issuer is attempting to invoke. The subscription agreement should also contain representations on the part of the subscriber with respect to its authority to execute the agreement.

Venture Capital Funds

A buyer/offeror whose transactions do not qualify for debt financing from a commercial bank, or where a private placement is not appropriate, might consider an institutional venture capital or buyout as a source of acquisition financing. The term *venture capital* has been defined in many ways, but refers generally to relatively high-risk, early-stage financing of young, emerging growth companies. The professional venture capitalist is usually a highly trained finance professional who manages a pool of venture funds for investment in growing companies on behalf of a group of passive investors. Another major source of venture capital available to buyer/offerors who meet certain minimum size requirements is a small-business investment company (SBIC). An SBIC is a privately organized investment company that is specially licensed under the Small Business Investment Act of 1958 to borrow funds through the Small Business Administration for subsequent investment in the small-business community. Finally, some private corporations and state governments manage venture capital funds that may be available sources of equity capital for acquisition financing.

The Investment Decision

Regardless of the buyer/offeror's particular stage of development, or the specific details of the proposed acquisition transaction, there are several key variables that all venture capital firms will consider in analyzing the acquisition plan presented. These variables generally fall into four categories: (1) the management team; (2) products and services offered; (3) the markets in which the target company and the buyer/offeror competes; and (4) the anticipated return on investment. In determining whether the growing company would qualify for venture capital, its management team must be prepared to answer the following questions:

Management Team

- What are the background, knowledge, skills, and abilities of each member?
- How is this experience relevant to the specific industry in which the buyer/offeror competes?
- How are the risks and problems often inherent in the buyer/offeror's industry handled by the members of the management team?

Products and Services

- At what stage of development are the buyer/offeror's products and services?
- What is the specific market opportunity which has been identified by the proposed transaction?
- How long will this window of opportunity remain open?
- What steps are necessary for the company to exploit this opportunity?
- To what extent are the company's products and services unique, innovative, and proprietary?

The Growing Company's Targeted Markets

- What is the stage in the life cycle of the industry in which the buyer/offeror plans to operate on a postclosing consolidated basis?
- What are the size and projected growth rate of the company's targeted market?
- What methods of marketing, sales, and distribution will be utilized in attracting and keeping customers?
- What are the strengths and weaknesses of each competitor, be they direct, indirect, or anticipated, in the targeted market?

Return on Investment

- What are the buyer/offeror's current and projected valuations and performance in terms of sales, earnings, and dividends?
- To what extent have these budgets and projections been substantiated?
- Has the company overestimated or underestimated the amount of capital that will be required for the growth and development of its acquisition plan?
- How much money and time have already been invested by the owners and managers?

Negotiating and Structuring the Investment

The negotiation and structuring of most venture capital transactions revolve around the need to strike a balance between the concerns of the buyer's management team (such as dilution of ownership and loss of control) and the concerns of the venture capitalist (such as return on investment and mitigating the risk of company failure). The typical end result of these negotiations is a *term sheet* that specifies the key financial and legal terms of the transaction and then serves as a basis for the negotiation and preparation of the definitive legal documentation.

The buyer/offeror should work with its legal counsel in order to understand the many traps and restrictions, such as contingent proxies and super majority voting provisions, that are typically found in venture capital financing documents. The term sheet may also contain rights and obligations, including an obligation to maintain an agreed valuation of the company; that the company will be responsible for certain costs and expenses in the event the proposed transaction does not take place; or an obligation to secure commitments for financing from additional sources prior to closing.

The initial negotiation of the term sheet, and eventually the definitive documents, will usually center on the types of securities to be used and the principle terms, conditions, and benefits offered by the securities. The type of security ultimately selected will usually fall within one of the following categories:

- *Preferred stock.* The most typical form of security issued in connection with a venture capital financing because of the many advantages offered to an investor, such as convertibility into common stock, dividend and liquidation preferences over the common stock, antidilution protection (allowing the venture capitalist to maintain its ownership position), mandatory or optional redemption schedules (allowing the company to repurchase the shares or the investors to "put" them back to the buyer), and special voting rights and preferences.

- *Convertible notes.* Often preferred by a venture capitalist in connection with higher-risk transactions because he or she is able to enjoy the senior position of a creditor over a shareholder until the risk of the company's failure has been mitigated.

- *Debt securities with warrants.* Also preferred by venture capitalists because they protect the downside by earning debt payments and protect the upside by including warrants to purchase common stock at favorable prices and terms. The use of a warrant enables the investor to buy common stock without sacrificing the position as a creditor, as would be the case if only convertible debt were used in the financing.

- *Common stock.* Rarely preferred by venture capitalists, especially at early stages of development, because it does not offer the investor any special rights or preferences, a fixed return on investment, special ability to exercise control over management, or liquidity to protect against downside risks. One of the few times that common stock might be selected is when there are tax advantages to preserving the buyer's Subchapter S status under the Internal Revenue Code. This might be jeopardized if a class of preferred stock (with different economic terms) were to be authorized by an amendment of the buyer's corporate charter.

Once the type of security is designated by the venture capitalist, steps must be taken to ensure that authorization and issuance of the security is properly made under applicable state corporate laws. For example, if the company's charter does not provide for a class of preferred stock, then the articles of amendment must be prepared, approved by the board of directors and shareholders, and filed with the appropriate state corporation authorities. The articles of amendment will include new provisions on voting rights, dividend rates and preferences, mandatory redemption provisions, antidilution protection (also called "ratchet clauses" because the price of the shares upon conversion is ratcheted down if the buyer's company issues shares below the conversion price), and related special rights and features. If debentures are selected, then negotiations will typically focus on term, interest rate and payment schedule, conversion rights and rates, extent of subordination, remedies for default, acceleration and prepayment rights, and underlying security for the instrument, as well as on the terms and conditions of any warrants granted along with the debentures.

The legal documents involved in a venture capital financing must reflect the end result of the negotiation process and must contain all of the legal rights and obligations. These documents generally include the following:

- Preferred stock or debenture purchase agreement (investment agreement)
- Stockholders' agreement
- Employment and confidentiality agreements
- Warrant (where applicable)
- Debenture or notes (where applicable)
- Preferred stock resolution to amend the corporate charter (where applicable)
- Contingent proxy
- Legal opinion of company counsel
- Registration rights agreement

The investment agreement describes all of the material terms and conditions of the financing. It also serves as a type of disclosure document because certain key historical and financial information is disclosed in the representations and warranties made to the investors. The representations and warranties (along with any exhibits) are designed to provide full disclosure to the investors, which will then provide a basis for evaluating the risk of the investment and structure of the transaction. The investment agreement will also provide for certain conditions precedent that must be met by the company prior to the closing. These provisions require the company to perform certain acts at, or prior to, closing as a condition to the investor providing the venture capital financing. The conditions to closing are often used in negotiations to mitigate or eliminate certain risks identified by the investor, such as a class action suit by a group of disgruntled employees. But usually they are more of an administrative checklist of actions that must occur at closing, such as the execution of the stockholders', employment, and confidentiality agreements.

The stockholders' agreement will typically contain certain restrictions on the transfer of the company's securities, voting provisions, rights of first refusal, and co-sale rights in the event of a sale of the founder's securities, antidilution rights, and optional redemption rights for the venture capital investors. Venture capitalists will often require the principle stockholders to become parties to the stockholders' agreement as a condition to closing on the investment. Any existing stockholders or buy/sell agreements will also be carefully scrutinized and may need to be amended or terminated as a condition to the investment. For example, the investors may want to reserve a right to purchase additional shares of preferred stock in order to preserve their respective equity ownership in the company in the event that another round of the preferred stock is subsequently issued. This is often accomplished with a contractual preemptive right, as opposed to such a right being contained in the corporate charter, which would make these rights available to all holders of the company's stock.

Employment and confidentiality agreements will be often be required of key members of the management team as a condition to the investment. These agreements define the obligations of each employee, the compensation package, the grounds for termination, the obligation to preserve and protect the company's intellectual property, and posttermination covenants, such as covenants not to compete or to disclose confidential information.

The contingent proxy provides for a transfer of the voting rights attached to any securities held by a key principal to the venture capitalist upon the death or disability of such personnel. The proxy may also be used as a penalty for breach of a covenant or warranty included in the investment agreement.

The registration rights agreement would require the venture capital investors to convert their preferred stock or debentures prior to the time that a registration statement is approved by the SEC.

This is often required, since these registration rights are limited to the company's common stock. Many venture capitalists view the eventual public offering of the company's securities (pursuant to a registration statement filed with the SEC under the Securities Act) as the optimal method of achieving investment liquidity and maximum return on investment. As a result, the venture capitalist will protect his or her right to participate in the eventual offering with a registration rights agreement. The registration rights may be in the form of *demand rights,* which are the investors' rights to require the company to prepare, file, and maintain a registration statement, or *piggyback rights,* which allow the investors to have their investment securities included in a company-initiated registration. The number of each type of demand or piggyback rights, the percentage of investors necessary to exercise these rights, the allocation of expenses of registration, the minimum size of the offering, the scope of indemnification, and the selection of underwriters and broker/dealers will all be areas of negotiation in the registration rights agreement.

A well-prepared acquisition plan, an understanding of the analysis conducted by the venture capitalist, and an understanding of the legal documents typically prepared in a venture capital financing will significantly increase the buyer/offeror's ability to gain access to this growing source of acquisition financing.

Chapter 10

The Purchase Agreement and Related Legal Documents

Once the due diligence has been completed, valuations and appraisals conducted, terms and price initially negotiated, and financing arranged, the acquisition team must work carefully with legal counsel to structure and begin the preparation of the definitive legal documentation that will memorialize the transaction. The drafting and negotiation of these documents will usually focus on the past history of the seller, the present condition of the business, and a description of the rules of the game for the future. They also describe the nature and scope of the seller's representations and warranties, the terms of the seller's indemnification of the buyer, the conditions precedent to closing of the transaction, the responsibilities of the parties during the time period between execution of the purchase agreement and actual closing, the terms and structure of payment, the scope of postclosing covenants of competition, the deferred or contingent compensation components, and any predetermined remedies for breach of the contract.

Case Study: GCC Acquires TCI

Again, we will use the two companies described in Chapter 6, Growth Co. Corp. (GCC) and Target Co., Inc. (TCI). GCC is concerned about unknown or contingent liabilities stemming from some prior product liability claims against TCI that may resurface. A *memorandum of understanding* is negotiated so GCC will acquire substantially all of the assets of TCI for $10 million. The financing arranged by GCC will come from the following sources:[1]

1. $2 million in cash from the internal capital reserves and retained earnings of GCC
2. $3 million in debt financing provided by Business Bank Corp. (BBC), which will be secured by the assets of TCI
3. $4.5 million in seller's take-back financing by TCI and in the securities of GCC, payable as follows:
   a. $2 million subordinated five-year promissory note
   b. $1 million in the common stock in Growth Co. Subsidiary Inc. (GCS), a new subsidiary established by GCC to manage and operate the assets being acquired
   c. $1.3 million as a target—it could be more, it could be less—in the form of a contingent earn-out based on the financial performance, such as a percentage of sales or net profits, of GCS over the next three years
   d. $200,000 in the form of a two-year consulting agreement at $100,000 per annum for the founding and majority shareholders of TCI[2]
4. $500,000 of TCI debt, which will be assumed by GCC

In structuring this deal, notice that GCC has created a new subsidiary to receive, manage, and operate the assets being acquired from TCI. This will help to insulate GCC assets in the event of a subsequent dispute and make the accounting for the earn-out component easier to calculate. GCC has also managed to shift the allocation of risk back to the seller by negotiating roughly 40 percent of the purchase price as being either contingent or deferred. From a liquidity and timing perspective, this deal is also favorable

1. This financing structure may be more complex than the typical asset acquisition at this level; however, it is designed to provide the reader with some different approaches for structuring such an acquisition.
2. Note that when part of the overall consideration to the seller will be a consulting agreement, there are often certain fiduciary issues that must be addressed in terms of a majority shareholder being favored over the minority shareholders. There are also certain tax advantages to the buyer when structuring the deal in this fashion.

to GCC, since it must use only 20 percent of its own funds to make the acquisition and has several years to repay the lion's share of its obligations to BBC and TCI. The officers of GCC have also managed to convince the shareholders of TCI to buy into the future business plan of GCS, since they have agreed to take 25 percent of their consideration stock in a consulting agreement and in the form of a contingent earn-out. Notwithstanding these attractive features for GCC/GCS, the TCI shareholders are not exactly in terrible shape, either. They receive 50 percent of their selling price in cash at closing, get $500,000 of their accounts payable assumed by GCS/GCC, and are second in line (behind BBC) with a security interest in the assets sold.

This transaction requires a wide variety of legal documents that must be prepared and negotiated in order to consummate the transaction.

- Asset purchase agreement (among GCC, GCS, and TCI)
- Intercreditor agreement (between BBC and TCI)
- Loan agreement (among BBC, GCC, and GCS)
- Promissory note, security agreement, and financing statements (for BBC loan)
- Promissory note, security agreement, and financing statements (for TCI take-back financing)
- Board of directors and shareholders resolutions of TCI approving the transaction
- Board of directors resolutions of GCC and GCS approving the transaction
- Certificates for the GCS common stock (for TCI shareholders)
- Assumption of liabilities agreement (also known as a liabilities undertaking) by GCS to TCI (whereby GCS, as the buyer, assumes responsibility for specific obligations of TCI as the seller), subject to the consent of the TCI creditors. In addition, TCI may want to obtain estoppel certificates or novation agreements from creditors covered by this agreement
- Bill of sale (for TCI assets sold to GCC and GCS)
- Bulk sales affidavits, if applicable under Article 6 of the state commercial code (from TCI to its creditors)

- Disclosure documents to TCI shareholders for issuance of GCS warrants, if required by federal or state securities laws
- Noncompetition and nondisclosure agreements (for TCI management team to GCC and GCS)
- Consulting agreement, which serves as part of the deferred compensation to the controlling TCI shareholder
- Employment agreements to the extent that any of TCI's employees will be hired
- Assignment of key contracts and third-party consent agreements (e.g., leases, loan agreements from TCI to GCS)
- Opinion of TCI counsel (to GCC and GCS)
- Lien search reports on TCI assets
- Certificates of compliance with representations, warranties, and conditions precedent (by TCI president and secretary)
- Earn-out agreement (may be included in main body of asset purchase agreement or be separate)
- Indemnification agreement (may be included in main body of asset purchase agreement or be separate)
- Escrow agreement, if negotiated; proceeds of sale price to be placed in escrow until certain postclosing conditions are met and postclosing adjustments are made by TCI, or as a contingency reserve fund in the event that representations and warranties are subsequently found to be untrue
- Resignation and release agreements (from TCC employees who will not be retained after the transaction)
- Personal guarantees (by key shareholders of GCC if demanded by BBC or TCI to secure the promissory notes)
- License agreements, if any (to the extent that intellectual property rights are being retained by TCI and exclusively licensed by GCS)
- Allocation certificates for federal, state, and local tax filings, as well as UCC filings where applicable
- List of schedules and exhibits to the asset purchase agreement (to be compiled and prepared by TCI and its counsel)

Note: Had the transaction been structured as a stock purchase rather than as an asset transaction, then TCI shareholders would also have to produce duly endorsed stock certificates, current corporate financial statements, certified copies of the corporate financial statements, certified copies of the corporate articles and bylaws, certificates of good standing, officer and director releases, termination and resignation agreements, termination of personnel and retirement plans (where applicable), and all other material corporate documentation at the closing.

Naturally, providing a detailed review of all these agreements would be a book unto itself—one that would likely put you quickly to sleep. For illustrative purposes, now, let's take a look at a few of these agreements in more detail.

The Asset Purchase (or Acquisition Agreement)

This document includes a statement of the parties to the transaction; the assets and liabilities that are being sold; the manner in which the assets and liabilities will be sold; the terms and conditions of the transaction; the amount and terms of payment of the consideration to be paid by the purchaser; the assurances of the seller as to the status and performance of the assets being sold; and the rights of each party if another party fails to perform as contemplated by the agreement or otherwise breaches its representations and warranties. It also addresses the timetable for the closing of the transaction.

The asset purchase agreement should be balanced to protect the interests of both parties. From the buyer's perspective, the asset purchase agreement should provide as much detail as possible concerning the status and performance of the business to be acquired. It should shift risk to the seller by establishing grounds for the buyer to terminate the transaction if the representations and warranties prove untrue as well as provide a basis for renegotiation if facts develop indicating that the transaction, as structured, is not what the buyer had bargained for. And it should provide a basis after closing for the buyer to seek monetary damages from the seller should the representations, warranties, and covenants of the agreement prove untrue.

The asset purchase agreement should provide a means for updating the information delivered to the purchaser by the seller and, if the transfer of the business is to occur on a date subsequent to the date on which the asset purchase agreement is signed, the asset purchase agreement should include covenants of the seller regarding its conduct of the business from the date of the asset purchase agreement through the closing or termination of the asset purchase agreement.

The initial draft of the asset purchase agreement is typically prepared by GCC's counsel, as purchaser who is responsible for ensuring that the purchaser acquires the assets and liabilities bargained for without assuming responsibility for any undisclosed obligations of the business or the seller.

Here is a list of the categories of issues that must be addressed in the GCC/TCI asset purchase agreement items.

1. Recitals identifying TCI and GCC, stating their relative roles, and the assets being sold.
2. Clauses that provide for the transfer of the assets being sold, the price to be paid, and the manner in which the price will be paid. In the event securities are being issued in payment of the purchase price, methods of valuing those securities might be appropriate in this section. And in connection with transfer of assets, there is provision for the buyer's assumption of liabilities.
3. Representations and warranties of TCI.
4. Representations and warranties of GCC.
5. A statement of the manner in which TCI will conduct the business, including restrictions on certain types of operations or merger purchases, prior to the closing.
6. Those conditions that are to precede the obligations of GCC to be performed at the closing.
7. Those conditions that are to precede the obligations of TCI to be performed at the closing.
8. A summary of the closing itself, the mechanics thereof, and the documents to be delivered at the closing.
9. Agreements and commitments relating to the relationship of the parties and the activities of the business sold after the closing.
10. Agreements relating to the survival of the representations and warranties of the parties and, importantly, the indemnification provisions to be provided by TCI and GCC.
11. For an asset transfer, provisions relating to bulk sales laws.

12. For a stock transfer, provisions relating to the securities laws and rights to resell securities issued pursuant to registration statements or otherwise.
13. A provision relating to brokers.
14. Provisions related to employee benefits.
15. Miscellaneous provisions including notices, the completeness of the agreement, the law governing the interpretation of the agreement, whether or not the provisions of the agreement will be severable, and other general provisions desired by the parties.

Legal counsel to GCC should also specify all conditions precedent to the obligations of the parties to close the transaction in the asset purchase agreement. Conditions are generally factors beyond either party's control, such as regulatory approval or consents, the existence or nonexistence of which will excuse one or both parties from its obligation to close the transaction. The asset purchase agreement should include remedies for losses, liabilities, damages, or expenses arising out of a party's breach either before or after the acquisition.

There are a wide variety of issues in the asset purchase agreement that will be hotly negotiated between TCI and GCC.

Indemnification

One of the most contested areas is the indemnification provisions, usually because GCC/GCS will want to be reimbursed for any transaction or occurrence that took place before closing that subsequently gives rise to some claim or liability. TCI shareholders, on the other hand, will want to make a clean break from liability attached to the assets being conveyed, including any responsibility for events that arose even before closing.

As discussed earlier in this book, one of the key aspects of an acquisition is the negotiation and allocation of the *risks* to each party both before and after closing. The goal is to allocate risk in a balanced and economically appropriate manner. The buyer is concerned with *core risks,* such as those raised by a misrepresentation or breach of covenant by the seller, and *collateral risks,* such as those raised by facts and circumstances that were not necessarily anticipated by the parties at the time of the negotiation. Buyers and their counsel will often seek a full indemnity from the seller against any specific liabilities that have not been assumed by the buyer as part of the transaction and any damages or losses (including costs and expenses) that were incurred owing to inaccuracy of representations, warranties, or agreements. The party claiming indemnity is required to provide specific written notice of those claims to the other party and permit the other party to contest the claim. The indemnity provisions should provide for mutual access to all personnel and material that may be relevant to the claim and that no claim would be settled without the written consent of the injured party.

Indemnity provisions, along with opinions of counsel, are usually among the most hotly negotiated items in a purchase agreement. The seller will usually be unwilling to provide a comprehensive set of indemnity provisions. Counsel for the seller may also try to negotiate a "basket" or a "trigger" as part of the tradeoff for cash adjustments and no personal liability for the buyer's stockholders.

In our example, if the aggregate claims for which GCC demanded to be indemnified did not exceed $250,000, and a basket of $250,000 had been agreed to, no indemnity could be sought and GCC would be entitled to indemnification only for amounts in excess of $250,000. If TCI's counsel suggests that a "trigger of $250,000" rather than a "basket" should be built into the indemnity, then the trigger would provide that GCC could not seek indemnity unless the aggregate amount for which it was to be indemnified exceeded the triggering amount—in the case of GCC, $250,000. However, once the amount for which the indemnity was sought did exceed $250,000, GCC/GCS would have the right under the indemnity provision to recover from TCI all monies from the first dollar involved. In such case, the indemnity section could be drafted to state that any remedies available to either party were cumulative, so that they could be exercised one on top of another, and that they could be exercised at any time.

TCI and its advisors will seek a wide variety of additional limitations on the indemnification provisions. In addition to the basket negotiations, TCI could seek to establish a ceiling on overall liability, a limitation on the types of claims for which seller can be held liable, a limitation on claims only to those for which the seller had actual knowledge (which makes the buyer's burden of proof much higher in the event of a subsequent dispute), a limitation on the types of assets that would be available to repay GCC in the event of a claim, an exclusion of certain parties who will be held liable for certain types of claims, and a limitation on the time after closing (survival) after which GCC/GCS may no longer proceed against the seller for a breach or misrepresentation. A sample negotiated indemnification provision (with a trigger) might look like that shown in Exhibit 10-1.

Representations and Warranties

TCI will be expected to make a wide range of written and binding representations and warranties to GCS. These provisions will include that the sale is not in breach of any other agreement or obligation of TCI, that the assets are free and clear of all clouds on title to the assets, that the assets are in good operating condition, that all material facts have been disclosed, and so forth. Naturally, GCC/GCS will want the scope of these representations and warranties to be as broad and comprehensive as possible, primarily because these clauses serve as a form of an insurance policy for GCS. It will be incumbent on TCI and its counsel to negotiate limitations on the scope of these provisions where necessary.

The scope of the representations and warranties contained in the definitive purchase agreement are among the most difficult aspects of closing a transaction. This is the section where the TCI shareholders must "represent and warrant" everything about the company that has been told or implied to GCC/GCS. Representations and warranties set forth the financial responsibility for existing problems that may arise in the future, but that may not exist or be known to the parties at closing. The buyer typically views postclosing events that reduce assets or increase liabilities as being the responsibility of the seller. These provisions set forth the financial responsibility of each party if certain unknown or unforeseen problems arise in the future owing to an existing situation.

In many of the representations and warranties, GCC may be willing to accept the phrase "to the best of the seller's knowledge" as a qualifier to certain provisions. In addition, some matters lend themselves to outside testing or evaluation by experts. Relying on the reports of outside experts may significantly reduce or even eliminate the need for certain areas to be addressed. In other cases, a time and/or dollar limit on a particular representation or warranty will be sufficient to allow the seller to provide assurances in situations where it would otherwise be unwilling to do so. For example, a dollar limit is often attached to environmental and product liability representations and warranties.

Sellers should make certain that their advisors are familiar with the types of representations and warranties they are likely to face and that the advisors are skilled in finding mutually acceptable positions. During actual negotiations, sellers should make a sincere attempt to understand the buyer's underlying motivation in requesting each warranty and representation, and point out any facts or circumstances that may be inconsistent with a given request.

In our example, TCI and their counsel should expect that GCC will insist on the following types of representations and warranties:

- The transaction is not in breach of any license or other agreement or violation of any order or decree of any court or other governmental body.

- TCI's business entity is properly organized under state corporate law, is in good standing, and is qualified to do the business it is doing in the states where it is doing business.

- TCI has clear title to all assets made part of the sale, and these assets are not subject to any undisclosed restrictions or claims and are in good operating condition.

- TCI has no knowledge or reason to know that its business relationship has changed with any customer or group of customers whose purchases constitute more than stated percent (usually 5 percent) of business sales for the previous year.

- TCI represents that all required tax returns have been filed and required payments have been made.

- Licenses, zoning, and other permissions necessary to conduct TCI's business as it is being conducted have been obtained, and benefits may be transferred to GCC/GCS.

- TCI will need to represent and warrant the following facts regarding the accuracy of its financial statements, as presented to GCC:

1. It has fairly presented the financial condition of the business as of date of the statements.
2. TCI is not subject to any material liability, including contingent liability, not reflected or noted in financial statements.
3. The statements are prepared in accordance with generally accepted accounting principles.
4. Since the date of the statements, TCI has not transferred any assets to or on behalf of any owner or employee other than in payment of customary salaries.

- TCI is not in default on any material contract or loan, nor is it aware of any claims pending or threatened against it.

- TCI owns specified patents, trademarks, trade names, and copyrights, and there is no knowledge of any claims of infringement pending or threatened.

- TCI is in compliance with all applicable local, state, and federal laws and no notice of any claimed violations.

- TCI has not engaged or authorized to act as broker or finder in connection with sale.

Conditions Precedent to Closing

This section is essentially a checklist of events that must occur as a condition to closing the transaction. Both GCS and TCI will have their share of items that must be accomplished and documents or consents that must be signed. The nature and scope of these conditions must be carefully considered since failure to satisfy them will give the opposing party the right to walk away from the transaction.

Conduct of Business Prior to Closing

TCI must have a contractual obligation to preserve the goodwill of the business and condition of the assets during the time period between execution of the purchase agreement and closing of the transaction. The parties should negotiate all affirmative and negative covenants that will be imposed on the conduct of TCI during this time period, as well as the penalties for noncompliance (e.g., reduction of purchase price, ability to walk away from deal by GCS).

Other Key Agreements in an Asset Purchase

In addition to the purchase agreement, there are a wide variety of other agreements that may need to be prepared and negotiated between buyer and seller, as well as by and among certain third parties. Examples of a few other agreements are discussed below.

Intercreditor Agreement

An intercreditor agreement is a contract among multiple lenders (in this case, TCI and BBC) to a particular borrower (GCC and GCS). The document governs the priority rights of the various lenders in the collateral (the assets acquired by GCC and GCS), otherwise known as *subordination*. Subordination and standby provisions govern "who gets what proceeds when" in the event of a default by the borrower. In the GCC/TCI transaction, it is likely that BBC and its counsel will prepare this agreement and demand that BBC receive the senior priority rights.

Noncompetition Agreements

Covenants against competition and disclosure of confidential information are commonly a key part of any business acquisition. This is especially true in situations like the GCC/TCI transaction, where the management team of the target may be left out of the transaction and its members therefore are likely candidates to be future competitors. Counsel to GCS will naturally want to include covenants that are broad in terms of the scope of subject matter, duration, and geographic territory. Although these agreements will be carefully scrutinized by the courts as potential restraints of trade, agreements prohibiting sellers from competing against buyers in a business purchase transaction are given considerably more latitude than in other agreements, such as employment or consulting agreements.

Earn-Out Agreements

When earn-out agreements are negotiated as part of the purchase price in an acquisition, part of the consideration payable to TCI essentially becomes contingent on the ability of GCS to meet its financial and growth projections. In the GCC/TCI transaction, TCI shareholders are betting on the ability of the GCS management team to manage and operate the assets being acquired in an efficient and profitable manner. If any other of the TCI shareholders will become members of the GCS management team, then the earn-out provides an incentive for performance from which both GCC and TCI can gain. The key terms of the earn-out agreement to be negotiated are the formula to be used (e.g., tied to gross sales, earnings), the duration of the earn-out, the floor and ceiling on the payout to be provided to TCI shareholders, the controls that TCI shareholders will have, if any, over the budgets and expenditures made by GCS or GCC, the effect of business distress or bankruptcy of GCS on the earn-out, and the tax implications of the transaction.

The typical earn-out provides additional consideration to the seller if certain financial and/or performance targets are met. But buyers may also want to consider *reverse earn-outs* as an additional penalty if performance targets are not met. For example, if the seller accepts a combination of cash and promissory notes, the principal of the note or the interest rate could be reduced if minimal performance criteria are not met, representations or warranties are breached, or if sales fall below a given level.

Earn-outs can be used as incentives, as equalizers, or as risk mitigators. As an incentive, the earn-out may be used as a sweetener to motivate the founding entrepreneur (as seller) to stay on board to help build the business after closing or to ensure that a technical or engineering team remains in place after closing. As an equalizer, it can be used to resolve differing views over the valuation of the seller's business, particularly when the seller feels that its stock or assets are being undervalued. As a risk mitigator, the earn-out can be used to hold a seller's feet to the fire regarding its representations of the future value of the company and to help ensure against overpayment if a buyer is unsure or unclear of the future value of the business.

The key issues to be addressed in the negotiation and structuring of the earn-out provisions include:

- The financial formula to be used to determine the contingent payments payable to the seller (e.g., specified minimum sales levels, net income before taxes).
- The limitations that the seller will request to ensure that financial targets are reached.
- The audit and inspection rights to be granted by the seller to ensure against underpayment by the buyer.
- The business plan and financial benchmarks that are fair and reasonable over the course of the earn-out period. These performance-driven milestones may be better measuring sticks for the payment of the earn-out than a strict financial formula, especially for high-tech businesses.
- Term of the earn-out period, the method and frequency of payment, and the form of consideration itself, such as cash, stock, notes, and warrants.
- The relationship of the earn-out to the other liability and risk allocation sections of the acquisition agreement.

Scope of the Assets

The typical buyer will want to specify a virtual laundry list of categories of assets to be purchased, but the classic seller will want to modify the list by using words like *exclusively* or *primarily*. The seller may want to exclude all or most of the cash on hand from the schedule of assets to be transferred. In some cases, the seller may want to license some of the technology rights in lieu of an outright sale or, at the very least, obtain a license-back of what has been sold.

Security for the Seller's Take-Back Note

When the seller is taking back a note from the buyer for all or part of the consideration, the issue of security for the note is always

---

Box 10-1. Sample Schedule of Documents to Be Exchanged at a Typical Closing

1. Deeds, bills of sale, and any other documents and instruments buyer deems sufficient to transfer title to seller's assets
2. Certificate by shareholders that representations are true as of closing date and that shareholders have met obligations under agreement
3. Certificate by officers of acquired corporation that representations and warranties are true as of closing date and that corporation has met its obligations under agreement
4. Duly endorsed stock certificates
5. Written opinion of seller's attorney to effect that to the best of attorney's knowledge all representations are true, agreement has been duly executed and constitutes valid obligation of seller, and noncompetition agreement is valid and enforceable
6. Employment agreements
7. Certified copy of duly adopted resolutions by board of directors and shareholders authorizing sale
8. Certified copy of articles of incorporation and bylaws
9. Incumbency certificate of each person executing documents relating to sale
10. Title insurance covering real estate
11. Releases of any claims officers or directors may have against seller or buyer
12. Written resignations of certain officers and directors
13. Letter from accountant certifying financial statements and that following inquiries, accountant has no knowledge of any material adverse change in business's financial position between date of financial statements and closing
14. Certificate of good standing from each state where corporation to be acquired has been doing business
15. Estoppel certificates from creditors whose debts have been assumed by buyer
16. Copy of bulk sales notice (for asset acquisitions)

---

a problem. Naturally, the seller will want noncontingent personal and corporate guaranties from the buyer and anyone else that it can manage to get. The buyer will be reluctant to offer such broad

security. Several "creative' compromises have been reached between the parties, including partial or limited guaranties, the acceleration of the note based on postclosing performance, the right to
repurchase the assets in the event of a default, the issuance of warrants or preferred stock in the event of default, commercial-lender-
like covenants to prevent the buyer from getting into a position
where it is unable to pay the note (such as dividend restrictions,
limitations on excessive salaries), or contingent consulting agreements in the event of a default.

The Financial Statements

The financial statements provided by the seller to the buyer in
connection with the due diligence and prior to closing are often a
hotly contested item. The timing and scope of the financial statements, as well as the standard to which they will be held, are at
issue. The buyer and its team may prefer a "hot-off-the-press" and
recently completed audited set of financials from a Big 6 accounting firm, and the seller will want to serve up a "best-efforts" unaudited and uncertified guesstimate. Somewhere in between is
where most deals wind up, with verbiage such as "of a nature
customarily reflected," and "prepared in substantial accordance
with GAAP," and "fairly present the financial condition" being
bantered around. The scope of the liabilities included on the statements and who will bear responsibility for unknown or undisclosed liabilities will also be negotiated in the context of the
financial statements overall discussion.

The Existence and Scope of the Noncompete

It is only natural for the buyer to expect that the seller will
agree to stay out of the business being sold for some reasonable
amount of time. Depending on the seller's stage of life and postclosing plans, which may include actual retirement, the parties are
likely to argue over the scope, duration, and geographic focus of
the covenant against noncompetition. The more difficult issues
often arise when a conglomerate is spinning off a particular division or line of business and the remaining divisions will continue
to operate in similar or parallel industries to the business being

---

Box 10-2. Playing With the Buzzwords

Any veteran transactional lawyer knows that there are certain key "buzz-words" that can be inserted into sections of the Purchase Agreement which will detract or enhance or even shift liability by and among the buyer and seller. Depending on which side of the fence you are on, look out for words or phrases like:

materially
to the best of our knowledge
could possibly
without any independent investigation
except for . . .
subject to . . .
reasonably believes . . .
ordinary course of business
to which we are aware . . .
would not have a material adverse effect on . . .
primarily relating to . . .
substantially all . . .
might (instead of "would")
exclusively
other than claims which may be less than $_____
have received no written notice of . . .
have used our best efforts (or commercially reasonable efforts) to . . .
endeavor to . . .

---

sold to the buyer. The allocation of the purchase price to a noncompete covenant raises certain tax issues that must be analyzed, and these covenants may have only limited enforceability under applicable state laws if their scope or duration is deemed unreasonable or excessive.

Allocation of Risk

As discussed earlier in this chapter, the heart and soul of the purchase agreement is, in many ways, merely a tool for allocating risk. On the one hand, the buyer will want to hold the seller accountable for any postclosing claim or liability that arose relating to a set of facts that occurred while the seller owned the company *or* that has occurred as a result of a misrepresentation or material omission by the seller. The seller, on the other hand, wants to bring as much finality to the transaction as possible to allow some degree of sleep at night. When both parties are represented by skilled negotiators, a middle ground is reached, both in general as well as on specific issues of actual or potential liability.

The buyer's counsel will want to draft changes, covenants, representations, and warranties that are strong and absolute and the seller's counsel will seek to insert phrases like "except insignificant defaults or losses which have not, or are not likely to, at any time before or after the closing, result in a material loss or liability to or against the buyer," leaving some wiggle room for insignificant or nonmaterial claims. The battleground will be the indemnification provisions and any exceptions, carve-outs, or baskets created to dilute these provisions. The weapons will be the buzzwords listed in Box 10-2.

A Sample Agreement

I have included as Exhibit 10-2 an abbreviated version of an asset purchase agreement for use in the GCC/TCI transaction. This sample agreement is provided to give the reader a feel for what the starting point or first draft of an agreement will look like before the negotiation process begins. Please remember to use it only as a guideline and not as a crutch.

Exhibit 10-1. Model Indemnification Provisions

INDEMNIFICATION BY THE SELLER

The Seller, TCI, and its shareholders, jointly and severally, covenents and agrees to indemnify, defend, protect and hold harmless GCC and GCS and their respective officers, directors, employees, stockholders, assigns, successors and affiliates (individually, an "Indemnified Party" and collectively, "Indemnified Parties") from, against and in respect of:

(a) all liabilities, losses, claims, damages, punitive damages, causes of action, lawsuits, administrative proceedings (including formal proceedings), investigations, audits, demands, assessments, adjustments, judgments, settlement payments, deficiencies, penalties, fines, interest (including interest from the date of such damages) and costs and expenses (including without limitation reasonable attorneys' fees and disbursements of every kind, nature and description, collectively, "Damages") suffered, sustained, incurred or paid by the GCC Indemnified Parties in connection with, resulting from or arising out of, directly or indirectly:

(i) any misrepresentation or breach of any warranty of the Sellers, set forth in this Agreement or any schedule or certificate, delivered by or on behalf of the Seller in connection herewith; or

(ii) any nonfulfillment of any covenant or agreement on the part of any of the Sellers set forth in this Agreement; or

(iii) the business, operations or assets of the Sellers prior to the Closing Date or the actions or omissions of the Sellers' directors, officers, shareholders, employees or agents prior to the Closing Date (except as to the Assumed Liabilities); or

(iv) failure to comply with country of origin marking requirements imposed by the Federal Trade Commission or the U.S. Customs Service, including without limitation damages arising out of breaches of any contract relating to failure to deliver product as required under any contract or delivery of non-conforming goods pursuant to any contract, fines or other penalties for violations of such requirements; or

(v) the Excluded Liabilities.

(b) any and all damages incident to any of the foregoing or to the enforcement of this Section 7.1.

LIMITATION AND EXPIRATION

Notwithstanding the above:

(a) there shall be no liability for indemnification under Section 7.1 unless, and solely to the extent that, the aggregate amount of damages exceeds $250,000 (the "Indemnification Threshold"); *provided, however,* that the Indemnification Threshold shall not apply to (i) adjustments to the Purchase Price; (ii) damages arising out of any breaches of the covenants of the Seller set forth in this Agreement or representations made in Sections 3.13 (environmental matters), 3.16 (inventory), 3.19 (employee benefit plans), 3.20 (conformity with law; litigation), 3.21 (taxes) or 3.26 (intellectual property), or (iii) the Excluded Liabilities;

(continues)

Exhibit 10-1. (continued)

(b) the indemnification obligations under this Section 7 or in any certificate or writing furnished in connection herewith shall terminate on the later of clause (i) or (ii) of this Section 7.2(b):

(i) (1) third anniversary of the Closing Date, or

(2) with respect to representations and warranties contained in Sections 3.14 (real and personal property), 3.19 (employee benefit plans), 3.21 (taxes), and the Excluded Liabilities, on (A) the date that is six (6) months after the expiration of the longest applicable federal or state statute of limitation (including extensions thereof), or (B) if there is no applicable statute of limitation, (x) ten (10) years after the Closing Date; or

(ii) the final resolution of a claim or demand (a "Claim") pending as of the relevant dates described in clause (i) of this Section 7.2(b) (such claim referred to as a "Pending Claim");

(c) for purposes of the indemnity in this Section 7, all representations contained in Section 3 are made without any limitations as to materiality; and

(d) for purposes of the Indemnification Threshold, all damages incurred by GCC or any of its affiliates under any of the related Acquisition Agreements shall be included within the Indemnification Threshold under this Agreement.

NOTE: The indemnification provision would then go on to address the procedures for making an indemnification claim.

Exhibit 10-2. Sample Asset Purchase Agreement

THIS ASSET PURCHASE AGREEMENT ("Agreement") is made and entered into this _____ day of _____, 19_____, by and among Growth Co. Corp., a Maryland corporation (the "Buyer"), and Target Co., Inc., a New York corporation (the "Seller"), and Jane C. Doe and John F. Doe individually (each a "Shareholder" and collectively, the "Shareholders").

WITNESSETH:

WHEREAS, the Seller is engaged in the equipment manufacturing business and activities related thereto (herein referred to as the "Business"); and

WHEREAS, Seller and the Shareholders (constituting all of the beneficial shareholders of the Seller), desire to sell, convey, transfer, assign and deliver to Buyer the Business and substantially all of the assets, properties and operations used in the Business, and Buyer desires to purchase the Business and such assets, properties and operations, on the terms and subject to conditions contained in this Agreement, and other agreements related hereto.

NOW, THEREFORE, in consideration of the mutual benefits to be derived from this Agreement, the receipt and sufficiency of which are hereby acknowledged, the parties hereto hereby agree as follows:

1. **SALE AND PURCHASE OF ASSETS**

    1.1   Sale of Assets to Buyer. Upon the terms and subject to the conditions herein set forth, at the Closing referred to in Section 3, Seller shall sell, transfer, assign, convey and deliver to Buyer, and Buyer shall purchase and acquire from Seller, all of the properties, assets and goodwill that are used in the Business, of whatever kind and nature, real or personal, tangible or intangible (including all rights of the Seller arising from its operation of the Business) and excluding only those assets referred to in Section 1.2 of this Agreement (collectively, the "Assets"), as those Assets exist on the Closing Date (as defined in Section 3). The Assets include, but are not limited to, the following:

    (a) all of Seller's machinery, equipment, equipment leases, chemicals, supplies, vehicles, furniture, fixtures, tools, computers and all other personal property, wherever located, which are used in the Business, including, but not limited to, the items listed on Schedule 1.1(a);

    (b) all interests of Seller in real property, including leases, options, rights of way, zoning and development rights and easements, described on Schedule 1.1(b);

    (c) all inventory of Seller used in the Business, wherever located, including, without limitation, the parts, chemicals and materials listed on Schedule 1.1(c);

    (d) all of Seller's computer software used in the Business, and all

(continues)

Exhibit 10-2. (continued)

rights, title and interest of Seller in, to and under all trademarks, trademark rights, trademark applications, patents, patent rights, patent applications, trade secrets, inventions, training and equipment manuals, technology, methods, manufacturing, engineering, technical and any other know-how, processes, projects in development, trade names, service marks, other intellectual property rights and other proprietary information of the Seller used in or relating to the Business. All material intellectual property, including all trade names and patents used or held by Seller, are listed on Schedule 1.1(d);

(e) all of Seller's rights under any written or oral contracts, unfilled service and/or purchase orders, agreements, leases, instruments, registrations, licenses, certificate, distribution agreements or other documents, commitments, arrangements or authorizations relating to the Business, including, but not limited to, the agreements and other instruments identified on Schedule 1.1(e) (the "Contracts"); provided, that nothing contained in this Agreement shall be construed as an attempt to agree to assign any contract which is by itself nonassignable without the consent of the other party or parties thereto, unless such consent shall be given;

(f) all rights in connection with all permits, certificates, licenses, approvals, registrations and authorizations of Seller which may be necessary or desirable in order to conduct the Business (the "Permits");

(g) all of Seller's rights under manufacturers' and vendors' warranties relating to those items included in the Assets and all of Seller's similar rights against third parties relating to items included in the Assets;

(h) all of Seller's accounts receivable, notes and other receivables, unbilled costs and fees, all prepaid items, amounts on deposit of Seller, and other current assets existing on the Closing Date, including, but not limited to, the receivables and other assets set forth on Schedule 1.1(h), but excluding cash and cash equivalents;

(i) all goodwill, customer and vendor lists, telephone numbers, and other intangible property, and all of Seller's rights to commence or maintain future and existing actions relating to the operation of the Business or the ownership of the Assets, for events occurring after the Closing Date, and the right to settle those actions and retain the proceeds therefrom;

(j) all shares of stock and partnership interests owned by Seller, if any;

(k) all of Seller's rights under the insurance or similar policies in effect on or prior to the Closing Date set forth on Schedule 1.1(k);

(l) all financial, operational, and any other files, logs, books and records and data of the Business of Seller, (collectively, "Books and Records") and including, without limitation, all correspondence, accounting records, personnel records, purchase orders and invoices, customer records, supplier records, advertising and promotional materials and files, and other business records which are owned by Seller relating to the Business.

1.2　Excluded Assets. The following assets (the "Excluded Assets") shall be retained by the Seller and shall not be sold or assigned to Buyer:

(a)　all cash on hand and cash equivalents (excluding the pre-paid proceeds from the Baxter Contract) and cash-value life and other split-life insurance policies of Seller;

(b)　the corporate minute books and stock books of Seller; and

(c)　any lease, commitment or other agreement listed on Schedule 1.2(c) with respect to which the Buyer does not desire to acquire concurrent with its purchase of the Assets under this Agreement, including any employee advance.

1.3　Method of Conveyance. The sale, transfer, conveyance and assignment by the Seller of the Assets to the Buyer in accordance with Section 1.1 hereof shall be effected on the Closing Date by the Seller's execution and delivery to the Buyer of a general assignment and bill of sale, in substantially the form attached hereto as Exhibit A (the "General Assignment and Bill of Sale"). At the Closing, all of the Assets shall be transferred by the Seller to the Buyer free and clear of any and all liens, encumbrances, mortgages, security interests, pledges, claims, equities and other restrictions or charges of any kind or nature whatsoever (collectively, "Liens") except for a lessor's interest in any leased assets or as otherwise listed in Schedule 4.5(a).

2.　**PURCHASE PRICE.** The purchase price to be paid by the Buyer for the Assets to be sold, transferred and conveyed by the Seller pursuant to this Agreement shall be:

(a)　cash in the amount of Three Million Dollars ($3,000,000), paid by cashier's check or wire transfer, subject to adjustment as described in Section 2.2; and

(b)　two promissory notes, one for the principal amount of Five Hundred Thousand Dollars ($500,000) (the "Short-Term Note"); and the second for the principal amount of Eight Hundred Thousand Dollars ($800,000) (the "Long-Term Note") and, together with the Short-Term Note (the "Notes"), each Note subject to adjustment as described in Sections 2.3(a) and 2.3(b), in the forms attached hereto as Exhibits B-1 and B-2, with the Short-Term Note secured by a pledge of marketable securities pursuant to a Pledge Agreement and a Stock Power in the forms attached hereto as Exhibit C and Exhibit D.

3.　**CLOSING**

3.1　Date of Closing. Subject to the terms and conditions set forth herein, the closing of the transactions contemplated hereby (the "Closing") shall be held at 10:00 a.m. at the offices of counsel for the Seller on or before _____, 19_____, provided that all conditions to the Closing have been satisfied, or at such other time, date and place as shall be fixed by agreement among the parties hereto. The date on which the Closing shall occur is referred to herein as the "Closing Date." At the Closing, the parties shall execute and deliver the documents referred to in Section 3.2.

(continues)

Exhibit 10-2. (continued)

3.2   Items to be Delivered at Closing. At the Closing and subject to the terms and conditions herein contained:

(a) Seller shall deliver or cause to be delivered to Buyer the following:

(i)   one or more Bills of Sale and such other good and sufficient instruments and documents of conveyance and transfer executed by Seller, in a form reasonably satisfactory to Buyer and its counsel, as shall be necessary and effective to transfer and assign to, and vest in, Buyer all of Seller's right, title and interest in and to the Assets, including without limitation, (A) good and valid title in and to all of the Assets owned by Seller, (B) good and valid leasehold interests in and to all of the Assets leased by Seller as lessee, and (C) all of the Seller's rights under all agreements, contracts, instruments and other documents included in the Assets to which Seller is a party or by which it has rights on the Closing Date;

(ii)   all third-party consents required to be delivered as a condition to Closing as set forth in Section 8.2(d), which may be necessary or desirable in connection with the transfer of the Assets, including the Contracts and the Permits;

(iii)   all of the agreements, contracts, commitments, leases, plans, computer programs and software, data bases whether in the form of computer tapes or otherwise, manuals and guidebooks, customer lists, supplier lists, and other documents, books, records, papers, files, office supplies and data belonging to the Seller which are part of the Assets;

(iv)   one or more Assignment and Assumption Agreements executed by Seller;

(v)   executed lease for the Seller's home offices (the "Darien Property"), attached hereto as Exhibit M and assignment of lease for the Seller's Wisconsin warehouse and office (the "Wisconsin Property"), transferring the leasehold and subleasehold interests in said properties to Buyer;

(vi)   a written opinion of Joseph P. Doe, Esq., counsel for Seller, dated the Closing Date, in the form of Exhibit F hereto;

(vii)   a certificate, signed by a duly authorized officer of the Seller and dated the Closing Date, representing that the conditions contained in Section 8.2(b) of this Agreement have been satisfied;

(viii)   certified copies of resolutions of the Seller's Board of Directors and its Shareholders with respect to the approval of this Agreement and the transactions contemplated hereby (Exhibit O);

(ix)   Employment Agreements, executed by Jane C. Doe and John F. Doe, respectively (Exhibits G and H, respectively); and

(x)   any other opinions, certificates or other documents and instruments required herein to be delivered by the Seller or the Shareholders.

(b) Buyer shall deliver to the Seller the following:

(i)   the Purchase Price pursuant to Section 2 hereof;

(ii)   a certificate, signed by a duly authorized officer of the Buyer and dated the Closing Date, representing that the conditions contained in Section 8.1(a) of this Agreement have been satisfied;

(iii)   certified copies of resolutions of the Manager of the Buyer with respect to the approval of this Agreement and the transactions contemplated hereby;

(iv)   executed counterparts of the lease amendments with respect to the Darien and Wisconsin Properties;

(v)   the executed Promissory Notes;

(vi)   the Operating Agreement of the Buyer, providing for the Equity Interest in the Buyer to be issued to Seller, in accordance with Section 2.1(c) hereof;

(vii)   the Pledge Agreement and the Pledged Collateral Account Agreement executed by the Pledgor in accordance with Section 8.1(f) hereof;

(viii) executed Employment Agreements as provided in Section 8.2(f); and

(ix)   any other certificates or other documents and instruments required herein to be delivered by Buyer.

4.   **REPRESENTATIONS AND WARRANTIES OF THE SELLER.** In order to induce the Buyer to enter into this Agreement and to consummate the transactions contemplated hereby, the Seller and each of the Shareholders, jointly and severally, hereby represents and warrants to the Buyer as follows:

4.1   Organization and Authority. Seller is a corporation duly organized, validly existing and in good standing under the laws of the State of Illinois. Seller has the full power and authority to enter into and perform this Agreement, to own, operate and lease its properties and assets, to carry on its business as it is now being conducted, and to execute, deliver and perform its obligations under this Agreement and consummate the transactions contemplated hereby. Each Shareholder has the full power and authority to enter into and perform this Agreement. Seller has delivered to the Buyer complete and correct copies of its Articles of Incorporation and Bylaws, each as amended to date. Seller is duly qualified to do business as a foreign corporation and in good standing in Anytown.

4.2   Authorization of Agreement. The execution, delivery and performance by the Seller of this Agreement and of each and every document and instrument contemplated hereby and the consummation of the transactions contemplated hereby and thereby have been duly and validly authorized and approved by all necessary corporate action of the Seller. This Agreement has been duly executed and delivered by the Seller and each of the Shareholders and constitutes (and, when executed and delivered, each such other document and instrument will constitute) a valid and bind-

(continues)

Exhibit 10-2. (continued)

ing obligation of the Seller and each of the Shareholders, enforceable against the Seller and each of the Shareholders in accordance with its terms.

4.3   Capitalization and Share Ownership of Seller. The Seller's authorized capital stock consists of 1,000 shares of common stock, no par value. There are 1,000 shares of the Seller's common stock presently outstanding, all of which shares are owned by the Shareholders, free and clear of all Liens. All of the Shareholders' shares have been duly authorized and validly issued, are fully paid and nonassessable. No equity securities (or debt securities convertible into equity securities) of the Seller, other than the Shareholders' shares, are issued and outstanding. There are no existing contracts, subscriptions, options, warrants, calls, commitments or other rights of any character to purchase or otherwise acquire any common stock or other securities of the Seller.

4.4   Non-Contravention; Consents and Approvals.

(a) Neither the execution and delivery by the Seller of this Agreement nor the consummation by the Seller or the Shareholders of the transactions contemplated hereby, nor compliance by the Seller or the Shareholders with any of the provisions hereof, will (i) conflict with or result in a breach of any provision of the Articles of Incorporation or Bylaws of the Seller, (ii) result in the breach of, or conflict with, any of the terms and conditions of, or constitute a default (with or without the giving of notice or the lapse of time or both) with respect to, or result in the cancellation or termination of, or the acceleration of the performance of any obligations or of any indebtedness under, any contract, agreement, lease, commitment, indenture, mortgage, note, bond, license or other instrument or obligation to which the Seller or any Shareholder is a party or by which the Seller, the Shareholders or any of the Assets may be bound or affected, (other than such breaches, conflicts and defaults set forth in Schedule 4.4(a) hereto, which shall have been waived at or prior to the Closing) (iii) result in the creation of any Lien upon any of the Assets, or (iv) violate any law or any rule or regulation of any administrative agency or governmental body, or any order, writ, injunction or decree of any court, administrative agency or governmental body to which the Seller, the Shareholders or any of the Assets may be subject.

(b) Except as set forth in Schedule 4.4(b) hereto, no approval, authorization, consent or other order or action of, or filing with or notice to any court, administrative agency or other governmental authority or any other person is required for the execution and delivery by Seller or the Shareholders of this Agreement or the consummation by the Seller and the Shareholders of the transactions contemplated hereby.

(c) A description of all Permits held by Seller and necessary or desirable for the operation of the Business are set forth in Schedule 4.4(c) hereto. All Permits listed in Schedule 4.4(c) are valid, and neither Seller nor any Shareholder has received any notice that any government authority intends to modify, cancel, terminate, or deny renewal of any Permit. No current or former stockholder, officer, director or employee of Seller or any affiliate of Seller owns or has any proprietary, financial or other interest in any Permit which Seller owns or uses. Seller has conducted the Business in compliance with the requirements, standards, criteria and conditions set forth in the Permits and other applicable orders, approvals, variances, rules and regulations and is not in violation of any of the foregoing. The transactions contemplated by this Agreement will not result in a default under or a breach of or violation of or adversely affect the rights and benefits afforded to the Seller by any Permits. Except as set forth in Schedule 4.4(c) hereto, no approval by a governmental authority is required for transfer to Buyer of such Permits.

　　　4.5　Ownership of Assets.

　　　　　(a) the Seller has and will have at the Closing good, valid and marketable title to each and every item of the tangible and intangible personal property and assets included in the Assets, and valid leasehold interests in all leases of tangible personal and real property included in the Assets, free and clear of any Liens except as set forth in Schedule 4.5(a). At the Closing, the Seller will transfer to Buyer good, valid and marketable title to the Assets, free and clear of any and all Liens, except as set forth in Schedule 4.5(a).

　　　　　(b) No affiliate of the Seller has, or has indirectly acquired, any right, title or interest in or to any of the Assets.

　　　　　(c) The Seller has not sold, transferred, assigned or conveyed any of its right, title and interest, or granted or entered into any option to purchase or acquire any of its right, title or interest, in and to any of the Assets or the Business. No third party has any option or right to acquire the Business or any of the Assets.

　　　4.6　Balance Sheet: Existing Conditions; Ordinary Course. Attached hereto as Schedule 4.6 are (i) the Seller's unaudited balance sheet (the "1996 Balance Sheet") as of December 31, 1996 (the "Balance Sheet Date"), together with the related unaudited statements of income, shareholders equity and cash flows for the year then ended, and (ii) the Seller's unaudited balance sheets as of December 1995 and 1994, together with the related unaudited statements of income, shareholders equity and cash flows for the years ended December 31, 1995 and 1994 (such unaudited financial statements for 1994, 1995 and 1996 being referred to herein collectively as the "Financial Statements"). The Financial Statements (i) are true, complete and correct, (ii) are in accordance with the books and records of the Seller, (iii) fairly, completely and accurately present the financial position of the Seller as of the respective dates thereof and the results of its operations for the periods presented and (iv) were prepared in conformity with generally accepted accounting principles consistently applied throughout the periods covered thereby. Since the Balance Sheet Date, except as set forth in Schedule 4.6 hereto, there has not been with respect to the Seller:

　　　　　(a) any material adverse change in the Assets or the Business of the Seller from their condition as set forth on the 1996 Balance Sheet;

　　　　　(b) any damage, destruction or loss, whether covered by insurance or not, materially and adversely affecting the Business or Assets of the Seller or

(continues)

Exhibit 10-2. (continued)

any sale, transfer or other disposition of the Assets other than in the ordinary course of business;

      (c) any declaration, setting aside or payment of any dividend, or any distribution with respect to the capital stock of the Seller or any direct or indirect redemption, purchase or other acquisition by the Seller of shares of its capital stock, or any payment to any affiliate of any intercompany payable or any transfer of Assets to any affiliate; or

      (d) except as set forth on Schedule 4.6(d), any increase in the compensation payable by the Seller to any Shareholder or any of the Seller's officers, employees or agents, or in the payment of any bonus, or in any insurance, payment or arrangement made to, for or with any such officers, employees or agents.

Since the Balance Sheet Date, Seller has conducted its Business in the ordinary course and has made no material change to its marketing, purchasing, collections or accounting procedures.

      4.7   Litigation. There is no litigation, suit, proceeding, action, claim or investigation, at law or in equity, pending or, to the best knowledge of the Seller or any Shareholder, threatened against, or affecting in any way the Assets, the Seller or any Shareholder's ability to own or operate the Business, or which questions the validity of this Agreement or challenges any of the transactions contemplated hereby or the use of the Assets after the Closing by the Buyer. Neither the Seller, nor any of the Shareholders, nor any of the Assets is subject to any judgment, order, writ, injunction or decree of any court or any federal, state, municipal or other governmental authority, department, commission, board, bureau, agency or other instrumentality.

      4.8   Compliance with Laws. Except as set forth in Schedule 4.8, the Seller's Business has at all times been conducted in compliance with all applicable laws, regulations, ordinances and other requirements of governmental authorities (including applicable federal, state and local laws, rules and regulations respecting occupational safety and health standards). Except as set forth in Schedule 4.8, neither the Seller nor any Shareholder has received any notice, advice, claim or complaint from any employee or governmental authority that the Seller has not conducted, or is not presently conducting, its business and operations in accordance with all applicable laws and other requirements of governmental authorities.

      4.9   Permits and Licenses. The Seller has all permits, certificates, licenses, approvals, registrations and authorizations required in connection with the conduct of the Business. The Seller is not in violation of, and has not violated, any applicable provisions of any such permits, certificates, licenses, approvals, registrations or authorizations. Except as set forth on Schedule 4.9, all permits, certificates, licenses, approvals, registrations and authorizations of the Seller which are necessary for the operation of the Seller's Business are freely transferable.

      4.10   Contracts.

      (a) Schedule 4.10(a) contains a true and complete list of all material contracts and agreements related to or involving the Business or the Assets or by which any of the Assets is subject or bound in any material respect, including, without limiting the generality of the foregoing, any and all: contracts and agreements for the purchase, sale or lease of inventory, goods, materials, equipment, hardware, supplies or other personal property; contracts for the purchase, sale or lease of real property; contracts and agreements for the performance or furnishing of services; joint venture, partnership or other contracts, agreements or arrangements involving the sharing of profits; employment agreements; and agreements containing any covenant or covenants which purport to limit the ability or right of the Seller or any other person or entity to engage in any aspects of the business related to the Assets or compete in any aspect of such business with any person or entity (collectively, the "Scheduled Contracts"). As used herein, the terms "contract" and "agreement" mean and include every material contract, agreement, commitment, arrangement, understanding and promise whether written or oral. A complete and accurate copy of each written Scheduled Contract has been delivered or made available to the Buyer or, if oral, a complete and accurate summary thereof has been delivered to the Buyer. Except as set forth on Schedule 4.10(a), the Scheduled Contracts are valid, binding and enforceable in accordance with their respective terms, are in full force and effect and were entered into in the ordinary course of business on an "arms-length" basis and consistent with past practices. The Seller is not in breach or default of any of the Standard Contracts and, except as set forth on Schedule 4.10(a), no occurrence or circumstance exists which constitutes (with or without the giving of notice or the lapse of time or both) a breach or default by the other party thereto. Neither the Seller nor any Shareholder has been modified or advised by any party to a Scheduled Contract of such party's intention or desire to terminate or modify any such contract or agreement. Neither the Seller nor any Shareholder has granted any Lien on any Scheduled Contract included in the Assets.

(b) Except as set forth on Schedule 4.10(b) and this Agreement, neither the Seller nor any Shareholder is a party to, and neither the Seller nor any Shareholder nor any of the Assets is subject or bound in any respect by, any written or oral contract and agreement related to or involving the Business which will affect in any manner the Buyer's ownership, use or operation of the Assets, including, without limitation any contracts or agreements (i) for the purchase, sale or lease of inventory, goods, equipment or for the performance or furnishing of services; (ii) for the furnishing of services for which the Seller has received payment in advance of furnishing such services and has not yet furnished such services; and (iii) containing any covenant or covenants which purport to limit the ability or right of the Seller or any other person or entity to engage in any aspects of the business related to the Assets or compete in any aspect of such business with any person or entity.

(c) Except as set forth on Schedule 4.10(c), all Scheduled Contracts included in the Assets will be fully and validly assigned to the Buyer as of the Closing.

(d) Except as set forth in Schedule 4.10(d), there is no Scheduled Contract or any other Contract included in the Assets which cannot be terminated without any further obligation, payment or penalty upon thirty-days notice or more to the other party or parties to such Contract.

(continues)

Exhibit 10-2. (continued)

4.11   Condition of Purchased Assets. Each and every one of the tangible Assets to be purchased by Buyer pursuant to this Agreement is in good operating condition and repair, ordinary wear and tear excepted, and is fit and suitable for the purposes for which they are currently used by Seller. The Assets include all of the properties and assets of Seller required, necessary or desirable to enable Buyer to conduct the operation of the Business in the same manner in which the Business has been conducted prior to the date hereof by Seller.

4.12   Customers. Seller has delivered to Buyer a complete and accurate list of all customers which has been included in Schedule 4.12. Except as set forth in Schedule 4.12, no current customer (i) has cancelled, suspended or otherwise terminated its relationship with the Seller or (ii) has advised the Seller or either Shareholder of its intent to cancel, suspend or otherwise terminate such relationship, or to materially decrease its usage of the services provided by Seller.

4.13   Employee Benefit Plans. Except as set forth in Schedule 4.13, there are not currently, nor have there ever been, any Benefit Plans (defined below) in place or established by Seller. "Benefit Plan" means any bonus, incentive compensation, deferred compensation, pension, profit sharing, retirement, stock purchase, stock option, stock ownership, stock appreciation rights, phantom stock, leave of absence, layoff, vacation, day or dependent care, legal services, cafeteria, life, health, accident, disability, workmen's compensation or other insurance, severance, separation or other employee benefit plan, practice, policy or arrangement of any kind, whether written or oral, including, but not limited to, any "employee benefit plan" within the meaning of Section 3(3) of ERISA. All group health plans of the Seller have been operated in compliance with all applicable federal and state laws and regulations.

4.14   Warranties. Schedule 4.14 sets forth a complete and correct copy of all of the Seller's standard warranties (collectively, the "Warranties" or individually a "Warranty") currently extended by the Seller to the customers of the Seller. There are no warranty claims outstanding against the Seller.

4.15   Trademarks, Patents, Etc. Except as set forth in Schedule 4.15, the Seller does not own or have any rights to any patents, trademarks, trade names, brand names, service marks, service names, copyrights, inventions or licenses and rights and applications with respect to the foregoing (collectively, the "Marks and Patents"). All the Marks and Patents are valid and have not been abandoned, and there are no prior claims, controversies, lawsuits or judgments which affect the validity of the Seller's rights to the Marks and Patents nor are there any legal proceedings, claims or controversies instituted, pending or, to the best knowledge of the Seller or the Shareholders, threatened with respect to any of the Marks and Patents, or which challenge the Seller's rights, title or interest in respect thereto. Except as set forth on Schedule 4.15, none of the Marks and Patents are the subject of any outstanding assignments, grants, licenses, Liens, obligations or agreements, whether written, oral or implied. All required renewal fees, maintenance fees, amendments and/or other filings or payments which are necessary to preserve and maintain the Marks and Patents have been filed and/or made. The Seller owns or has the right to use all Marks and Patents and the like necessary to conduct its Business as presently conducted and without conflict with any patent, trade name, trademark or the like of any other person or entity.

4.16 Insurance. Set forth in Schedule 4.16 is a complete and accurate list of all insurance policies which the Seller maintains with respect to its Business or the Assets. Such policies are in full force and effect. Such policies, with respect to their amounts and types of coverage, are adequate to insure fully against risks to which the Seller, the Business or the Assets are normally exposed in the operation of the Business. There has not been any material adverse change in the Seller's relationship with its insurers or in the premiums payable pursuant to such policies. The insurance coverage provided by the Seller's insurance policies shall not be affected by, and shall not lapse or otherwise be terminated by reason of, the execution of this Agreement. Neither the Seller has or either Shareholder received any notice respecting the cancellation of such insurance policies.

4.17 Environmental Matters.

(a) Except as set forth on Schedule 4.17(a) attached hereto, Seller has obtained all permits, licenses, and other authorizations (collectively, the "Licenses") which are required in connection with the conduct of the Business under all applicable Environmental Laws (as defined below) and regulations relating to pollution or protection of the environment, including Environmental Laws and regulations relating to emissions, discharges, releases or threatened releases of pollutants, contaminants, chemicals, or industrial, toxic or hazardous substances or wastes into the environment (including without limitation, ambient air, surface water, groundwater, or land) or otherwise relating to the manufacture, processing, distribution, use, treatment, storage, disposal, transport, or handling of pollutants, contaminants, chemicals, or industrial, toxic or hazardous substances or wastes.

(b) Except as set forth in Schedule 4.17(b), Seller is in substantial compliance in the conduct of the Business with all terms and conditions of the Licenses and is in substantial compliance with all other limitations, restrictions, conditions, standards, prohibitions, requirements, obligations, schedules and timetables contained in the Environmental Laws or contained in any regulation, code, plan, order, decree, judgment, injunction, notice (written or verbal) or demand letter issued, entered, promulgated or approved thereunder.

(c) Except as set forth on Schedule 4.17(c), neither Seller nor any Shareholder is aware of, nor has Seller received any written or verbal notice of, any past, present or future events, conditions, circumstances, activities, practices, incidents, actions or plans which may interfere with or prevent compliance or continued compliance with any Environmental Laws or any regulations, code, order, decree, judgment, injunction, notice (written or verbal) or demand letter issued, entered, promulgated or approved thereunder, or which may give rise to any common law or legal liability, or otherwise form the basis of any claim, action, demand, suit, proceeding, hearing, study or investigation, based on or related to the Seller's,

(continues)

Exhibit 10-2. (continued)

processing, storage, distribution, use, treatment, disposal, transport, or handling, or the emission, discharge, release or threatened release into the environment, of any pollutant, contaminant, chemical, or industrial, toxic or hazardous substance or waste.

(d) There is no civil, criminal or administrative action, suit, demand, claim, hearing, notice or demand letter, notice of violation, investigation, or proceeding pending or threatened against Seller or the Shareholders in connection with the conduct of the Business relating in any way to any Environmental Laws or regulation, injunction, notice or demand letter issued, entered, promulgated or approved thereunder.

(e) For purposes of this Agreement, "Environmental Laws" means collectively, all federal, state and local environmental laws, common law, statutes, rules and regulations including, without limitation, the Comprehensive Environmental Response, Compensation and Liability Act (42 U.S.C. Sec. 9061 et seq.), as amended, the Hazardous Materials Transportation Act (49 U.S.C. Sec. 1801 et seq.), as amended, the Resource Conservation and Recovery Act (42 U.S.C. Sec. 6901 et seq.), as amended, the Federal Water Pollution Control Act (33 U.S.C. Sec. 1251 et seq.), as amended, the Safe Drinking Water Act (42 U.S.C. Sec. 300f et seq.), as amended, the Clean Air Act (42 U.S.C. Sec. 7401 et seq.), as amended, the Toxic Substances Control Act (15 U.S.C. Sec. 2601 et seq.), as amended, the Federal Emergency Planning and Community Right-to-Know Act ((42 U.S.C. Sec. 11001 et seq.), as amended, any so-called "superfund" or "super-lien" law and such statutes and ordinances as may be enacted by state and local governments with jurisdiction over any real property now owned or leased by the Seller or any real property upon which the Seller now conducts its Business and any permits, licenses, authorizations, variances, consents, approvals, directives or requirements of, and any agreements with, any governments, departments, commissions, boards, courts, authorities, agencies, officials and officers applicable to such real property or the use thereof and regulating, relating to, or imposing liability or standards of conduct concerning any pollutant, contaminant, chemical, or industrial, toxic or hazardous substance or waste.

4.18   Notes, Accounts or Other Receivables. Set forth on Schedule 1.1(h) is a complete list of Seller's notes, accounts or other receivables included in the Assets as existing on the Closing Date and included in the Estimated Accounts Receivable valuation pursuant to Section 2.2. All of the Seller's notes, accounts or other receivables included on Schedule 1.1(h) are properly reflected on the books and records of the Seller, and are in their entirety valid accounts receivable arising from bona fide transactions in the ordinary course of business.

4.19   Real Estate.

(a) The Seller does not own any real property.

(b) The Seller has valid leasehold interests in all of the real property which it leases or purports to lease, free and clear of any Liens, other than the interests of the lessors, including the Darien Property and the Anytown Property.

(c) The Seller enjoys peaceful and undisturbed possession under all of the leases pursuant to which Seller leases real property (the "Real Property Leases"). All of the Real Property Leases are valid, subsisting and in full force and effect and there are no existing defaults, or events which with the passage of time or the giving of notice, or both, would constitute defaults by the Seller or, by any other party thereto.

(d) Neither Seller nor any Shareholder received notice of any pending condemnation, expropriation, eminent domain or similar proceedings affecting all or any portion of any real property leased by the Seller and no such proceedings are contemplated.

(e) The Shareholders enjoy peaceful and undisturbed possession of the Darien Property and have the right to lease and collect all rents on the Darien Property and clear of any Liens.

4.20   No Guarantees. The Seller has not guaranteed or pledged any Assets with respect to any obligation or indebtedness of any person or entity and no person or entity has guaranteed any obligation or indebtedness of the Seller.

4.21   Taxes.

(a) The Seller has timely filed or will timely file all requisite federal, state and other Tax (defined below) returns, reports and forms ("Returns") for all periods ended on or before the Closing Date, and all such Tax Returns are true, correct and complete in all respects. Neither the Seller nor any Shareholder has any knowledge of any basis for the assertion of any claim relating or attributable to Taxes which, if adversely determined, would result in any Lien on the assets of such Seller or any Shareholder or otherwise have an adverse effect on the Seller, the Assets or the Business.

(b) For purposes of this Agreement, the term "Tax" shall include any tax or similar governmental charge, impost, or levy (including, without limitation, income taxes, franchise taxes, transfer taxes or fees, sales taxes, use taxes, gross receipts taxes, value added taxes, employment taxes, excise taxes, ad valorem taxes, property taxes, withholding taxes, payroll taxes, minimum taxes or windfall profits taxes) together with any related penalties, fines, additions to tax or interest imposed by the United States or any state, county, local or foreign government or subdivision or agency thereof.

4.22   Labor Matters. Schedule 4.22 sets forth a true and complete list of all employees of Seller together with a brief summary of their titles, duties, terms of employment and compensation arrangements, including the salary and any bonus, commission or other compensation paid to each employee during the twelve (12) month period prior to the date hereof and the current employment and compensation arrangements with respect to each such employee. Further, with respect to employees of and service provided to Seller:

(a) Seller is not a party to any collective bargaining or similar labor agreements, no such agreement determines the terms and conditions of employment of any employee of Seller, no collective bargaining or other labor agent

(continues)

Exhibit 10-2. (continued)

has been certified as a representative of any of the employees of the Seller, and no representation campaign or election is now in progress with respect to any of the employees of the Seller;

(b) Seller is and has been in compliance in all material respects with all applicable laws respecting employment and employment practices, terms and conditions of employment and wages and hours, including without limitation, any such laws respecting employment discrimination and harassment, workers' compensation, family and medical leave, the Immigration Reform and Control Act, and occupational safety and health requirements, and has not and is not engaged in any unfair labor practice;

(c) there is not now, nor within the past three years, has there been, any unfair labor practice complaint against Seller, pending or to Seller's best knowledge, threatened before the National Labor Relations Board or any other comparable authority; nor any labor strike, slowdown or stoppage actually ending or, to Seller's best knowledge, threatened against or directly affecting Seller; there exist no other labor disputes with regard to Seller's employees or relative to Seller's Employee Technician Manual ("Manual"), including, without limitation, any reports of harassment, substance abuse, disciplinary, safety or punctuality problems in contravention of Seller's Manual, or other acts or omissions filed or recorded by or against any employee of Seller. Seller's cessation of operations will not violate any laws, rules, regulations or employment policies applicable to its employees.

(d) As of the Closing Date, each employee of the Seller has received any pay owed him or her with respect to vacation, compensatory or sick time and any other employee benefits due employee, except as otherwise set forth in Schedule 4.22(d).

4.23 <u>Absence of Undisclosed Liabilities</u>. Neither the Seller nor any Shareholder has any material liabilities or obligations with respect to the Business, either direct or indirect, matured or unmatured or absolute, contingent or otherwise, other than (a) those reflected in the 1996 Balance Sheet and (b) those liabilities or obligations incurred, consistently with past business practice, in or as a result of the normal and ordinary course of business since the Balance Sheet Date.

4.24 <u>Liabilities</u>. The liabilities to be assumed by Buyer pursuant to this Agreement consist solely of liabilities of Seller under Contracts included in the Assets which relate solely to the operation of the Business and the Assumed Liabilities in Schedule 1.2.

4.25 <u>Accuracy of Documents and Information</u>. The information provided to the Buyer by the Seller and the Shareholders with respect to the Seller, the Assets and the Business, including the representations and warranties made in this Agreement and in the Schedules attached hereto, and all other information provided to the Buyer in connection with their investigation of the Seller, does not (and will not at the Closing Date) contain any untrue statement of a material fact and does not omit (and will not omit at the Closing Date) to state any material fact necessary to make the statements or facts contained herein or therein not misleading.

4.26 Brokers and Agents. Neither Seller nor any Shareholder has employed or dealt with any business broker, agent or finder in respect of the transactions contemplated hereby.

5. **NON-COMPETITION.** Each of the Shareholders agrees that for a period of six (6) years from the date of this Agreement, he or she shall not, directly or indirectly: (a) engage in competition with the Buyer in any manner or capacity (e.g., as an advisor, consultant, independent contractor, principal, agent, partner, officer, director, stockholder, employee, member of any association, or otherwise) or in any phase of the business conducted by the Buyer during the term of this Agreement in any area where the Buyer is conducting or initiating operations during the period described above; provided, however, that ownership by a Shareholder as a passive investment, of less than one percent (1%) of the outstanding shares of capital stock of any corporation listed on a national securities exchange or publicly traded in the over-the-counter market shall not constitute a breach of this provision; (b) hire or engage or attempt to hire or employ any individual who shall have been an employee of the Buyer at any time during within one (1) year prior to such action taken by a Shareholder, whether for or on behalf of such Shareholder or for any entity in which such Shareholder shall have a direct or indirect interest (or any subsidiary or affiliate of any such entity), whether as a proprietor, partner, co-venturer, financier, investor or stockholder, director, officer, employer, employee, agent, representative or otherwise; or (c) assist or encourage any other person in carrying out, directly or indirectly, any activity that would be prohibited by the above provisions of this Section if such activity were carried out by Shareholder, either directly or indirectly; and in particular each Shareholder agrees that he or she will not, directly or indirectly, induce any employee of the Buyer to carry out, directly or indirectly, any such activity. In the event of any conflict between this provision and the terms of an Employment Agreement in full force and effect, the Employment Agreement will govern.

6. **REPRESENTATIONS AND WARRANTIES OF THE BUYER.** In order to induce the Seller to enter into this Agreement and to consummate the transactions contemplated hereby, each of the Buyer, jointly and severally, hereby represents and warrants to the Seller as follows:

6.1 Buyer's Organization. The Buyer is a limited liability company duly organized, validly existing and in good standing under the laws of the State of Maryland. The Buyer has all requisite power and authority to own and operate and lease its properties and assets, to carry on its business as it is now being conducted and to execute, deliver and perform its obligations under this Agreement and consummate the transactions contemplated hereby.

(continues)

Exhibit 10-2. (continued)

6.2 <u>Authorization of Agreement</u>. The execution, delivery and perform-ance by the Buyer of this Agreement and of each and every agreement and docu-ment contemplated hereby and the consummation of the transactions contemplated hereby and thereby have been duly authorized by all necessary corporate action of the Buyer. This Agreement has been duly and validly executed and delivered by Buyer and constitutes (and, when executed and delivered, each such other agree-ment and document will constitute) a valid and binding obligation of the Buyer, en-forceable against the Buyer in accordance with its terms.

6.3 <u>Non-Contravention; Consents</u>. Neither the execution and delivery by the Buyer of this Agreement nor the consummation by the Buyer of the transactions contemplated hereby, nor compliance by the Buyer with any of the provisions hereof, will (i) conflict with or result in a breach of any provision of the Articles of Organiza-tion or Operating Agreement of the Buyer, (ii) result in the breach of, or conflict with, any of the terms and conditions of, or constitute a default (with or without the giving of notice or the lapse of time or both) with respect to, or result in the cancellation or termination of, or the acceleration of the performance of any obligations or of any indebtedness under any contract, agreement, commitment, indenture, mortgage, note, bond, license or other instrument or obligation to which the Buyer is now a party or by which the Buyer or its respective properties or assets may be bound or affected (other than such breaches, conflicts and defaults as shall have been waived at or prior to the Closing) or (iii) violate any law or any rule or regulation of any administrative agency or governmental body, or any order, writ, injunction or decree of any court, administrative agency or governmental body to which the Buyer may be subject. No approval, authorization, consent or other order or action of, or filing with or notice to any court, administrative agency or other governmental authority or any other person is required for the execution and delivery by the Buyer of this Agree-ment or consummation by the Buyer of the transactions contemplated hereby (other than such consents as shall have obtained at or prior to the Closing).

6.4 <u>Litigation</u>. There is no litigation, suit, proceeding, action, claim or investigation, at law or in equity, pending, or to the best knowledge of the Buyer, threatened against, or affecting in any way, the Buyer's ability to perform its obliga-tions as contemplated by this Agreement.

6.5 <u>The Equity Interest</u>. The Equity Interest has been duly authorized and issued in accordance with the terms hereof and the Operating Agreement.

6.6 <u>Accuracy of Financial Statements</u>. The Financial Statement for Stu-art Savanuck, set forth in <u>Schedule 6.6</u>, is true and correct in all material respects.

7.   **FURTHER AGREEMENTS OF THE PARTIES**

7.1 <u>Operation of the Business</u>. From and after the Balance Sheet Date until the Closing Date, except to the extent contemplated by this Agreement or other-wise consented to in writing by the Buyer, the Seller shall have continued to operate its Business in substantially the same manner as presently conducted and only in the ordinary and usual course and substantially consistent with past practice and in substantial compliance with (i) all laws and (ii) all leases, contracts, commitments and other agreements, and all licenses, permits, and other instruments, relating to the operation of the Business, and will use reasonable efforts to preserve intact its present business organization and to keep available the services of all employees, representatives and agents. The Seller and each of the Shareholders shall have continued to use its, his or her reasonable efforts, consistent with past practices, to promote the Business and to maintain the goodwill and reputation associated with the Business, and shall not take or omit to take any action which causes, or which is likely to cause, any material deterioration of the Business or the Seller's relationships with material suppliers or customers. Without limiting the generality of the foregoing, (a) the Seller will have maintained all of its equipment in substantially the same condition and repair as such equipment was maintained prior to the Balance Sheet Date, ordinary wear and tear excepted; (b) the Seller shall not have sold, transferred, pledged, leased or otherwise disposed of any of the Assets, other than in the ordinary course of business; (c) the Seller shall not have amended, terminated or waived any material right in respect of the Assets or the Business, or do any act, or omit to do any act, which will cause a breach of any material contract, agreement, commitment or obligation by it; (d) the Seller shall have maintained its books, accounts and records in accordance with good business practice and generally accepted accounting principles consistently applied; (e) the Seller shall not have engaged in any activities or transactions outside the ordinary course of business; (f) the Seller shall not have declared or paid any dividend or make any other distribution or payment of any kind in cash or property to the Shareholder or other affiliates; and (g) the Seller shall not have increased any existing employee benefits, established any new employee benefits plan or amended or modified any existing Employee Plans, or otherwise incurred any obligation or liability under any employee plan materially different in nature or amount from obligations or liabilities incurred in connection with the Employee Plans.

7.2 <u>Consents; Assignment of Agreements</u>. Seller shall obtain, at the earliest practicable date, all consents and approvals of third parties (whether or not listed on Schedule 4.4) which are necessary or desirable for the consummation of the transactions contemplated hereby (including, without limitation, the valid and binding transfer of the Assets to Buyer) (the "Consents"). The Consents shall be written instruments whose form and substance are reasonably satisfactory to Buyer. The Consents shall not, without Buyer's express consent, impose any obligations on Buyer or create any conditions adverse to Buyer, other than the conditions or obligations specified in this Agreement.

7.3 <u>No Discussions</u>. The Seller shall not enter into any substantive negotiations or discussions with any third party with respect to the sale or lease of the Assets or the Business, or the sale of any capital stock of the Seller, or any other merger, acquisition, partnership, joint venture or other business combination until the earlier to occur of the (a) Closing Date or (b) the termination of this Agreement.

(continues)

Exhibit 10-2. (continued)

7.4   Employee Matters. The Seller shall permit the Buyer to contact and make arrangements with the Seller's employees for the purpose of assuring their employment by the Buyer after the Closing and for the purpose of ensuring the continuity of the Business, and the Seller agrees not to discourage any such employees from being employed by or consulting with the Buyer. Nothing herein shall obligate the Buyer to employ or otherwise be responsible for any of the Seller's employees, (other than the persons with whom the Buyer has entered or will enter into an employee agreement in accordance with Section 8.2 hereof) or pay any employee any compensation or confer any benefit earned or accrued prior to the Closing Date, except as set forth in Schedule 4.22(d).

7.5   Notice Regarding Changes. The Seller shall promptly notify the Buyer in writing of any change in facts and circumstances that could render any of the representations and warranties made herein by the Seller materially inaccurate or misleading.

7.6   Furnishing of Information. The Seller will allow Buyer to make a complete examination and analysis of the Business, Assets and records, financial or otherwise, of the Seller. In connection with the foregoing review, Seller agrees that it shall furnish to the Buyer and Buyer's representatives all such information concerning the Seller's Business, Assets, operations, properties or affairs as may be reasonably requested.

7.7   Notification of Customers. At the Buyer's request and in a form approved by the Buyer, the Seller agrees to notify all customers of the Business identified by Buyer and all customers of the Business during the year preceding the Closing as identified by Buyer, either separately or jointly with the Buyer, of the Buyer's purchase of the Business and Assets hereunder and that all further communications or requests by such customers with respect to the Business and Assets shall be directed to the Buyer. Without limiting the foregoing, promptly following the Closing, the Seller shall send a letter, in a form approved by the Buyer, to each debtor with respect to the notes, accounts or other receivables included in the Assets directing that all payments on account of such receivables made after the Closing shall be made to the Buyer.

7.8   Collection of Receivables. The Seller agrees that it will reasonably cooperate with the Buyer in collecting the notes, accounts and other receivables included in the Assets from any customers and will immediately deliver to the Buyer the amount paid on any and all receivables it collects after the Closing Date in connection with the Business, less out-of-pocket expenses incurred by Seller at the request of Buyer.

7.9   Brokers and Agents. Buyer, on the one hand, and the Seller, on the other hand, agree to indemnify and hold the other harmless from and against all fees, expenses, commissions and costs due and owing to any other broker, agent or finder on account of or in any way resulting from any contract or understanding existing between the indemnifying party and such person.

8. **CONDITIONS PRECEDENT TO CLOSING**

8.1   Conditions Precedent to the Obligations of Seller. Seller's and Shareholders' obligations to consummate the transactions contemplated by this Agreement shall be subject to the fulfillment, at or prior to Closing, of each of the following conditions (any or all of which may be waived in writing, in whole or in part, by the Seller and the Shareholders):

(a) The Buyer shall have performed and complied in all material respects with each obligation and covenant required by this Agreement to be performed or complied with by them prior to or at the Closing.

(b) The representations and warranties of the Buyer contained herein shall be true and correct in all material respects at and as of the Closing Date as if made at and as of such time.

(c) Buyer shall have delivered to the Seller the items set forth in Section 3.2(b) of this Agreement.

(d) No action, suit or proceeding by any person shall have been commenced and still be pending, no investigation by any governmental or regulatory authority shall have been commenced and still be pending, and no action, suit or proceeding by any person shall have been threatened against the Buyer, the Seller or the Shareholders, (a) seeking to restrain, prevent or change the transactions contemplated hereby or questioning the validity or legality of any such transactions or (b) which if resolved adversely to any party, would materially and adversely affect the business or condition, financial or otherwise, of the Buyer, or the Seller.

(e) All proceedings to be taken by the Buyer in connection with the transactions contemplated hereby and all documents incident thereto shall be reasonably satisfactory in form and substance to the Seller and its counsel, and the Seller and said counsel shall have received all such counterpart originals or certified or other copies of such documents as it or they may reasonably request.

(f) Buyer shall have delivered to the Seller the Pledge Agreement together with the marketable securities and other collateral securing the Note.

(g) Buyer shall have delivered to the Seller all such other certificates and documents as the Seller and its counsel shall have reasonably requested.

8.2   Conditions Precedent to the Obligations of the Buyer. The obligation of the Buyer to consummate the transactions contemplated by this Agreement shall be subject to the fulfillment, at or prior to Closing, of each of the following conditions precedent (any or all of which may be waived in writing, in whole or in part, by the Buyer):

(a) The Seller shall have performed and complied in all material respects with each obligation and covenant required by this Agreement to be performed or to be complied with by it on or prior to the Closing Date.

(b) The representations and warranties of the Seller and the Shareholders contained herein or in any Schedule attached hereto shall be true and correct in all material respects at and as of the Closing Date as if made at and as of such time.

(continues)

Exhibit 10-2. (continued)

(c)   The Seller and the Shareholders shall have delivered or caused delivery of the items set forth in Section 3.2(a) hereof.

(d)   Except as otherwise set forth in this Agreement, the Buyer shall have received written evidence, in form and substance satisfactory to it, that all material consents, waivers, authorizations and approvals of, or filing with or notices to, governmental entities and third parties required in order that the transactions contemplated hereby be consummated have been obtained or made.

(e)   There shall not have occurred since the Balance Sheet Date any material damage or loss by theft, casualty or otherwise, whether or not insured against by the Seller or the Shareholders, of all or any material portion of the Assets, or any material adverse change in or interference with the Business or the properties, assets, condition (financial or otherwise) or prospects of the Seller.

(f)   Buyer shall have entered into an employment agreement with Jane C. Doe and John F. Doe, in substantially the forms attached hereto as Exhibit G and Exhibit H, respectively.

(g)   No action, suit or proceeding by any person shall have been commenced and still be pending, no investigations by any governmental or regulatory authority shall have been commenced and still be pending, and no action, suit or proceeding by any person shall have been threatened against the Buyer, the Seller or the Shareholders, (a) seeking to restrain, prevent or change the transactions contemplated hereby or questioning the validity or legality of any such transactions or (b) which if resolved adversely to any party, would materially and adversely affect the business or condition, financial or otherwise, of the Buyer, or the Seller.

(h)   All proceedings to be taken by the Seller and the Shareholders in connection with the transactions contemplated hereby and all documents incident thereto shall be reasonably satisfactory in form and substance to the Buyer and its counsel, and the Buyer and said counsel shall have received all such counterpart originals or certified or other copies of such documents as it or they may reasonably request.

(i)   Seller shall have delivered to the Buyer all such other certificates and documents as the Buyer or its counsel shall have reasonably requested.

9.   **INDEMNIFICATION; SURVIVAL OF REPRESENTATIONS AND WARRANTIES**

9.1   Indemnification by Seller and Shareholders. Each of the Sellers and the Shareholders, jointly and severally, covenants and agrees to indemnify, defend, protect and hold harmless the Buyer and any of the Buyer's officers, directors, stockholders, representatives, affiliates, assigns, successors in interest, and current and former employees, each only in their respective capacities as such (collectively, the "Buyer Indemnified Parties"), from, against and in respect of:

(a)   any and all liabilities, claims, losses, damages, punitive damages, causes of action, lawsuits, administrative proceedings, demands, judgments, settlement payments, penalties, and costs and expense (including, without limitation, reasonable attorneys' fees, travel expenses, expert witness fees and disbursements of every kind, nature and description) (collectively, "Damages"), suffered, sustained, incurred or paid by Buyer or any other Buyer Indemnified Party in connection with, resulting from or arising out of, either directly or indirectly:

(i)   any misrepresentation or breach of any warranty of the Seller or any Shareholder set forth in this Agreement or any Schedule or certificate delivered by or on behalf of the Seller or any Shareholder in connection herewith; or

(ii)   any nonfulfillment of any covenant or agreement on the part of the Seller or any Shareholder set forth in this Agreement; or

(iii)   the Business, operations or Assets of the Seller prior to the Closing Date or the actions or omissions of the Seller's directors, officers, shareholders, employees, or agents prior to the Closing Date (except with respect to the Assumed Liabilities); or

(iv)   the Excluded Liabilities.

(b) any and all Damages incident to any of the foregoing or to the enforcement of this Section 10.1.

9.2   Limitation and Expiration. The indemnification obligations under this Section 10 or in any other certificate or writing furnished in connection with the transactions contemplated hereby shall terminate on the later of (i) the date that is six (6) months after the expiration of the longest applicable federal or state statute of limitation (including extensions thereof), or (b) if here is no applicable statute of limitation, four years after the Closing Date, or (c) the final resolution of a claim or demand (a "Claim") as of the relevant dates described above in this Section.

9.3   Indemnification by Buyer. The Buyer covenants and agrees to indemnify, defend, protect and hold harmless the Shareholders, the Seller and any of the Seller's officers, directors, stockholders, representatives, affiliates, assigns, successors in interest, and current and former employees, each only in their respective capacities as such (collectively, the "Seller Indemnified Parties"), from, against and in respect of:

(a) any and all Damages sustained, incurred or paid by Seller or any other Seller Indemnified Party in connection with, resulting from or arising out of, either directly or indirectly:

(i)   any breach of any warranty of the Buyer set forth in this Agreement or any Schedule or certificate delivered by or on behalf of the Buyer in connection herewith; or

(ii)   any nonfulfillment of any covenant or agreement on the part of the Buyer set forth in this Agreement; or

(iii)   the ownership of the purchased Assets or the operation of the Business by the Buyer following the Closing Date.

(b) any and all Damages incident to any of the foregoing or to the enforcement of this Section 10.3.

(continues)

Exhibit 10-2. (continued)

9.4   Notice Procedures; Claims. The obligations and liabilities of the parties under this Section with respect to, relating to, caused (in whole or in part) by or arising out of claims of third parties (individually, a "Third Party Claim" and collectively, "Third Party Claims") shall be subject to the following conditions:

(a) The party entitled to be indemnified hereunder (the "Indemnified Party") shall give the party obligated to provide the indemnity (the "Indemnifying Party") prompt notice of any Third Party Claim (the "Claim Notice"); provided that the failure to give such Claim Notice shall not affect the liability of the Indemnifying Party under this Agreement unless the failure materially and adversely affects the ability of the Indemnifying Party to defend the Third Party Claim. If the Indemnifying Party promptly acknowledges in writing its obligation to indemnify in accordance with the terms and subject to the limitations of such party's obligation to indemnify contained in this Agreement with respect to that claim, the Indemnifying Party shall have a reasonable time to assume the defense of the Third Party Claim at its expense and with counsel of its choosing, which counsel shall be reasonably satisfactory to the Indemnified Party. Any Claim Notice shall identify, to the extent known to the Indemnified Party, the basis for the Third Party Claim, the facts giving rise to the Third Party Claim, and the estimated amount of the Third Party Claim (which estimate shall not be conclusive of the final amount of such claim or demand). The Indemnified Party shall make available to the Indemnifying Party copies of all relevant documents and records in its possession.

(b) If the Indemnifying Party, within a reasonable time after receipt of such Claim Notice, fails to assume the defense of any Third Party Claim in accordance with Section 10.4(a), the Indemnified Party shall (upon further notice to the Indemnifying Party) have the right to undertake the defense, compromise or settlement of the Third Party Claim, at the expense and for the account and risk of the Indemnifying Party.

(c) Anything in this Section 10.4 to the contrary notwithstanding, (i) the Indemnifying Party shall not without the written consent of the Indemnified Party, settle or compromise any Third Party Claim or consent to the entry of judgment which does not include as an unconditional term thereof the giving by the claimant or the plaintiff to the Indemnified Party of an unconditional release from all liability in respect of the Third Party Claim; (ii) if such Third Party Claim involves an issue or matter which the Indemnified Party believes could have a materially adverse effect on the Indemnified Party's business, operations, assets, properties or prospects of its business, the Indemnified Party shall have the right to control the defense or settlement of any such claim or demand, at the expense of the Indemnified Party without contribution from the Indemnifying Party; and (iii) the Indemnified Party shall have the right to employ its own counsel to defend any claim at the Indemnifying Party's expense if (x) the employment of such counsel by the Indemnified Party has been authorized by the Indemnifying Party, or (y) counsel selected by the Indemnifying Party shall have reasonably concluded that there may be a conflict of interest between the Indemnifying Party and the Indemnified Party in the conduct of the defense of such action or (z) the Indemnifying Party shall not have employed counsel to assume the defense of such claim in accordance with Section 10.4(a).

(d) In the event that the Indemnified Party should have a claim against the Indemnifying Party hereunder which does not involve a claim or demand being asserted against or sought to be collected from it by a third party, the Indemnified Party shall promptly send a Claim Notice with respect to such claim to the Indemnifying Party. If the Indemnifying Party does not notify the Indemnified Party within thirty (30) calendar days that it disputes such claim, the amount of such claim shall be conclusively deemed a liability of the Indemnifying Party hereunder.

(e) Nothing herein shall be deemed to prevent any Indemnified Party from making a claim hereunder for potential or contingent claims or demands, provided that (i) the Claim Notice sets forth (A) the specific basis for any such potential or contingent claim or demand and (B) the estimated amount thereof (to the extent then feasible) and (ii) the Indemnified Party has reasonable grounds to believe that such a claim or demand will be made.

9.5   Survival of Representations Warranties and Covenants. All representations, warranties and covenants made by the Seller, the Shareholders, and the Buyer in or pursuant to this Agreement or in any document delivered pursuant hereto shall be deemed to have been made on the date of this Agreement (except as otherwise provided herein) and, if a Closing occurs, as of the Closing Date. The representations of the Seller and the Shareholders will survive and the Closing and remain in effect until, and will expire upon, the termination of the relevant indemnification obligation as provided in Section 10.2. The representations of Buyer will survive and remain in effect until and will expire upon, the later of the third anniversary of the Closing Date or the satisfaction in full of any payment obligation pursuant to the Promissory Note.

9.6   Indemnification Trigger. Notwithstanding the provisions of Section 10.1 or 10.3 above, neither Seller nor Buyer shall be liable to the other for any indemnification under this Section 10 unless and until the aggregate amount of Damages due to an Indemnified Party exceeds Two Hundred Thousand Dollars ($200,000) (the "Trigger Amount"). Once the Trigger Amount has been exceeded, the Indemnified Party shall be entitled to indemnification for all Damages, including the amount up to the Trigger Amount and any amount in excess thereof. The foregoing trigger provision shall not apply, however, with respect to any Damages suffered, sustained, incurred or paid by an Indemnified Party related to Taxes or assessments by any governmental authority, or with respect to any claim of actual fraud or intentional misrepresentation relating to a breach of any representation or warranty in this Agreement.

9.7   Remedies Cumulative. The remedies set forth in this Section 10 are cumulative and shall not be construed to restrict or otherwise affect any other remedies that may be available to the Indemnified Parties under any other agreement or pursuant to statutory or common law.

(continues)

Exhibit 10-2. (continued)

10. **POST-CLOSING MATTERS**

10.1   Transition Services. The Seller agrees to provide reasonable assistance to the Buyer in connection with the transition of the Business to the Buyer. The Shareholders will provide assistance to Buyer in accordance with their respective Employment Agreement.

10.2   Further Assurances. The Seller and each of the Shareholders hereby covenants and agrees to (a) make, execute and deliver to the Buyer any and all powers of attorney and other authority which the Seller may lawfully make, execute and deliver, in addition to any such powers and authorities as are contained herein, which may reasonably be or become necessary, proper or convenient to enable the Buyer to reduce to possession, collect, enforce, own or enjoy any and all rights and benefits in, to, with respect to, or in connection with, the Assets, or any part or portion thereof, and (b) upon the Buyer's request, to take, in the Seller's name, any and all steps and to do any and all things which may be or become lawful and reasonably necessary, proper, convenient or desirable to enable the Buyer to reduce to possession, collect, enforce, own and enjoy any and all rights and benefits in, to, with respect to, or in connection with, the Assets, and each and every part and portion thereof. The Seller and each of the Shareholders also covenants and agrees with the Buyer, its successors and assigns, that the Seller and each of the Shareholders will do, execute, acknowledge and deliver, or cause to be done, executed, acknowledged and delivered, any and all such further reasonable acts, instruments, papers and documents as may be necessary to carry out and effectuate the intent and purposes of this Agreement. From and after the Closing Date, Seller will promptly refer all inquiries with respect to ownership of the Assets or the Business to Buyer.

10.3   Payment of Liabilities; Discharge of Liens. The Seller shall satisfy and discharge as the same shall become due, all of Seller's liabilities, obligations, debts and commitments including but not limited to Tax liabilities, in accordance with this Agreement, other than the Assumed Liabilities.

10.4   Transfer of Permits; Additional Consents. Subsequent to the Closing, Seller shall use its reasonable efforts to effectively transfer to Buyer all Permits which were not so transferred at or prior to the Closing and to obtain all approvals, consents and authorizations with respect to such transfers. In addition, subsequent to the Closing, to the extent requested by Buyer, Seller shall use its reasonable efforts to obtain any required consents of the other parties to the Scheduled Contracts included in the Assets to the assignment thereof to the Buyer which were not obtained at or prior to the Closing.

10.5   Inspection of Documents, Books and Records; Financial Reports. Subsequent to the Closing, Buyer shall make available for inspection by Seller or its authorized representatives during regular business hours and upon reasonable notice, any original documents conveyed to Buyer under this Agreement. Upon reasonable notice to the Buyer, for five years from the Closing Date forward, Seller or its representatives shall be entitled, at Seller's expense, to audit, copy, review and inspect the Buyer's books and records at the Buyer's offices during reasonable business hours. For so long as any payment obligation is outstanding under this Agreement, Buyer shall make available to Seller and its representatives, copies of Buyer's annual corporate tax returns and any quarterly financial statements or reports prepared or compiled by or for Buyer.

10.6 Acceleration of Notes. In the event that Buyer shall subsequently sell, convey, transfer or assign assets of the Buyer, to a non-affiliated third party (other than as collateral under a lien or security arrangement), the value of which is greater than twenty-five percent of the total assets of the Buyer at the time of the transfer, all amounts of principal and interest then outstanding under both Notes shall become immediately due and payable.

11. **RISK OF LOSS.** Prior to the Closing, the risk of loss (including damage and/or destruction) of all of the Seller's property and assets, including without limitation the Assets, shall remain with the Seller, and the legal doctrine known as the "Doctrine of Equitable Conversion" shall not be applicable to this Agreement or to any of the transactions contemplated hereby.

12. **MISCELLANEOUS**

12.1 Entire Agreement. This Agreement, and the Exhibits and Schedules to this Agreement constitute the entire agreement between the parties hereto with respect to the subject matter hereof and supersede all prior negotiations, agreements, arrangements and understandings, whether oral or written, among the parties hereto with respect to such subject matter, (including, without limitation, the letter of intent dated January 17, 1997, as amended, between the Seller and the Buyer).

12.2 No Third Party Beneficiary. Nothing expressed or implied in this Agreement is intended, or shall be construed, to confer upon or give any person, firm, corporation, partnership, association or other entity, other than the parties hereto and their respective successors and assigns, any rights or remedies under or by reason of this Agreement.

12.3 Amendment. This Agreement may not be amended or modified in any respect, except by the mutual written agreement of the parties hereto.

12.4 Waivers and Remedies. The waiver by any of the parties hereto of any other party's prompt and complete performance, or breach or violation, of any provision of this Agreement shall not operate nor be construed as a waiver of any subsequent breach or violation, and the failure by any of the parties hereto to exercise any right or remedy which it may possess hereunder shall not operate nor be construed as a bar to the exercise of such right or remedy by such party upon the occurrence of any subsequent breach or violation.

(continues)

Exhibit 10-2. (continued)

12.5 Severability. If any term, provision, covenant or restriction of this Agreement (or the application thereof to any specific persons or circumstances) should be held by an administrative agency or court of competent jurisdiction to be invalid, void or unenforceable, such term, provision, covenant or restriction shall be modified to the minimum extent necessary in order to render it enforceable within such jurisdiction, consistent with the expressed objectives of the parties hereto. Further, the remainder of this Agreement (and the application of such term, provision, covenant or restriction to any other persons or circumstances) shall not be affected thereby, but rather shall be enforced to the greatest extent permitted by law.

12.6 Descriptive Headings. Descriptive headings contained herein are for convenience only and shall not control or affect the meaning or construction of any provision of this Agreement.

12.7 Counterparts. This Agreement may be executed in any number of counterparts and by the separate parties hereto in separate counterparts, each of which shall be deemed to be one and the same instrument.

12.8 Notices. All notices, consents, requests, instructions, approvals and other communications provided for herein and all legal process in regard hereto shall be in writing and shall be deemed to have been duly given (a) when delivered by hand, (b) when received by facsimile transmission, with printed confirmation of transmission and verbal (telephonic) confirmation of receipt, (c) one day after being sent by a nationally-recognized overnight express service or (d) five (5) days after being deposited in the United States mail, by registered or certified mail, return receipt requested, postage prepaid, as follows:

    If to the Seller: Target Co., Inc.
                       16602 Side Avenue
                       Anytown, USA 01206
                       Attn: President

    If to Buyer: Growth Co. Corp.
                       12345 Main Street
                       Anytown, USA 01234
                       Attn: Chief Executive Officer

or to such other address as any party hereto may from time to time designate in writing delivered in a like manner.

12.9 Successors and Assigns. This Agreement shall be binding upon and shall inure to the benefit of the parties hereto and their respective successors and assigns. None of the parties hereto shall assign any of its rights or obligations hereunder except with the express written consent of the other parties hereto.

12.10 Applicable Law. This Agreement shall be governed by, and shall be construed, interpreted and enforced in accordance with, the internal laws of the State of Maryland.

12.11 <u>Expenses</u>. Each of the parties hereto agrees to pay all of the respective expenses incurred by it in connection with the negotiation, preparation, execution, delivery and performance of this Agreement and the consummation of the transactions contemplated hereby.

12.12 <u>Confidentiality</u>. Except to the extent required for any party to obtain any approvals or consents required pursuant to the terms hereof, no party hereto shall divulge the existence of the terms of this Agreement or the transactions contemplated hereby without the prior written approval of all of the parties hereto, except and as to the extent (i) obligated by law or (ii) necessary for such party to defend or prosecute any litigation in connection with the transactions contemplated hereby.

12.13 <u>Attorney Fees</u>. In the event any suit or other legal proceeding is brought for the enforcement of any of the provisions of this Agreement, the parties hereto agree that the prevailing party or parties shall be entitled to recover from the other party or parties upon final judgment on the merits reasonable attorneys' fees and expenses, including attorneys' fees and expenses for any appeal, and costs incurred in bringing such suit or proceeding.

IN WITNESS WHEREOF, the parties have executed and delivered this Agreement on the date first above written.

GROWTH CO. CORP.

By: _____

_____, President

TARGET CO., INC.

By: _____

_____, President

Chapter 11

Postclosing Challenges

The closing of a merger or acquisition usually brings a great sigh of relief to the buyer, seller, and their respective advisors. Everyone has worked hard to ensure that the process went smoothly and that all parties are happy with the end result. But the term *closing* can be misleading in that it suggests a sense of finality, when in truth the hard work, particularly for the buyer, has just begun.

Often one of the greatest challenges for the buyer is the post-closing integration of the two companies. The integration of human resources, the corporate cultures, the operating and management information systems, the accounting methods and financial practices, and related matters are often the most difficult part of completing a merger or acquisition. The consequences of a rocky transition will be the buyer's inability to realize the true value of the transaction, wasted time and resources devoted to solving postclosing problems, and in some cases even litigation.

The focus of this chapter is on understanding and anticipating the nature and types of postclosing challenges faced by both buyer and seller *after* the deal is completed. The seller must facilitate a smooth transition of ownership and management to the buyer's team without ego, emotion, or politics. The buyer must have procedures in place to prevent the seller undermining these transitional efforts and assume control of the company—also without ego, emotion, or politics. Postclosing challenges may arise in a wide variety of subject areas, which are addressed in this chapter—e.g., operations, finance, personnel, and information systems. As we

I would like to gratefully acknowledge and thank Richard Guenther for his significant contributions to this chapter.

will see, a series of emotional and psychological factors must be considered, and strong leadership is needed to guide affected employees through the process.

A Time of Transition

Postclosing challenges raise a wide variety of human fears and uncertainties that must be understood and addressed by both buyer and seller. The fear of the unknown experienced by the employees of the seller must be confronted and put to rest; otherwise, the employees' stress and trauma will affect the seller's performance and the viability of the transaction. The need to quickly integrate the two corporate cultures also raises personal and psychological issues that must be addressed. Once word of a deal leaks out to employees, there is likely to be widespread insecurity and fear of job loss from the executive suite all the way down to the shop floor.

Many of the fears experienced by the employees of *both* buyer and seller result from expectations of downsizing to cut waste, avoid duplication, and enjoy the economies of scale created from the transaction. The trend toward these layoffs, however, seems to be declining. For example, there was a record $658.8 billion worth of merger transactions in 1996. But instead of laying off employees, companies held on tight, according to Chicago-based outplacement firm Challenger, Gray & Christmas. Only 8.9 percent of the 477,147 job cuts in 1996 were related to mergers. That's down 46 percent from 1995, when 16.4 percent of 439,882 cuts were merger driven.

Another common problem is the psychological consequences of "seller's remorse," particularly when the seller remains on-site in a consulting capacity or even as a minority owner. The seller can be so accustomed to managing the business that it may not be open to changes in strategies or policies implemented by the buyer. The seller undermines or meddles in the buyer's efforts or contradicts its authority. These sellers often want the *benefit* of the bargain but seem unwilling to accept the *burden* of the bargain and relinquish control of the company. These problems are particularly common in mergers where the management and flow of the deal may be one of shared objectives and values as opposed to an acquisition that more clearly has a designated quarterback.

In attempting to realize the true value of a merger or acquisition, the buyer must coordinate a smooth and efficient postclosing process. Important issues that need to be managed fall into three areas—people, places, and things. Some issues are addressed in the closing documents. Most require some forethought in order to anticipate potential pitfalls. The bottom line is that if the buyer doesn't plan to address the following issues, the chances for failure or for not fully realizing success are greatly increased.

Staffing Levels and Other People Problems

One of the primary areas that an acquiring company looks to in order to realize the projected return on its investment is the new company's level of staffing. If a certain number of employees can be eliminated, it is more likely that financial projections will be met or exceeded. The hard part is deciding who stays, and in what positions, and who goes. Much of this depends on the nature of the acquisition. On the one hand, if the terms dictate that the acquired firm is to maintain its independence, it is much more difficult to reduce staffing levels. On the other hand, if the acquired firm is absorbed into the acquirer, staff cutbacks are probably necessary.

The first step in determining staffing levels is to divide the workforce into management and labor. These two groups must be distinguished because the terms of employment are often quite different. Management is often party to employment contracts, and

---

Box 11-1. Strategic Postclosing Issues

1. Who should lead the transition team?
2. Which changes should be made and how quickly?
3. How will the changes be presented and sold?
4. How can the seller's transition from owner to employee status be managed?
5. How can "turfmanship be avoided?"

receives deferred compensation, stock options, and other issues, while labor is often protected by union contracts and/or federal or state employment laws.

Management

In many ways, management staffing is a much easier problem to resolve. Most employment agreements and/or management benefits can be quantified to determine the cost of such decisions. This should have been examined during the due diligence process and worked into the pricing for the transaction.

The primary task of resolving the level of management staffing is to determine where there are redundancies and who are the most qualified candidates. Such a process is normally driven by the acquiring company, but it is not a bad idea to involve the acquired company as well. Only in this way can a true evaluation be made. Failure to consider all candidates fairly potentially results in a lower return on the investment.

All candidates must be evaluated as objectively as possible. It is often difficult to do so because emotions often cloud the judgment of the evaluators. For the acquiring company, it is much easier to just stick with the team it knows and has worked with for years. No one likes change. But failure to embrace the change inherent with acquisitions reduces the chances of success.

Labor

Labor is often protected by union contracts and labor laws. This limits the options available when deciding who should stay and who should go. However, it should not prevent the buyer from evaluating all employees. By evaluating first and then worrying about possible protections, the buyer gains a much better sense of the quality of the workforce that does ultimately remain.

The same rules apply to evaluating labor as to evaluating management. Be objective. Be balanced. Be honest. The buyer short-changes itself by not doing so. Develop a selection methodology by targeting certain employees for layoff or retention based on performance and experience. Make sure that the applied criteria are documented and objective and are supported by a performance evaluation and that any review of personnel files and performance evaluations is confidential. This may require the formation of a review committee made up of representatives from each organization to ensure that the terminations occur according to agreed upon procedures.

Once the selections are made, they must be examined in light of the law. The following is a list of legal considerations to be examined:

- Employment agreements that may contain conditions that are unacceptable to the buyer or conditions that may be triggered in the event of a merger or acquisition.

- Employees on family leave, pregnancy leave, workers' compensation, or disability who have certain rights to comparable positions upon their return to work, which may or may not be consistent with staffing plans after the acquisition.

- Whistle-blowers who could bring claims of wrongful discharge.

- WARN (Workers Adjustment and Retraining Notification) notices, which must be sent 60 days in advance by the seller to its employees if there is a plan to close facilities.

- Union contracts that could fall under the National Labor Relations Act (NLRA), which protects the rights of union, as well as nonunion, employees on matters of wages, hours, and working conditions.

- Race, religion, or sex discrimination for which the buyer may be held accountable under civil rights legislation, even if claims are filed based on events that occurred before the acquisition.

- Age discrimination under the Age Discrimination in Employment Act (ADEA) and/or Older Workers Benefit Protection Act (OWBPA), which protects workers against changes in the workforce or changes in benefit plans that would discriminate against workers over forty or make age-based distinctions.

- Compliance with the Americans with Disabilities Act (ADA), which, among other things, requires a review of job descriptions to ensure that there is a distinction between essential and nonessential duties and a review of property leases to determine who is responsible (the lessee or the lessor) for renovations required under the ADA.

▪ Violations of the Fair Labor Standards Act (FLSA) or Equal Pay Act, especially concerning the determination of exempt versus nonexempt positions; a violation in this area could lead to substantial payments to current and former employees for overtime worked but not paid.

▪ Problems that could develop under the Occupational Health and Safety Act (OSHA) if current compliance is not verified and the cost of future compliance is not factored into operating results.

▪ If the employees being acquired are legally able to work in the United States; the burden of compliance is on the employer under the Immigration Reform and Control Act (IRCA).

▪ If there is compliance with the Drug-Free Work Place Act and various government contract laws, since lack of compliance can lead to suspended payments or terminated contracts for a seller that is a federal government contractor.

▪ Whether state law counterparts to federal employment laws have precedence.

The bottom line is that the buyer needs to conduct a thorough labor and employment review. This entails all manner of documents related to such issues. Each transaction is unique in that the above issues will apply in differing degrees.

Customers

When a buyer acquires a business, a key component that probably makes the company attractive is its customer base. In order to meet the needs of that customer base, the company needed good vendors. As a result, the continued success of the company, and hence the success of the merger, hinges on maintaining the key customers and suppliers.

The hard part is determining which customers are worth keeping. This is often a financial decision. It makes little sense to keep a customer if it is not possible to make a profit on the relationship, unless the customer enables the merged company to penetrate a new market. However, even in that case, there is a limit to the amount of losses that make financial sense. In addition, the customer may be a direct competitor of the buyer or of one of the buyer's customers. As a result, it is important to evaluate the seller's customer base. It may be necessary to discount the value of the acquisition to account for a customer base that is unprofitable or duplicative and that provides little additional strategic value.

Perhaps more important, however, is for the seller to transfer the goodwill of its customers to the buyer. A disgruntled employee can very quickly destroy this goodwill and perhaps jeopardize a significant income stream on which the value of the acquisition was based. The key steps to transferring this goodwill are:

- Personal introductions to customer contacts
- Social events to acquaint customers with the new owners
- Letters from both the seller and buyer that thank customers for their business and announce the new management and plans for the merged entity

Vendors

Suppliers are much more often overlooked than customers. After all, any vendor can easily be replaced. Since this is often true, it is necessary for the buyer to conduct a thorough review of the existing suppliers to ensure that the seller is getting the best prices and terms. However, there are certain suppliers whose replacement would cause significant disruption. This can occur in situations where there is only one supplier of a given product or service, or if the supplier is an integral part of a just-in-time inventory system. Essential vendors are a key component of the continued success and uninterrupted operations of a company.

Of special importance are suppliers that provide professional services—in particular, bankers, accountants, and lawyers. The standard assumption is that the combined company will use the buyer's professional suppliers, but this may not always be desirable or feasible. If a buyer is purchasing a business in a different industry, the bankers may not feel comfortable. The legal counsel of the seller may be better suited to deal with certain local matters or be more cost-effective. The accountants of the seller may be providing outsourcing of certain tasks for which it may not be practical to change immediately. These factors should be considered carefully before any key relationships, and it may be best to continue to use both firms for certain purposes, subject to any potential conflicts of interests being resolved.

Problems Involving Places

Often one of the larger expenses on the income statement, rent and/or lease payments are a natural place for a buyer to focus when evaluating the efficiencies to be gained by a merger. It would seem to be an easy issue to resolve: In acquiring this company, we can reduce the staff by x percent, which means that we need x percent less of square footage in which to work. In addition, the staff has x percent more square footage per employee than our company. As a result, total square footage can be reduced by x percent, thereby saving $\$x$. But very few decisions in a merger or acquisition can be resolved with a simple mathematical equation. There usually are people involved, and with people come emotions and unpredictability. This has to be accounted for when looking at space, just as much as when examining staffing levels.

When examining the space requirements of the combined entity, it is certainly helpful to consider the square footage. The space should be evaluated to determine if the rent is more or less expensive than other company space and if the amount of space is more than is needed. This will go a long way toward helping to cut expenses in order to reach the target return.

However, there must also be human considerations. How long have the employees been in this space? How does the commute compare to where they might be relocated? How much interaction is required between the staff being relocated and staff in a different location? How much reconfiguration of the office and facilities of each company will be required to accommodate additional staff or functions? How much productivity can be expected from these people during the course of the move?

Failure to explore these and other related questions can open up a can of worms. Location is a factor that can effect the overall integration of the buyer by the seller and can lead to significant turnover. It is taken very personally by many employees. This, of course, does not mean that you should not take steps to maximize the efficiency of the space or to dispose of property when appropriate. But it does mean that these other factors need to be taken into consideration, communicated properly, and implemented thoughtfully.

Problems Involving Attitudes and Corporate Culture

The mating dance was fun. The due diligence was outright friendly. The negotiations were cordial. All has gone well. Now, let's get on with the business. And by the way, I think we'll do things our way. After all, we are the buyer.

This is a perfect example of how to ruin months of goodwill with the seller and its employees. It is a perfect example of how to cause problems on the level of corporate culture. Many of the problems associated with mergers and acquisitions are rooted in a lack of sensitivity to the cultures of the combining entities.

There are four keys steps to make sure that such issues don't cloud the success of an otherwise wonderful marriage. First, allow cultural differences to play a part when determining the value of the deal. Second, realize that the cultures of both companies are important. Third, admit that it is not in either company's interest to maintain both cultures. And fourth, figure out how to combine the two cultures in a way that will prevent the deal from exploding.

If cultural differences are not uncovered during the due diligence process and incorporated into the terms of the deal, there will usually be disappointment in the return on the investment. The primary reason this issue can affect the value of the deal is that cultural differences often spell decreased productivity, which leads to lower revenues and income, and hence a lower value on the deal. As a result, it is often wise to place a conservative value on at least the first year's earnings and cash flow. After that, the value should depend on the experience the buyer has obtained as a result of prior acquisitions. If this is the first acquisition and there is no staff with experience in such matters, the buyer would be well served to be conservative in future years as well!

Because of the longevity of the companies that are now seeking to create a single operating entity, the culture of each is usually deeply ingrained. If this were not the case, the companies would probably not be successful and hence not be attractive merger candidates. In many cases, company employees are unaware of the strength of the culture and how it impacts daily activities.

Recognizing that it is not feasible to keep both cultures seems obvious. This would translate into having two different ways to perform each function. This is a clear recipe for chaos and lack of unity, factors that are normally noticed by outsiders even though efforts are made to hide them. The bottom line is that if the two companies don't act as one, the chances of success are greatly minimized. There will be internal problems—low morale, uncommon goals, redundancy—and external ones—poor customer service, disenchanted investors, negative press.

The most difficult part of merging two corporate cultures is to identify the common ground. Believe it or not, this usually exists. Look not at the operational level but at the philosophical level. Once a common primary goal can be agreed upon, and referenced back on many occasions, the true process of merging the cultures can begin. This primary goal must be agreed upon at the top and communicated to all levels. Only then can functional-level details be worked out.

Corporate culture is such a nebulous, personal concept that it can often be difficult to get your arms around it. This makes it even more difficult to plan for and incorporate it into any merger planning. But if it is ignored, it is an issue that can linger for years and ultimately contribute to disappointment on many levels, not to mention return on investment!

Benefit and Compensation Plans

With the advent of the Employee Retirement Income Security Act (ERISA), and other legislation concerned with compensation and benefits, managing the merging of benefit and compensation plans has taken on added importance. All of the issues concerned with benefit and compensation plans should be worked out in the course of negotiations. Failure to do so, especially as concerns pension plans, can result in costly surprises that cannot be readily addressed afterwards.

As a result of the elaborate structure of such plans, the primary concern should be the ERISA-covered plans—in particular, defined benefit pension plans. The options available for ERISA-covered pension plans (defined benefit as well as defined contribution) include terminating the existing plan, freezing the benefits accrued up to the acquisition, merging the two companies' plans, maintaining two plans, or converting to an entirely different plan. Each of these options has benefits and pitfalls, but the primary issue is the potential costs. The costs include required contributions, the amount of unfunded liabilities (in the case of defined benefit plans), and cash flow requirements. Only after evaluating the magnitude of these costs can an educated decision be made as to the course to take.

Another issue to consider is the integration of other compensation and benefit components, such as medical, life, and disability insurance; severance policies; and reimbursement of medical and child care expenses. As with ERISA-covered plans, the options available are similar—maintain separate systems, choose one system over the other, or choose a combination of the two systems. The method of integration chosen is often driven by the costs involved, but it should also take into account the overall compensation and benefits philosophy.

Believe it or not, making the above choices is the easy part. The hard part comes with the closing of the transaction and the need to integrate the plans of the two companies. The first step is to set the objectives of the integration. The objectives should cover such factors as the cost, funding, adequacy, and competitive position of the plan.

Once the objectives have been set, the pre-merger plans of both organizations should be reviewed relative to the objectives outlined for the choice made. In addition, the option chosen should be compared to the general marketplace. Finally, the plan should be evaluated by a representative group of employees. Assuming the plan has passed all of the above tests, it is now time to implement. As with most postclosing issues, implementation spells the success or failure of the plan. The key function in a successful implementation of benefit and compensation plans is communication. Without good communication of the plan's objectives and details, implementation will be moderately successful, at best. The importance of benefit and compensation plans at every level of the workplace means that without successful implementation of such plans, no matter how well other aspects of the consolidation may be handled, the situation can spell disaster for employee morale and the ability of the combined entity to work as one.

Corporate Identity

Now that the two companies have become one, it only stands to reason that the merged entity is different from what existed before. Yet this is a point that can often be forgotten when it comes to corporate identity. Since there is essentially a *new* company, it may be important to consider a new corporate identity in the form of the company name and/or logo.

This may seem obvious, but the real issue goes much deeper. A corporate identity defines what makes a corporation unique. The company name and logo are merely manifestations of that identity. Before such issues can be decided, it must be determined what the corporation stands for, where it is going, and how it is different from other corporations. Only then does it make sense to put a name on it and identify an image with it.

There are several aspects of a corporation that go into its identity. These include market share, industry group identification, customer base, employees, and direction. Most, if not all, of these aspects are altered in some way as the result of a merger or acquisition. The key is to identify what changes have occurred and respond to them by shaping the image or identity that is communicated to the public.

Legal Issues

Following the closing of the transaction, there are many legal and administrative tasks that must be accomplished by the acquisition team to complete the transaction. The nature and extent of these tasks will vary, depending on the size and type of the financing method selected by the purchaser. The parties to any acquisition must be careful to ensure that the jubilation of closing does not cause any postclosing matters to be overlooked.

In an *asset acquisition,* these postclosing tasks typically include the following:

- Final verification that all assets acquired are free of liens and encumbrances
- Recording of financing statements and transfer tax returns
- Recording of any assignments of intellectual property with the Library of Congress or Patent and Trademark Office
- Notification of the sale to employees, customers, distributors, and suppliers
- Adjustments to bank accounts and insurance policies

In addition to the above, a *stock acquisition* may also include the following:

- Filing articles of amendment to the corporate charter or articles of merger
- Completion of the transfer of all stock certificates
- Amendments to the corporate bylaws
- Preparation of all appropriate postclosing minutes and resolutions

Such actions require legal counsel familiar with the issues of corporate governance and intellectual property. While the buyer's legal counsel attends to these matters, management can more readily focus on the other aspects of the business combination for which they are better qualified and more effective.

Minimizing the Barriers to Transition

No matter how hard you try and how well you anticipate the issues that need to be addressed, the natural response of most people is to avoid change. As a result, it is important to be aware of the various aspects of change management and address them as well. The primary emotion that will be encountered in dealings with various groups will be *fear.* There will be fear on the part of employees, as relates to such things as job security, workplace location, and reporting structure. But you may also have to deal with fear on the part of customers (the buyer may discontinue a product line) and suppliers (the buyer may already have someone to supply that good).

Communication

The primary tool for dealing with fear, and many of the other emotions that surface during the course of acquisition transition, is communication. If a merger is thought of as the beginning of a marriage, think of the amount of communication that is necessary in the first few weeks and months of such a relationship. As with any relationship, a lack of communication typically means a lack of success.

In a merger, the two keys to effective communication are to determine (1) the importance of the information and (2) who should communicate it. Information should be communicated in the order of its importance. This means that you want to first communicate that information that affects people directly, including changes in:

- The organization, especially who is staying and who is going
- Reporting structures
- Job descriptions and responsibilities
- Grade, title, compensation, and benefits
- Job location and operating procedures

As a result of the importance of this information, the person doing the communicating is also important. A trusted person from the seller's side, along with an important person from the buyer's side, works best. This will assist in the transition and add credibility to the process.

The next most important information is the introduction of the new management team and the transition to new managers and employees. It is a bit disconcerting to walk the halls in an organization and not know people. Think of how it feels on the first day of a new job. Well, that's how it feels for all the employees of an acquired company. By making an effort to introduce the key players, people are more comfortable. They can place a name with a face and know who is being referred to in discussions. This can help overall efficiency because employees will be focusing on doing their job rather than wondering who someone is and how that person might affect their career. It also helps in the socialization process among the employees, which in turn contributes to efficiency! This, of course, is more difficult as organizations grow larger. You can, however, introduce those people that are most likely to run into each other.

Finally, communicate the new reporting structure and have individual managers introduce the two sides when there will be day-to-day interaction. If possible, have the prior manager make some kind of handover to the new. Some kind of group meeting or social gathering among the employees of various departments, especially those that interact regularly, can go a long way in making everyone more comfortable with the new faces, functions, and procedures.

Postmerger Task Force

One of the tools through which communication can be made more effective is a *postmerger task force.* Such an entity should be composed of a representative group from both sides of the transaction and should be formed after due diligence and during the negotiation process. The role of such a group, which needs to be defined and communicated early, is to uncover, evaluate, and resolve postmerger problems.

The importance of effectively communicating the role of the task force cannot be emphasized enough. Failure to do so will limit its effectiveness and call into question the resolve of the new organization. In a very real sense this is the first operating decision to be seen by the seller's employees and thus it will greatly influence the new employees' perception of the acquiring organization.

The composition of the task force has a bearing on its effectiveness and the integrity of the buyer, as viewed by the seller's employees. As a result, the CEO should probably avoid making him or herself a member. An honest assessment of those being considered for the task force will go a long way toward establishing its credibility. If one of the members from the seller's side is an employee who is not respected by the majority of the workforce, people will not take the task force seriously.

The role of the task force is best kept simple. It can serve as a conduit from labor to management to resolve problems that arise during the course of the merger. In this way, a dialogue can be opened and people will get the impression that actions are being taken to address concerns. The task force can also be used to organize the information that needs to be communicated to the new employees. The amount of information to be communicated can be overwhelming, and the way it is communicated can also cause problems. The task force can serve to communicate the issues in order of importance and to address them accurately. This helps prevent the grapevine from disseminating erroneous information. Creating the dialogue and organizing the information serve to help reduce or eliminate the fear discussed earlier.

Once its work is completed, the task force must be dissolved. This is easier said than done, as it is much easier to say when the merger activity begins than to define when it is over. The first sign that the end of the task force's life is near is when all the information deemed to be important in relation to the merger has been disseminated. An additional indication is the amount of information flowing back from the employees to the task force. Nonetheless, it is often helpful to give the task force a set life at its beginning—sixty or ninety days—and to evaluate the situation at that time. The final call will come from the CEO, when it is determined that the value of the task force has been expended and it is now time to get to work to realize the true value of the combination.

The importance of a well-planned and smooth postclosing transition cannot be emphasized enough. Without the proper attention to these matters, the value of the transaction may never be realized. This will require assembling a team with proven implementation skills and a desire to see the transaction work. The sheer number of issues that need to be addressed can seem overwhelming at first glance. But the importance of these issues in the success of a business combination cannot be overemphasized. By planning properly, paying attention to the details, and picking the right people for the job, a buyer will gain confidence in its ability to successfully integrate such a transaction. This will serve to encourage further growth through mergers and acquisitions.

Chapter 12

Alternatives to Mergers and Acquisitions

We established in Chapter 1 that mergers and acquisitions, at least from the buyer's perspective, were internal growth strategies. The buyer's acquisition plan identifies one or more transactions that will enhance market share, create economies of scale, penetrate new geographic and categorical markets, and provide a basis for raising additional capital. Hopefully, at this point you feel comfortable with the logistics, challenges, and mechanics of this strategy as well as the legal, financial, and strategic aspects of mergers and acquisitions.

However, there are a wide variety of alternative strategies focusing on the building of *external* relationships that achieve these same objectives. The primary differences among these strategies is the *degree of control* that results between the parties after the consummation of the relationship. Box 12-1 shows mergers and acquisitions appearing to the far left as being the growth strategy that results in the strongest level of control—ownership doesn't get much stronger than 100 percent! As you move your way to the right, you will see strategies such as joint ventures, franchising, licensing, strategic alliances, and distributorships. These are alternatives to mergers and acquisitions; while all of them envision a dynamic and synergistic working relationship, they fall short of a metamorphosis. In some cases, these strategies and relationships are designed to be long-term and truly independent; in other cases, the relationships are slightly more noncommittal and merely have shared objectives. Let's take a look at a few of these alternatives.

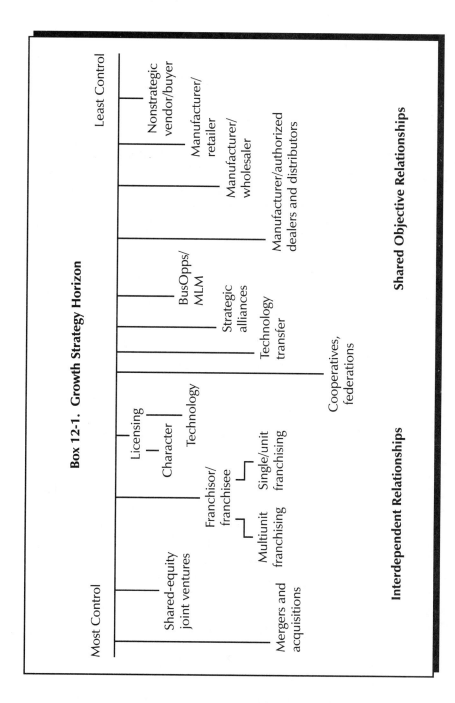

Box 12-1. Growth Strategy Horizon

Joint Ventures

One strategic alternative to an acquisition available to today's small and growing companies is a legal structure known as a joint venture. A joint venture is typically structured as a partnership or as a newly formed co-owned corporation where two or more parties are brought together to achieve a series of strategic and financial objectives on a short- or long-term basis. Growing companies who wish to explore this strategy should give careful thought to the type of partner they are looking for and what resources they will be contributing to the newly formed entity. As in raising a child, each parent makes its respective contribution of skills, abilities, and resources.

Joint ventures, strategic partnering, cross-licensing, and technology transfer agreements are all strategies designed to obtain one or more of the following:

1. Direct capital infusion in exchange for equity and/or intellectual property or distribution rights
2. A "capital substitute," where the resources that would otherwise be obtained with the capital are obtained through joint venturing
3. A shift of the burden and cost of development (through licensing) in exchange for a potentially more limited upside

The search for a joint venture partner is a bit like the search for an appropriate spouse. Take care to conduct a thorough review of prospective candidates, and make sure that extensive due diligence is done on the final few being considered. Develop a list of key objectives and goals to be achieved by the joint venture or licensing relationship, and compare this list with the objectives and goals of your final candidates. Take the time to understand the corporate culture and decision-making process within each company, and consider the following issues:

1. How do the culture and processes fit with your own processes?
2. What about each prospective partner's previous experi-

ences and track record with other joint venture relationships?

3. Why did these previous relationships succeed or fail?

In many cases, smaller companies looking for joint venture partners wind up selecting a much larger Goliath, which offers a wide range of financial and nonfinancial resources that allow the smaller company to achieve its growth plans. Under these circumstances, the motivating factor for the larger company is to gain access and distribution rights to new technologies, products, and services. In turn, the larger company offers access to pools of capital, research and development, personnel, distribution channels, and general contacts that the small company desperately needs.

But if yours is a small company, proceed carefully. The politics, red tape, and different management practices in place at a larger company will be foreign to many smaller firms, and you need to be sensitive to them. Try to distinguish between what is being promised and what will actually be delivered. If your primary motivating force is really only capital, consider whether alternative (and perhaps less costly) sources of money have been thoroughly explored. Ideally, the larger joint venture partner offers a lot more than money. If the primary motivating force is access to technical personnel, consider whether it might be better to purchase these resources separately than to enter into a partnership where you give up a certain measure of control. Also, consider whether strategic relationships or extended payment terms with vendors and consultants can be arranged in lieu of the joint venture.

Why Consider a Joint Venture or Strategic Alliance?

1. Develop a new market (domestic/international).
2. Develop a new product.
3. Develop/share technology.
4. Combine complementary technology.
5. Pool resources to develop a production/distribution facility.
6. Acquire capital.
7. Execute a government contract.

8. Access a distribution network or sales/marketing capability.

For example, suppose a small business named ProductCorp has the patents to protect the technology necessary to produce a wide range of new consumer products. It could commence a search for a "capital-rich" partner that will invest money in the construction of a manufacturing facility to be owned and operated by the newly established entity. Or it could enter into a joint venture with a larger competitor that already has the manufacturing capability to produce the products.

Each strategy has its respective advantages and disadvantages. The capital-rich joint venture partner brings the necessary financial resources to achieve the smaller company's objectives, but

---

Box 12-2. The Difference Between Joint Ventures and Strategic Alliances

	Joint Ventures	*Strategic Alliances*
Term	Usually medium- to long-term.	Short-term
Strategic objective	Often serves as the precursor to a merger.	More flexible and noncommittal
Legal agreements and structure	Actual legal entity formed.	Contractually driven
Extent of commitment	Shared equity	Shared objectives
Capital and resources	Each party makes a capital contribution of cash or intangible assets.	No specific capital contributions (may be shared budgeting even on cross-investment)
Tax ramifications	Be on the lookout for double taxation unless pass-through entities are utilized.	No direct tax ramifications

it cannot contribute experience in the industry. On the other hand, while the larger competitor offers certain operational and distribution synergies and economies of scale, it may seek greater control over ProductCorp's management decisions.

Unlike franchising, distributorships, and licensing, which are almost always vertical in nature, joint ventures are structured at *either* horizontal or vertical levels of distribution. At the horizontal level, the joint venture is almost an alternative to a merger, in which two companies operating at the same level in the distribution channel join together (either by means of a partnership-type agreement or by joint ownership of a specially created corporation) to achieve certain synergies or operating efficiencies. Consider the following key strategic questions before and during joint venture or strategic alliance negotiations:

- *Exactly what types of tangible and intangible assets will each party contribute to the joint venture?* Who will have ownership rights in the property contributed during the term of the joint venture and thereafter? Who will own property developed as a result of joint development efforts?

- *What covenants of nondisclosure or noncompetition will be expected of each joint venturer during the term of the agreement and thereafter?*

- *What timetables or performance quotas for completion of the projects contemplated by the joint venture will be included in the agreement?* What are the rights and remedies of each party if these performance standards are not met?

- *How will issues of management and control be addressed in the agreement?* What will be the respective voting rights of each party? What are the procedures in the event of a major disagreement or deadlock? What is the fallback plan?

Once you have discussed all of the preliminary issues with the joint venturer, prepare a formal joint venture agreement or corporate shareholders' agreement with the assistance of counsel. The precise terms of the agreement between the joint venturer and the company naturally depend on the specific objectives of the parties. At a minimum, however, the following topics should be addressed in as much detail as possible:

- *Nature, purpose, and trade name for the joint venture.* To prevent future disputes, clearly state the legal nature of the parties' relationship along with a clear statement of purpose. If a new trade name is established for the venture, provisions should be made as to the use of the name and any other trade or service marks should the project be terminated.

- *Status of the respective joint venturers.* Clearly indicate whether each party is a partner, shareholder, agent, independent contractor, or any combination thereof.

- *Representations and warranties of each joint venturer.* Standard representations and warranties will include obligations of due care and due diligence as well as mutual covenants governing confidentiality and anticompetition restrictions.

- *Capital and property contributions of each joint venturer.* Establish a clear schedule of all contributions, whether in the form of cash, shares, real estate, or intellectual property. Detailed descriptions will be particularly important if the distribution of profits and losses are to be based on overall contributions. The specifics of allocation and distribution of profits and losses among the venturers should also be clearly defined.

- *Management, control, and voting rights of each joint venturer.* If the proposed venture envisions joint management, it will be necessary to specifically address, in addition to responsibility for administrative and overhead expenses, the keeping of books, records, and bank accounts; the nature and frequency of inspections and audits; and insurance and cross-indemnification obligations.

- *Rights in joint venture property.* Each party must be mindful of intellectual property rights, and the issues of ownership use and licensing entitlements should be clearly addressed, not only for the venturers' currently existing property rights but also for future use of rights (or products or services) developed in the name of the venture itself.

- *Default, dissolution, and termination of the joint venture.* The obligations of the venturers and the distribution of assets should be clearly defined along with grounds for default and procedures in the event of bankruptcy.

Franchising

Over the last two decades, franchising has emerged as a popular expansion strategy for a variety of product and service companies, especially for smaller businesses that cannot afford to finance internal growth. Recent Department of Commerce statistics demonstrate that retail sales from franchised outlets comprise nearly 45 percent of all retail sales in the United States, estimated at more than $800 billion and employing some 8 million people in 1996. Notwithstanding these impressive figures, franchising as a method of marketing and distributing products and services is really only appropriate for certain kinds of companies. Despite the favorable media attention it has received over the past few years, franchising is not for everyone. That is because there are a host of legal and business prerequisites that must be satisfied before any company can seriously consider it as a method for rapid expansion.

Some companies prematurely select franchising as a growth alternative and then haphazardly assemble and launch the franchising program. Others are urged to choose this strategy by unqualified consultants or advisors, who may be more interested in professional fees than in the long-term success of the franchising program. This has caused financial distress and failure at both the growing company and franchisee level, usually resulting in litigation. Current and future members of the franchising community must be urged to take a responsible view towards the creation and development of their franchising programs.

Reasons for Franchising

Successful growing companies cite a wide variety of reasons for selecting franchising as a method of growth and distribution. These reasons include:

- Operating efficiencies and economies of scale
- More rapid market penetration at a lower capital cost
- Reaching the targeted consumer more effectively through cooperative advertising and promotion
- Ability to sell products and services to a dedicated distributor network

- Replacement of internal personnel with motivated owner/ operators
- Shift in the primary responsibility for site selection, employee training and personnel management, local advertising, and other administrative concerns to the franchisee, licensee, or joint venture partner with the guidance or assistance of the growing company

In the typical franchising relationship, the franchisee shares the risk of expanding the market share of the growing company by committing its capital and resources to the development of satellite locations modeled after the proprietary business format of the growing company. For the growing company, the risk of business failure is further reduced by the improvement in competitive position, reduced vulnerability to cyclical fluctuations, the existence of a captive market for its proprietary products and services (due to the network of franchisees), and reduced administrative and overhead costs.

The Foundation for Franchising

Responsible franchising is the *only* way that growing companies and franchisees will be able to harmoniously coexist in the twenty-first century. By *responsible,* we mean franchising based on a secure foundation from which the franchising program is launched. Any company considering franchising as a method of growth and distribution or any individual considering franchising as a method of getting into business must understand the key components of this foundation. They are:

- A *proven prototype* location (or chain of stores) that will serve as a basis for the franchising program. The store or stores must have been tested, refined, and operated successfully, and they must be consistently profitable. The success of the prototype should not be too dependent on the physical presence or specific expertise of the founders of the system.
- A *strong management team* made up of internal officers and directors (as well as qualified consultants) who understand both

the particular industry in which the company operates and the legal and business aspects of franchising as a method of expansion.

• *Sufficient capitalization* to launch and sustain the franchising program so that the growing company can provide initial as well as ongoing support and assistance to franchisees (a lack of a well-prepared business plan and inadequate capital structure are often the principal causes for the demise of many early-stage franchisors).

• A *distinctive and protected trade identity* that includes federal- and state-registered trademarks as well as a uniform trade appearance, signage, slogans, trade dress, and overall image.

• Proprietary and proven *methods of operation and management* that can be reduced to writing in a comprehensive operations manual that competitors cannot easily duplicate. These methods should be able to maintain their value to the franchisees over an extended period of time and be enforced through clearly drafted and objective quality control standards.

• A *comprehensive training* program for franchisees—both on-site at the franchisee's proposed location and at company headquarters—at the outset of the relationship and on an ongoing basis.

• *Field support staff* of skilled trainers and communicators who must be available to visit, inspect, and periodically assist franchisees, as well as monitor quality control standards.

• A set of comprehensive *legal documents* that reflect the company's business strategies and operating policies. Offering documents must be prepared in accordance with applicable federal and state disclosure laws, and franchise agreements should strike a delicate balance between the rights and obligations of the growing company and franchisee.

• A demonstrated *market demand* for the growing company's products and services that will be distributed through the franchisees. These products and services should meet certain minimum quality standards, not be subject to rapid shifts in consumer preferences (*e.g.*, fads), and be proprietary in nature. Market research and analysis should be sensitive to trends in the economy and the specific industry, the plans of direct and indirect competitors, and shifts in consumer preferences.

- A carefully developed set of uniform *site selection criteria and architectural standards* that can be readily and affordably secured in today's competitive real estate market.

- *A genuine understanding of the competition* (both direct and indirect) that the growing company will face in marketing and selling franchises to prospective franchisees as well as what the franchisee will face when marketing products and services.

- *Relationships* with suppliers, lenders, real estate developers, and related key resources as part of the operations manual and system.

- A *franchisee profile and screening system* to identify the minimum financial qualifications, business acumen, and understanding of the industry that will be required to be a successful franchisee.

- An effective system of *reporting and record keeping* to maintain the performance of the franchisees and ensure that royalties are reported accurately and paid promptly.

- *Research and development* capabilities for the introduction of new products and services on an ongoing basis to consumers through the franchised network.

- A *communication system* that facilitates a continuing and open dialogue with the franchisees, reducing the chances for conflict and litigation with the franchise network.

- National, regional, and local *advertising, marketing, and public relations programs* designed to recruit prospective franchisees as well as consumers to the sites operated by franchisees.

Regulatory Issues

The offer and sale of a franchise are regulated at both the federal and state level. At the federal level, the Federal Trade Commission (FTC) in 1979 adopted its trade regulation Rule 436 (FTC Rule), which specifies the minimum amount of disclosure that must be made to a prospective franchisee in any of the fifty states. In addition to the FTC Rule, more than a dozen states have adopted their own rules and regulations for the offer and sale of franchises within their borders. These states, known as the "registration states," generally follow a more detailed disclosure format, known as the Uniform Franchise Offering Circular (the UFOC).

Each registration state has slightly different procedures and requirements for the approval of a growing company prior to offers and sales being authorized. In all cases, however, the package of disclosure documents is assembled, consisting of a UFOC, franchise agreement, supplemental agreements, financial statements, franchise roster, an acknowledgment of receipt form, and the special disclosures required by each state—corporation verification statements, salesperson disclosure forms, and consent to service of process documents. The specific requirements of each state should be checked carefully by the growing company and its counsel.

Structuring and Preparing Franchise Agreements

The franchise agreement is the principal document that sets forth the binding rights and obligations of each party to the franchise relationship. The franchise agreement contains the various provisions, which will be binding on the parties for the life of their relationship, and therefore must maintain a delicate balance of power. On one hand, the franchisor must maintain enough control in the franchise agreement to enforce uniformity and consistency throughout the system; at the same time, it must be flexible enough to anticipate changes in the marketplace and modifications to the franchise system and to meet the special considerations or demands caused by the franchisee's local market conditions.

The franchise agreement can and should reflect the business philosophy of the franchisor and set the tenor of the relationship. If well drafted, it will reflect the culmination of literally thousands of business decisions and hundreds of hours of market research and testing. The length, term, and complexity will (and should) vary from franchisor to franchisor and from industry to industry. Many start-up franchisors make the critical mistake of "borrowing" terms of a competitor's franchise agreement. Such a practice can be detrimental to the franchisor and the franchisee, since the agreement will not accurately reflect the actual dynamics of their unique relationship. Early-stage franchisors should resist the temptation to copy from a competitor or to accept the "standard form and boilerplate" from an inexperienced attorney or consultant. The relationship between the franchisor and franchisee is far too complex for such a compromise to be accepted in the preparation of such a critical document.

Regardless of the size, stage of growth, industry dynamics, or specific trends in the marketplace, all basic franchise agreements should address the following key topics:

- *Recitals.* The recitals or "introduction to the purpose of the agreement" essentially set the stage for the discussion of the contractual relationship. This section provides the background information regarding the development and ownership of the franchisor's proprietary rights that are being licensed to the franchisee. The recitals should always contain at least one provision specifying the obligation of the franchisee to operate the business format in strict conformity with the operations manual and quality control standards provided by the franchisor.

- *Grant, term, and renewal.* The typical initial section of the franchise agreement is the grant of a franchise for a specified term. The length of the term is influenced by a number of factors including market conditions, the franchisor's need to periodically change certain material terms of the agreement, cost of the franchise and franchisee's expectations in relation to start-up costs, length of related agreements (e.g., leases and bank loans) necessary to the franchisee's operations, and anticipated consumer demand for the franchised goods and services.

The renewal rights granted to a franchisee, if included at all, will usually be conditioned upon the franchisee's being in good standing (e.g., no material defaults by franchisee) under the agreement. Other issues that must be addressed in any provision regarding renewal include renewal fees, obligations to execute the "then-current" form of the franchise agreement, and any obligations of the franchisee to upgrade its facilities to the "latest" standards and design. The franchisor's right to relocate the franchisee, adjust the size of any exclusive territory granted, or change the fee structure should also be addressed.

- *Territory.* The size of the geographic area granted to the franchisee by the franchisor must be specifically discussed in conjunction with what exclusive rights, if any, will be granted to the franchisee with respect to this territory. These provisions address whether the size of the territory is a specific radius, city, or county and whether the franchisor will have a right to operate company-owned locations and/or grant additional franchises within the territory. After conducting market research, some franchisors will designate a specific territory that could be successful without market oversaturation, and then will sell that exact number of franchises, without regard to specific location selected within the geographic area. Any rights of first refusal for additional locations, advertising restrictions, performance quotas relating to territory, and policies of the franchisor with regard to territory are addressed in this part of the agreement.

▪ *Site selection.* The responsibility for finding the specific site for the operation of the franchised business will rest with either the franchisor or the franchisee. If the franchisee is free to choose its own site, then the franchise agreement will usually provide that the decision be subject to the approval of the franchisor. Some franchisors provide significant assistance in site selection in terms of marketing and demographic studies, lease negotiations, and the securing of local permits and licenses, especially if a "turn-key" franchise is offered. Site selection, however, can be the most difficult aspect of success as a franchisee; as a result, most franchisors are reluctant to take on full responsibility for this task contractually. For additional protection and control, once an acceptable site has been selected, some franchisors will insist on being designated landlord to the franchisee through a mandatory sublease arrangement. A somewhat less burdensome method of securing similar protection is to provide for an automatic assignment of the lease to the franchisor upon termination of the franchise.

▪ *Services to be provided by the franchisor.* The franchise agreement should clearly delineate which products and services will be provided to the franchisee by the franchisor or its affiliates, both in terms of the initial establishment of the franchised business (preopening obligations) and any continuing assistance or support services provided throughout the term of the relationship (post-opening services).

The preopening obligations generally include a trade secret and copyright license for use of the confidential operations manual; recruitment and training of personnel; standard accounting and bookkeeping systems; inventory and equipment specifications and volume discounts; standard construction, building, and interior design plans; and grand opening promotion and advertising assistance. The quality and extent of the training program are clearly the most crucial preopening services provided by the franchisor, and should include classroom as well as on-site instruction.

Postopening services provided to the franchisee on a continuing basis generally include field support and troubleshooting, research and development for new products and services, development of national advertising and promotional campaigns, and the arrangement of group purchasing programs and volume discounts.

• *Franchise, royalty, and related fees payable to the franchisor; reporting.* The franchise agreement should clearly set forth the nature and amount of fees that will be payable to the franchisor by the franchisee, both initially and on a continuing basis.

The initial franchise fee is usually a nonrefundable lump sum payment due upon execution of the franchise agreement. Essentially, this fee is compensation for the grant of the franchise, the trademark and trade secret license, the preopening training and assistance, and the initial opening supply of materials, if any, to be provided to the franchisee.

A second category of fees is the continuing fee, usually in the form of a specific royalty on gross sales. This percentage can be fixed or based on a sliding scale for different ranges of sales achieved at a given location. Often a minimum royalty payment will be required, regardless of the franchisee's actual performance. These fees should be payable either weekly or monthly and submitted to the franchisor together with some standardized reporting form for internal control and monitoring purposes. A weekly or monthly payment schedule generally allows the franchisee to budget for this payment from a cash flow perspective (as well as provide the franchisor with an early warning system if there is a problem) and to react before past due royalties accrue to a virtually uncollectible sum.

The third category of recurring fees is usually in the form of a national cooperative advertising and promotion fund. The promotion fund may be managed by the franchisor, an independent advertising agency, or even a franchisee association. Either way, the franchisor must build into the franchise agreement a certain amount of control over the fund in order to protect the company's trademarks and ensure consistency in marketing efforts.

Other categories of fees payable to the franchisor may include the sale of proprietary goods and services to the franchisee, consulting fees, audit and inspection fees, lease management fees (where the franchisor is to serve as sublessor), and renewal or transfer fees. The obligations of the franchisee to provide periodic weekly, monthly, quarterly, and annual financial and sales reports to the franchisor should also be addressed in the franchise agreement.

▪ *Quality control.* A well-drafted franchise agreement always includes a variety of provisions designed to ensure quality control and consistency throughout the franchise system. Such provisions often take the form of restrictions on the franchisee's sources of products, ingredients, supplies, and materials, as well as of strict guidelines and specifications for operating procedures. These operating procedures usually specify standards of service, trade dress and uniform requirements, condition and appearance of the facility, hours of business, minimum insurance requirements, guidelines for trademark usage, advertising and promotional materials, accounting systems, and credit practices. Any restrictions on the ability of the franchisee to buy goods and services or requirements to purchase from a specific source should be carefully drafted within the perimeters of applicable antitrust laws. If the franchisor is to serve as the sole supplier or manufacturer of one or more products to be used by the franchisee in the day-to-day operation of the business, then such exclusivity must be justified by a product that is truly proprietary or unique, such as the eleven special herbs and spices that have been protected for many decades by KFC.

▪ *Insurance, record keeping, and other related obligations of the franchisee.* The minimum amounts and types of insurance that must be carried by the franchisee in connection with its operation of the franchised business should also be discussed. Typically the franchisor is named as an additional insured under these policies. Other related obligations of the franchisee that must be set forth in the franchise agreement include keeping proper financial records (which must be made available for inspection by the franchisor upon request); maintaining and enforcing quality control standards with its employees and vendors; complying with all applicable employment laws, health and safety standards, and related local ordinances; upgrading and maintaining the franchisee's facilities and equipment; continuing to promote the products and services of the franchisor; reasonably processing requests by patrons for franchising information; refraining from producing goods and services that do not meet the franchisor's quality control specifications or that may be unapproved for offer at the franchisee's premises (e.g., video games at a fast-food restaurant or X-rated material at a bookstore); refraining from soliciting customers outside its designated territory; personally participating in the day-to-day operation of the franchised business (required by many but not all franchisors); and generally refraining from any activity that might reflect adversely on the reputation of the franchise system.

▪ *Protection of intellectual property and covenants against competition.* The franchise agreement should always contain a separate section on the obligations of the franchisee and its employees to protect licensed trademarks and trade secrets against misuse or disclosure. The franchisor should provide for a clause clearly setting forth that the trademarks and trade names being licensed are the exclusive property of the franchisor and that any goodwill established is to inure to the sole benefit of the franchisor. It should also be made clear that the confidential operations manual is "on loan" to the franchisee under a limited use license and that the franchisee or its agents are prohibited from the unauthorized use of the trade secrets both during and after the term of the agreement. To the extent that such provisions are enforceable in local jurisdictions, the franchise agreement should contain covenants against competition by a franchisee—both during the term of the agreement and following termination or cancellation.

▪ *Termination of the franchise agreement.* One of the most important sections is the section discussing how a franchisee may lose its rights to operate the franchised business. The various "events of default" should be carefully defined and tailored to meet the needs of the specific type of business being franchised. Grounds for termination can range anywhere from the bankruptcy of a franchisee to failure to meet specified performance quotas or strictly abide by quality control standards. Certain types of defaults will be grounds for immediate termination, while other types of defaults will provide the franchisee with an opportunity to fix its mistakes within a certain time period prior to termination. This section should address the procedures under which the franchisor will provide notice to the franchisee of the default(s) and clearly explain how much time it will have to rectify the problem, as well as the alternative actions that the franchisor may pursue to enforce its rights to terminate the franchise agreement. Such clauses must be drafted in light of certain state regulations that limit franchise terminations to "good cause" and must have minimum procedural requirements that must be followed. The obligations of the franchisee upon default and notice of termination must also be clearly spelled out, such as the duty to return all copies of the operations manuals, pay all past due royalty fees, and immediately cease the use of the franchisor's trademarks.

▪ *Miscellaneous provisions.* As with any well-prepared business agreement, the franchise agreement should include a notice provision, a governing law clause, severability provisions, an integration clause, and a provision discussing the relationship of the parties. Some franchisors may want to add an arbitration clause, a "hold harmless" and indemnification provision, a reservation of the right to injunctions and other forms of equitable relief, specific representations and warranties of the franchisee, attorney fees for the prevailing party in the event of dispute, and even a contractual provision acknowledging that the franchisee has reviewed the agreement with counsel and has conducted an independent investigation of the franchise and is not relying on any representations other than those expressly set forth in the agreement.

Technology and Merchandise Licensing

Licensing is a contractual method of developing and exploiting intellectual property by transferring rights of use to third parties *without* the transfer of ownership. Virtually any proprietary product or service may be the subject of a license agreement, ranging from the licensing of the Mickey Mouse character by Walt Disney Studios in the 1930s to modern-day licensing of computer software and high technology. From a legal perspective, licensing involves complex issues of contract, tax, antitrust, international, tort, and intellectual property law. From a business perspective, licensing involves a weighing of the economic and strategic advantages of licensing against other methods of bringing the product or service to the marketplace, such as direct sales, distributorships, or franchises.

Many of the benefits of licensing to be enjoyed by a growing company closely parallel the advantages of franchising, namely:

- To spread the risk and cost of development and distribution
- To achieve more rapid market penetration
- To earn initial license fees and ongoing royalty income
- To enhance consumer loyalty and goodwill
- To preserve the capital that would otherwise be required for internal growth and expansion
- To test new applications for existing and proven technology
- To avoid or settle litigation regarding a dispute over ownership of the technology

The disadvantages of licensing are also similar in nature to the risks inherent in franchising, such as:

- A somewhat diminished ability to enforce quality control standards and specifications
- A greater risk of another party infringing upon the licensor's intellectual property
- A dependence on the skills, abilities, and resources of the licensee as a source of revenue
- Difficulty in recruiting, motivating, and retaining qualified and competent licensees
- The risk that the licensor's entire reputation and goodwill may be damaged or destroyed by the act or omission of a single licensee
- The administrative burden of monitoring and supporting the operations of the network of licensees

Failure to consider all of the costs and benefits of licensing could easily result in a regrettable strategic decision by the licensor. Or the licensor might be stuck with the terms of an unprofitable license agreement due to either an underestimation of the licensee's need for technical assistance and support or an overestimation of the market demand for the licensor's products and services. In order to avoid such problems, a certain amount of due diligence should be conducted by the licensor prior to engaging in any serious negotiations with a prospective licensee. This preliminary investigation generally includes market research, legal steps to fully protect intellectual property, and an internal financial analysis of the technology with respect to pricing, profit margins, and costs of production and distribution. It also includes a more specific analysis of the prospective licensee with respect to its financial strength, research and manufacturing capabilities, and reputation in the industry. Once the decision to enter into more formal negotiations has been made, the terms and conditions of the license agreement should be discussed. Naturally, these provisions will vary, depending on whether the license is for merchandising an entertainment property, exploiting a given technology, or distributing a particular product to an original equipment manufacturer or value-added reseller.

There are two principle types of licensing: (1) technology licensing, where the strategy is to find a licensee for exploitation of industrial and technological developments, and (2) merchandise and character licensing, where the strategy is to license a recognized trademark or copyright to a manufacturer of consumer goods in markets not currently served by the licensor.

Technology Licensing

The principal purpose behind technology transfer and licensing agreements is to make a marriage between the technology proprietor, as licensor, and the organization that possesses the resources to properly develop and market the technology, as licensee. This marriage is made between companies and inventors of all shapes and sizes, but it often takes place in the context of an entrepreneur that has the technology but lacks the resources to adequately penetrate the marketplace, as licensor, and the larger company, which has sufficient research and development, production, human resources, and marketing capability to make the best use of the technology, as licensee. The industrial and technological revolutions have histories of very successful entrepreneurs who have relied on the resources of larger organizations to bring their products to market, such as Chester Carlson (xerography), Edwin Land (Polaroid cameras), Robert Goddard (rockets), and Willis Carrier (air-conditioning). As the base for technological development becomes broader, large companies look not only to entrepreneurs and small businesses for new ideas and technologies but also to each other, foreign countries, universities, and federal and state governments to serve as licensors of technology.

In the typical licensing arrangement, the proprietor of intellectual property rights (patents, trade secrets, trademarks, and knowhow) permits a third party to make use of these rights pursuant to a set of specified conditions and circumstances that are set forth in a license agreement. Licensing agreements can be limited to a very narrow component of the proprietor's intellectual property rights, such as one specific application of a single patent, or be much broader in context, such as in a classic "technology transfer" agreement, where an entire bundle of intellectual property rights are transferred to the licensee in exchange for initial fees and royalties. The classic technology transfer arrangement is actually closer to a sale of the intellectual property rights, with a right by the licensor to get the intellectual property back if the licensee fails to meet its obligations under the agreement. An example of this type of transaction might be bundling a proprietary environmental cleanup system together with technical support and training services to a master overseas licensee, with reversionary rights in the event of a breach of the agreement or the failure to meet a set of performance standards.

Merchandise and Character Licensing Agreements

The use of commonly recognized trademarks, brand names, sports teams, athletes, universities, television and film characters, musicians, and designers to foster the sales of specific products and services is at the heart of today's merchandise and character licensing environment. Manufacturers and distributors of a wide range of products and services license these words, images, and symbols, which range from clothing to housewares to toys and posters. Certain brand names and characters have withstood the test of time, while others fall prey to fads, consumer shifts, and stiff competition.

The trademark and copyright owners of these properties and character images are motivated to license for a variety of reasons. Aside from the obvious desire to earn royalty fees and profits, many manufacturers view this licensing strategy as a form of merchandising to promote the underlying product or service. The licensing of a trademark for application on a line of clothing helps to establish and reinforce brand awareness at the consumer level. For example, when R. J. Reynolds Tobacco Company licenses a leisure apparel manufacturer to produce a line of Camel wear, the hope is to sell more cigarettes, appeal to the lifestyle of its targeted consumers, maintain consumer awareness, *and* enjoy the royalty income from the sale of the clothing line. Similar strategies have been adopted by manufacturers in order to revive a mature brand or failing product. In certain instances, the spinoff product that has been licensed has been almost as financially successful as the underlying product it was intended to promote.

Brand-name owners, celebrities, and academic institutions must be very careful not to grant too many licenses too quickly. The financial rewards of a flow of royalty income from hundreds of different manufacturers can be quite seductive, but these rewards must be weighed against the possible loss of quality control and dilution of the name, logo, or character. The loyalty of the licensee network is also threatened when too many licenses are granted in closely competing products. Retailers will also become cautious when purchasing licensed goods from a licensee if they fear that quality control has suffered or that the popularity of the licensed character, celebrity, or image will be short-lived. This may result in smaller orders and an overall unwillingness to carry inventory. This is especially true in the toy industry where purchasing decisions are being made, or at least influenced, by the whims of a five-year-old child who may strongly identify with a character image one week and then turn his attention to a totally different character image the next week. It is incumbent on manufacturers and licensees to develop advertising and media campaigns to hold the consumer's attention for an extended period of time. Only then will the retailer be convinced of the potential longevity of the product line. This will require a balancing of the risks and rewards between licensor and licensee in the character licensing agreement in the areas of compensation to the licensor, advertising expenditures by the licensee, scope of exclusivity, and quality control standards and specifications.

In the merchandise licensing community, the name, logo, symbol, or character is typically referred to as *the property*, and the specific product or product line (e.g., T-shirts, mugs, posters) is referred to as *the licensed product*. This area of licensing offers opportunities and benefits to both the owners of the properties and the manufacturers of the licensed products. For the owner of the property, brand recognition, goodwill, and royalty income are strengthened and expanded. For the manufacturer of the licensed products, there is an opportunity to leverage the goodwill of the property to improve sales of the licensed product. The manufacturer has an opportunity to hit the ground running in the sale of merchandise by gaining access to and use of an already established brand name or character image.

Naturally, each party should conduct due diligence on the other. From the perspective of the owner of the property, the manufacturer of the licensed product should demonstrate an ability to meet and maintain quality control standards, possess financial stability, and offer an aggressive and well-planned marketing and promotional strategy. From the perspective of the manufacturer of the licensed product, the owner of the property should display a certain level of integrity and commitment to quality, disclose its future plans for the promotion of the property, and be willing to participate and assist in the overall marketing of the licensed products. For example, if a star basketball player is unwilling to appear for promotional events designed to sell his own specially licensed line of basketball shoes, this presents a major problem and would likely lead to a premature termination of the licensing relationship. As a general rule, any well-drafted license agreement should address the following topics:

- *Scope of the grant.* The exact scope and subject matter of the license must be initially addressed and carefully defined in the license agreement. Any restrictions on the geographic scope, rights of use, permissible channels of trade, restrictions on sublicensing, limitations on assignability, or exclusion of improvements to the technology covered by the agreement should be clearly set forth in this section.

- *Term and renewal.* The commencement date, duration, renewals and extensions, conditions to renewal, procedures for providing notice of intent to renew, grounds for termination, obligations upon termination, and licensor's reversionary rights in the technology should all be included in this section.

- *Performance standards and quotas.* To the extent that the licensor's consideration will be dependent on royalty income calculated from the licensee's gross or net revenues, the licensor may want to impose certain minimum levels of performance in terms of sales, advertising and promotional expenditures, and human resources to be devoted to the exploitation of the technology. Naturally, the licensee will argue for a "best efforts" provision that is free from performance standards and quotas. In such cases, the licensor may want to insist on a minimum royalty level that will be paid regardless of the licensee's actual performance.

- *Payments to the licensor.* Virtually every type of license agreement includes some form of initial payment and ongoing royalty to the licensor. Royalty formulae vary widely, however, and may be based upon gross sales, net sales, net profits, fixed sum per product sold, or a minimum payment to be made to the licensor over a given period of time. Or they may include a sliding scale in order to provide some incentive to the licensee as a reward for performance.

- *Quality control assurance and protection.* Quality control standards and specifications for the production, marketing, and distribution of the products and services covered by the license must be set forth by the licensor. In addition, the agreement should include procedures that allow the licensor an opportunity to *enforce* these standards and specifications, such as a right to inspect the licensee's premises; a right to review, approve, or reject samples produced by the licensee; and a right to review and approve any packaging, labeling, or advertising materials to be used in connection with the exploitation of the products and services that are within the scope of the license.

- *Insurance and indemnification.* The licensor should take all necessary and reasonable steps to ensure that the licensee has an obligation to protect and indemnify the licensor against any claims or liabilities resulting from the licensee's exploitation of the products and services covered by the license.

- *Accounting, reports, and audits.* The licensor must impose certain reporting and record-keeping procedures on the licensee in order to ensure an accurate accounting for periodic royalty payments. Further, the licensor should reserve the right to audit the records of the licensee in the event of a dispute or discrepancy, along with provisions as to who will be responsible for the cost of the audit in the event of an understatement.

- *Duties to preserve and protect intellectual property.* The obligations of the licensee, its agents, and employees to preserve and protect the confidential nature and acknowledge the ownership of the intellectual property being disclosed in connection with the license agreement must be carefully defined. Any required notices or legends that must be included on products or materials distributed in connection with the license agreement (such as to the status of the relationship or actual owner of the intellectual property) are also described in this section.

- *Technical assistance, training, and support.* Any obligation of the licensor to assist the licensee in the development or exploitation of the subject matter being licensed is included in this section of the agreement. The assistance may take the form of personal services or of documents and records. Either way, any fees due to the licensor for such support services over and above the initial license and ongoing royalty fee must also be addressed.

- *Warranties of the licensor.* A prospective licensee may demand that the licensor provide certain representations and warranties in the license agreement. These may include warranties regarding the ownership of the technology, such as absence of any known infringements of the technology or restrictions on the ability to license the technology, or guaranties that the technology has the features, capabilities, and characteristics previously represented in the negotiations.

- *Infringements.* The license agreement should contain procedures under which the licensee must notify the licensor of any known or suspected direct or indirect infringements of the subject matter being licensed. The responsibilities for the cost of protecting and defending the technology should also be specified in this section.

Distributorships and Dealerships

Many growing product-oriented companies choose to bring their wares to the marketplace through independent third-party distributors and dealerships. This type of arrangement is commonly used by manufacturers of electronic and stereo equipment, computer hardware and software, sporting goods, medical equipment, and automobile parts and accessories. These dealers are generally more difficult to control than a licensee or franchisee; as a result, the agreement between manufacturer and distributor will be much more informal than a franchise or license agreement.

In developing distributor and dealership agreements, growing companies must be careful to avoid being included within the broad definition of a "franchise" under the FTC Rule, which requires the preparation of a disclosure document. To avoid such a classification, the agreement must impose minimal controls over the dealer; the sale of products must be at bona fide wholesale prices without any form of initiation fee; and the growing company must provide minimal assistance in the marketing or management of the dealer's business. A well-drafted distributorship agreement should, however, address the following key issues:

- What is the scope of the appointment? Which products is the dealer authorized to distribute, and under what conditions? What is the scope, if any, of the exclusive territory to be granted to the distributor? To what extent will product, vendor, customer, or geographic restrictions be applicable?

- What activities will the distributor be expected to perform in terms of manufacturing, sales, marketing, display, billing, market research, maintenance of books and records, storage, training, installation, support, and servicing?

- What obligations will the distributor have to preserve and protect the intellectual property of the manufacturer?

- What right, if any, will the distributor have to modify or enhance the manufacturer's warranties, terms of sale, credit policies, or refund procedures?

- What advertising literature, technical and marketing support, training seminars, or special promotions will be provided by the manufacturer to enhance the performance of the distributor?

- What sales or performance quotas will be imposed on the dealer as a condition to its right to continue to distribute the manufacturer's products or services? What are the rights and remedies of the manufacturer if the dealer fails to meet these performance standards?

- What is the term of the agreement, and under what conditions can it be terminated? How will posttermination transactions be handled?

Differences Between Distributors and Sales Representatives

Distributors are often confused with sales representatives. There are many critical differences which must be understood. Typically, a distributor buys the product from the manufacturer at wholesale prices, with the intent to resell to a retailer or directly to the customer. There is usually no actual fee paid by the distributor for the grant of the distributorship, and the distributor is typically permitted to carry competitive products. A distributor is expected to maintain some retail location or showroom where the manufacturer's products can be displayed. A distributor must maintain its own inventory storage and warehousing capabilities. A distributor looks to the manufacturer for technical support, advertising contributions, supportive repair, maintenance and service policies, new product training, volume discounts, favorable payment and return policies, and brand-name recognition. The manufacturer looks to a distributor for in-store and local promotion, adequate inventory controls, financial stability, preferred display and stocking, prompt payment, and qualified sales personnel. Although the distributorship network offers a viable alternative to franchising, it is not a panacea. The management and control of distributors may be even more difficult than that involved in franchising (especially without the benefit of a comprehensive franchise agreement), and the termination of these relationships is regulated by many state and anti-termination statutes.

A sales representative or sales agent is an independent marketing resource for the manufacturer. Unlike a distributor, a sales representative typically does not actually purchase the merchandise for resale, nor is it typically required to maintain inventories or retail locations or engage in any special price promotions unless instigated by the manufacturer.

Index